REEL SHAME

Bad Movies and the Hollywood Stars Who Made Them

Scott Hamilton & Christopher Holland

with a foreword by Freeman "Dr. Freex" Williams

A Stomp Tokyo Book

Reel Shame: Bad Movies and the Hollywood Stars Who Made Them

by Christopher Holland and Scott Hamilton

Copyright © 2003 by Stomp Tokyo

ISBN 0-9718356-0-8 (softcover)

Library of Congress Control Number: 2002104069

All rights reserved. No part of this book may be reproduced or transmitted in any form or by any means, electronic or mechanical, including photocopying, recording, or by an information storage and retrieval system – except by a reviewer who may quote brief passages in a review – without permission in writing from the publisher. For information, contact Stomp Tokyo, 6822 22nd Avenue North #278, St. Petersburg FL, 33710. Phone/fax 530-937-2827 or find our current contact information at **www.stomptokyo.com.**

Printed in the U.S.A. by Morris Publishing
3212 E. Hwy 30
Kearney, NE 68847
800-650-7888

Quantity discounts on bulk purchases of this book are available. For more information please contact Stomp Tokyo Sales Division, 6822 22nd Avenue North #278, St. Petersburg FL, 33710. Phone/fax 530-937-2827. E-mail: books@stomptokyo.com.

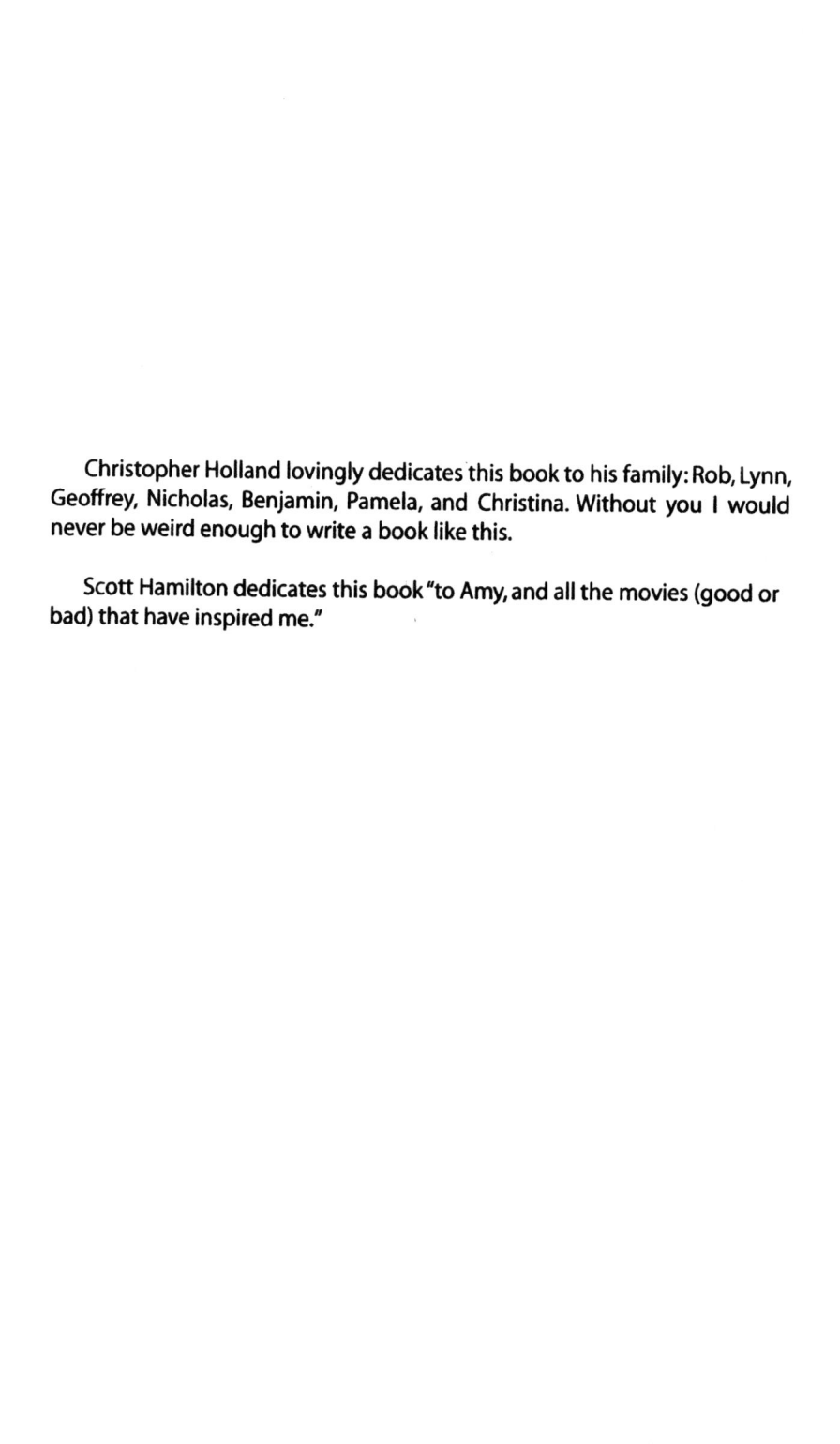

Christopher Holland lovingly dedicates this book to his family: Rob, Lynn, Geoffrey, Nicholas, Benjamin, Pamela, and Christina. Without you I would never be weird enough to write a book like this.

Scott Hamilton dedicates this book "to Amy, and all the movies (good or bad) that have inspired me."

Contents

Foreword by Freeman Williams ix

Part One: You Gotta Start Somewhere

Introduction	3
Girls Just Want to Have Fun	5
Cutting Class	8
High School Horror	10
The Lonely Lady	11
Pia Zadora	13
Are You In The House Alone?	14
I'm Talking to You!	16
Tammy and the T-Rex	17
Dinostars	19
Cyborg 2	20
Post-Apocalyptic Robots	22
Hercules Goes Bananas	23
Whose Voice is That?	25
Critters 3	26
Die, Leo, Die!	28
Texas Chainsaw Massacre: The Next Generation	29
Mazes and Monsters	32
Graduation Day	35
Zombie High	37
King Kong	39

Reel Shame **v**

Part Two: I Need A New Agent!

Introduction	47
Getting In	49
*Don't Put **Friends** in Your Movies*	51
Amityville 3-D	52
Now in 3-D!	54
Trancers	55
Trancers II	58
They Call Me Tim	60
Trancers III: Deth Lives	61
But Wait, There's More	63
Anaconda	64
Bite of the Snake Movie	66
The Tower	67
No Way Back	70
Shakes the Clown	73

Part Three: Sex Sells

Introduction	79
The Turning	81
Caligula	83
Embrace of the Vampire	85
Blindfold: Acts of Obsession	88
Shannen Doherty's Many Faces	90
Private Resort	91
Bikini Cinema	93
Zapped!	94
Magical Mystery Sex Comedies	96
Sizzle Beach U.S.A.	97
Kevin Costner vs. Bruce Campbell	100

Poison Ivy	101
More Poison, Not So Much Ivy	103
Zandalee	104
The Temp	106
Barb Wire	108
Cruel Intentions 2	110

Part Four: I Wanted to Try Something Different

Introduction	119
Tentacles	121
Killer Sea Beasts	123
Witchery	124
Curse of the Witch Movie	127
Carnosaur	128
Roger Corman, King of the Rip-Off Artists	130
Starcrash	131
Alone in the Dark	134
Didn't We Just See This Movie?	136
The Last Chase	137
Zardoz	140
Raise the *Titanic!*	143
Sir Alec Guinness	146
The Star Wars Holiday Special	147
Where Do I Get My Copy?	150

Appendix A: Movies Mentioned	153
Appendix B: Recommended Reading	164
Appendix C: B-Movie Web Sites	174
Index	177

Acknowledgments

Any book is a work made possible not only by its authors, but also by an army of editors, advisors, friends, colleagues, relatives, and random influences. This book is no different.

Our humblest of thanks to our team of editors, who went unpaid but not unappreciated. To Amy Morrison, for being our #1 fan, tireless champion, and merciless critic and proofreader. To Chris Magyar, for corrections in style and for unbridled opinion, which was usually right on the money. To Freeman Williams, for gentle course corrections, good advice, and the occasional bit of flattery. To Lisa McInnis, for her publishing knowledge, constant encouragement, and a kick-ass index. To Ken Begg, whose generosity is even more expansive than his prose. To Mark "Apostic" Hurst, who titled the book more effectively than we could have. To Marilyn Taylor, Betsy Boynton, and Laurinda Frye, who lent us their graphics expertise. To Jeff "Filmboy" Stanford, who always makes us laugh on the inside. To Robert Holland, who gave us extra pushes when we needed them in a number of ways.

To all those who suffered through some of these movies with us, especially the Movie Night crowd in incarnations past and present: Amy E., Amy M., Bryan, Christina, Heather, Jyotika, Tanya, Trent, and Loren. To the B-Masters Cabal for inspiration and cameraderie: Andrew, Keith, Scott, Lyz, Ken, Nathan, Apostic, Freex, and Joe. To the entire crew at stomptokyo.com: Jeff, Joe, Chris, Freex (again!), Lisa, Skip, Keith, Chad, and Mike. To our families, for allowing us to live to adulthood. To the folks at the B-Movie Message Board, for good conversation. To our readers.

Also to those people who provided inspiration and amusement: Steve Ryfle, Joal Ryan, Bruce Campbell, Kevin Smith, Kevin Murphy, Joel Hodgson, Mike Nelson, Frank Conniff, Trace Beaulieu, and all the creators of *Mystery Science Theater 3000*, Roger Ebert, John Bloom, Tim Thomerson, Sam Raimi, Jackie Chan, and a host of others. To the organizers of festivals like B-Fest and The New Orleans Worst Film Festival, for giving us a place to congregate with our own kind. To everyone who ever made a bad movie, for providing us with the raw material for our work.

To Christina Holland and Amy Eisenman, for their love, tolerance, support, and occasional smart-ass remarks.

Foreword
by Freeman "Dr. Freex" Williams

At one point in my critical career, I stated that it should be a law – or at least, an ironclad tradition – that every big-time big-name actor or actress must start out in a skeevy little movie with a budget of $1.98. To be sure, I was referring to Frank Bonner, whose major contribution to culture has been the unctuous Herb Tarlek in *WKRP in Cincinnati*, but the point remains the same for actors of a higher visibility and/or income.

To come from humble beginnings is one of the ways we judge the character of our public figures. The stirring rags-to-riches story has long been a staple of English literature. To see a movie star disembark from a limousine onto a glamorous red carpet, waving to the cheering schlubs held in check by velvet rope, is to taste from the heady vineyards of fame; to see that same star laboring in a no-budget clunker (possibly under a different name) is to realize that the glittering creature in the formal attire is no different from the cheering schlubs, or you or I. They were once looking for a job, that first entrance into a career, and they took that crummy job washing dishes in the back room of a Denny's.

The difference is: their back rooms are available on video.

Then there is the opposite side of that coin: the once-viable actor or actress who has fallen from grace, either through age, individual peccadilloes, or simple bad luck. It is harrowingly clear in these instances that all notions of art or craft have gone out the nearest window in favor of that most essential of commodities, the paycheck. Once again, we find ourselves sharing the same life as these luminous creatures: they too, have to pay rent or mortgages, and buy groceries.

And somewhere between the two sides of this increasingly thick metaphorical coin is the Unthinkable: the Big Budget Bad Movie in which matinee idols willingly appear, producing an indelible and entertaining stain on their resumes. The poster child for this phenomenon is *Ishtar*, the yardstick for Overblown Bad Movies for more than a decade. While it did not end the careers of Dustin Hoffman or Warren Beatty, it possesses a dreadful half-life of its own; the fact that the troubled money pit *Waterworld* was mockingly referred to as "Fishtar" before its release attests to the staying power of a particularly bad film.

I can think of no better guides into this realm of cinematic desperation than Chris Holland and Scott Hamilton. Friends since before the Crimean War, these two men devour movies like rubber-suited monsters consume unsuspecting cities. Their viewing habits are not constrained by mere notions of genre or nationality; just when you think you have their viewing habits figured out, they will begin ranting about the musical numbers in Indian pictures or discussing the relative merits of Pia Zadora versus Maria Ford.

This omnivorous appetite for offbeat cinema of all flavors begat a thriving empire, Stomp Tokyo (www.stomptokyo.com), wherein they expound upon their various cinematic findings. Whereas many movie critics eventually become jaded, grumbling misanthropes under the sheer weight of the product unspooling before them, Scott and Chris still carry with them a love for the art form that is contagious. If a high-profile big-budget picture is particularly horrid, they will tell you that; but if an impoverished, badly-shot little mongrel of a movie has some entertainment value, they'll tell you that, too. They're trustworthy that way.

And so, my little Dante, I must now entrust you to your twin Platos, that you may wander the netherworld of Movies That Stars Would Prefer You Forget. And if, in the future, you find yourself watching re-runs of *Mad About You* and find yourself thinking, "Tim Thomerson was a much better match for Helen Hunt than Paul Reiser," well, is that such a bad thing?

Freeman Williams is also known as Dr. Freex, creator of The Bad Movie Report (www.badmoviereport.com). He wrote and appeared in a movie called **Forever Evil**, *which is available in the back rooms of video stores everywhere.*

PART ONE

You Gotta Start Somewhere

2 *Reel Shame*

"You Gotta Start Somewhere"

Watching the early work of nearly any movie star underscores the differences between the type of person who becomes an actor and just about anyone else. When given the opportunity to be the butt of repeated jokes, dispense with one's modesty, and face certain humiliation which will be recorded and played back for the amusement of others, most people will politely decline. Aspiring actors not only seek out this sort of abuse, they return for multiple helpings. This is called "breaking into the business." It is the sort of treatment that inspires lawsuits in other professions, but in Hollywood it is an accepted ritual, a sort of fraternity hazing to which young would-be stars subject themselves in the hopes of earning more respectable roles. The logic of this is hazy at best ("Look at that young man stick his head in that toilet! I wonder if he's available to play Hamlet?"), but the system seems to work. Even the most respectable and dignified actors working today have at least one skeleton lurking in their cinematic closets, and it doesn't stop any of them from winning Oscars or making millions of dollars per picture.

One happy result of this system is that every rising star faces a moment on a TV talk show during which the host will grin mischeviously before showing a particularly heinous clip from the actor's past. We like to think that this teaches humility, but more likely it merely affords viewers the opportunity for a good laugh. Another fortunate consequence is that those of us who have acquired a taste for such detractive evidence of celebrity origins will never run out of entertainment.

In the 1952 musical *Singin' in the Rain*, Gene Kelly's character, Don Lockwood, regales the attendees of a '20s film premiere with the story of his rise to fame. The watchword he and his stage partner used was: "Dignity. *Always* dignity." As he reveals the proud details of their success story, the film shows us that their actual beginnings involved small-town vaudeville theaters, goofball slapstick stage antics, and repeated physical abuse as stunt doubles in budget Western movies. Don Lockwood never had to contend with video, which has laid bare the goofball antics of our modern stars and revealed just how little dignity has to do with any nascent movie career.

In this chapter, we present to you some of the most wretched examples of Hollywood careers being born. Since their lowly beginnings, some of these actors have produced the most popular and profitable movies ever made. Some of them have become the stars who are merely famous for being famous. Others have seen their careers peak only to decline again, and still others have their best work ahead of them. All of them, however, began at the bottom – and none of them could ever stand in front of an audience to intone: "Dignity. *Always* dignity."

Girls Just Want to Have Fun

(1985, Director: Alan Metter)

Let us consider a trio of Hollywood actresses.

Helen Hunt is quite the veteran of b-movies, with three *Trancers* films to her credit. More recently, she endured the run of a sitcom with Paul Reiser, starred in a blockbuster disaster flick, and won Best Actress at the Academy Awards for portraying a woman of thirty-five who falls in love with a sixty year-old Jack Nicholson.

Sarah Jessica Parker – who once played the Squarest of Pegs, rubbed elbows with aliens in *Flight of the Navigator*, and brought new meaning to the word "flighty" in *L.A. Story* – now eats men alive as Manhattan's sexiest journalist in HBO's *Sex and the City*. How Matthew Broderick lucked into marrying this woman is one of life's greatest mysteries.

Shannen Doherty was the bitch queen of teen prime-time drama and suffered death at the hands of Winona Ryder before floundering in a rash of trash flicks and TV movies, after which she redeemed herself by appearing in Kevin Smith's *Mallrats*. Some folks just can't get past her asymmetrical facial features, but her continued ability to get screen work means she must be doing something right.

What these disparate talents have in common, as you've likely guessed by now, is the 1985 "dance classic" movie *Girls Just Want to Have Fun*. For those of you fortunate enough not to have memories of the '80s, the film's title comes from the first hit song of pop star Cyndi Lauper. But that's about where the relationship ends; it's not as if Lauper appears in the film, nor does the song have much of a plot to appropriate. Moreover, the song as used in the movie isn't even Lauper's version. As an unofficial web site for the film quips, the soundtrack is composed of "songs you know by artists you don't know." *Girls* came just at the time that *Footloose*'s soundtrack, full of pop hits performed by the original artists, was one of the best-selling albums on Billboard's charts, so this was probably one of the last movies to use this type of cheap, *faux*-hit music. Producers would soon figure out they could pay for needle-drop rights to actual pop songs and then make their money back on soundtrack albums.

The film itself is a bit like watching the Muppet Babies sequence from *The Muppets Take Manhattan*. All of the faces are familiar, but look! How cute and ridiculous they are! That the movie takes place in the '80s, surely the most amusing decade of the Twentieth century (especially when it comes to teen fashion), is but icing on this most cheesy of cakes. First from our trio of actresses to appear is Janey Glenn (Parker), who hiccups her way through her introductory speech at her new Catholic girls' school in Chicago – the latest in a long line for this Army brat, although "the uniforms are always the same – even on Guam."

When she mentions her love of dancing and her desire to be on *Dance TV* (a version of *Soul Train* for white kids which is, whuddayaknow, taped right there in Chicago), she endears herself to Lynne (Hunt), who functions as the wacky, rebellious catalyst figure for Janey's pent-up passions. No, not *those* kinds of passions! Lynne talks Janey into entering the big *Dance TV* contest, during which a pair of new *Dance TV* regulars will be chosen. She also shows Janey her inimitable babysitting style, which involves placing the baby in the center of a pizza, but this detail is less crucial to the plot.

Meanwhile, a similar scene is playing out across town between two teenaged boys. As Jeff (Lee Montgomery, something of a teen screen fixture in the '70s and '80s) and his pal Drew (a squeaky-voiced Jonathan Silverman!) shoot hoops in Jeff's driveway, Drew unveils his plan to enter Jeff into the contest and make money selling bootleg *Dance TV* merchandise. You'll want to watch closely here folks, because Shannen Doherty makes her entrance as Jeff's sister Maggie, who has a hopeless crush on Drew. Why? We don't know. *Girls Just Want to Have Fun* is full of little mysteries.

Janey feels that her life is turning around. Inspired by Lynne's encouraging words, she gushes to her parents, "I have a best friend for the first time!" Janey honey, your best friend is Helen Hunt.

You've been screwed. Of course, later in life Parker will start hanging out with Kim Cattrall, so we suppose all these things are relative. So inspired is Janey that she actually attends the first round of the *Dance TV* competition and is selected as a finalist! And the hunky Jeff is selected as her partner! Oh, God! We're so *happy* for her!

Uh, we mean . . . *Lynne* is so happy for her. Lynne herself was rubbed out of the competition by an inconsiderate dance partner who stomped her leg – an "accident" which, it is later discovered, was engineered by the evil Natalie Sands, rich bitch and aspiring *Dance TV* regular. Lynne also had two other strikes against her, namely that she was wearing a big stuffed grasshopper on her hat, and she doesn't have Janey's ability to replace herself with a trained dancer in long shots.

Naturally, Jeff and Janey will go on to win the *Dance TV* spots, but only after their different backgrounds tear them apart, and then they realize they love each other, etc. and so on. *Girls Just Want to Have Fun* proudly declares itself an '80s movie by also including a scene in which the terrible trio of girls arrange for Natalie's very upscale coming-out party to be crashed by refugees from Billy Idol's backup band. And what '80s movie would be complete without the working-class dad who's sensitive to how much his son's dreams mean to him? Sometimes we just sit around feeling happy about the many years separating us from that decade.

If, unlike us, you have some twisted fascination with the ten years that brought us leg warmers and President Reagan, you'll probably enjoy the film a bit more than we did. With the exception of Michael Jackson's fashion and musical antics, *Girls* is crammed full of all the things that made the '80s unique: big hair, New Wave and punk rockers, and ALF! No, wait, we made up that last one. There's no ALF in this movie. Even if you're fairly neutral towards the '80s, you might get some sort of entertainment here, because at least it's got a beat you can dance to – even if the lead actors can't.

Cutting Class

(1989, Director: Rospo Pallenberg)

Cutting Class asks us to believe that its good-girl heroine is so desirable that Roddy McDowall would make a fool of himself to catch a glimpse up her skirt. While McDowall (rest his soul) was never above making a fool of himself for several thousand dollars, you'll have to forgive us if we are skeptical at the sight of him playing a perverted heterosexual school principal in a genre-conforming high school slasher flick.

Enter Paula Carson (Jill Schoelen), the all-American schoolgirl. Her grades are good, she is admittedly quite cute, and she has Brad Pitt for a boyfriend. No kidding: Pitt (who even dated Schoelen briefly after the film was made) makes his "feature film" debut in *Cutting Class*, and it must have been before the acting lessons. Pitt's character Dwight is the bad boy to whom our good girl is inexplicably attracted. He drives a red convertible with reckless abandon, defies every form of authority, and even tries to make it with Paula. "Not until your grades improve," she tells him. That particular line of dialogue reveals Paula isn't really even that good of a girl; she just has her price. Wanna break into the school's student records, to which Paula somehow holds a key? It's gonna cost you that family ring of yours, buster.

What Paula doesn't know is that Dwight has a shadowy past, including some involvement with Brian Woods (Donovan Leitch Jr.), the creepy student who recently returned from a mental asylum, where he was committed after the mysterious death of his father. Although Paula's father, the local district attorney (Martin Mull), believes Brian intentionally cut the brakes on the car that killed the senior Woods, no evidence came to light. Brian was quietly shuffled off to the loony bin and has recently returned to school with the rest of the loonies – er, teenagers. Paula catches Brian's fancy, and the flirting begins, much to the distress of Dwight.

You probably don't need much help guessing what happens next: people begin to die mysteriously, and Brian is the prime suspect. Paula notices some odd behavior on Dwight's part, however, casting some suspicion on him as well. Is Brian the killer, or is Dwight trying to frame him for horning in on his girlfriend? Or is there some third party responsible for the mayhem?

Sadly, there are no surprises waiting for us in this dismal little movie. The writer picks one of the two prime suspects and goes with him as the killer, despite the availability of at least two other wacked-out characters in the film. We would have liked to see the custodian revealed as the killer, especially after his inspired delivery of the now-hackneyed "respect your high school janitor" speech.

```
Shultz: I'm the custodian of your f---ing destiny!
```

Instead, the killer is revealed to be one of the two boys, and Paula must join forces with the other to fight off the true madman. Here we get the other line of good dialogue, which is doled out like a precious gem: "I am a murderer! Not as prestigious as a lawyer or a doctor, but the hours are good!"

Thrown in with the main plot is the recurring subplot concerning the Odious Comic Relief™. Mull's character is ambushed while on a hunting trip and the film visits him periodically as he stumbles through the swamp, an arrow through his chest. While an arrow through Martin Mull's chest would normally qualify as a good start, here it merely gives him an excuse to gesticulate wildly and make stupid faces at the camera. We can only assume that psychotic killer standards are slipping, as any true nut-job would have finished the job properly.

The real letdown is that *Cutting Class* has no reason to exist. We've told you the only interesting lines in the film, and the acting isn't nearly good enough to make up for the rest of the script. For a horror flick it's remarkably unscary, and though the allegedly humorous appearances of a dying Martin Mull suggest *Cutting Class* might have been intended to be a comedy, there isn't much to laugh about in the film either. People of Hollywood: Please, please if you're going to make a slasher flick, make sure you have either a funny script or a director adept at suspense! A lot of movies like this are made every year. Apparently there's a lot of cutting class in film school, too.

> There's no mystery to the fact that so many horror films are set in high schools: film producers know that teenagers are the primary consumers of slasher flicks and have guessed, rightly, that these viewers would enjoy the sight of a psychopathic killer roaming the halls of a high school like the ones they see every day. Should the killer/beast/whatever actually *be* a high school student, so much the better.
>
> In the 1950s and '60s, this meant a string of flicks that either combined *Rebel Without a Cause*-like teen angst with classic Universal horror traditions (*I Was a Teenage Werewolf*, *Blood of Dracula*) or pitted plucky young whitebread teens against monsters that threatened to eat their schoolmates (*Earth vs. the Spider*, *The Blob*).
>
> In later decades, teens gained an appetite for gore that pushed aside pyschological horror in favor of high body counts and unstoppable killers. Though this trend was arguably started by John Carpenter's *Halloween*, it's plain to see that horror movies concentrated more on splashing around buckets of fake blood than on atmosphere. Even initially imaginative film franchises like *A Nightmare on Elm Street* degenerated into "run and scream" stories featuring stars who weren't so much characters as potential victims.
>
> Remaining at the centers of these movies were teenagers, who were naturally ignored when they tried to warn their elders against the onslaught of the latest bad guy. No wonder teenagers flock to these films: they're just like the hapless experiences of high school, except for the fact that the adults in such movies usually lay in bloody pieces at the end of ninety minutes. The first *Prom Night* even put a teenager in charge of dispensing mayhem, although by the end of the series (*Prom Night IV: Deliver Us from Evil*) the franchise hit rock bottom by discarding the prom portion of the plot!
>
> Other teen horror flicks vacillated from peer-pressure-induced revenge horror (*Massacre at Central High*, *Slaughter High*) to supernatural monster movies (*Pumpkinhead II*, *The Addiction*) to campy horror "spoofs" like *Zombie High*. And let us not forget the rash of "self-aware" horror films in the '90s like *Scream*, which purported to deconstruct horror movie conventions even as the characters fell prey to them.
>
> Teen horror films can recycle their ideas because their audiences grow up and are replaced by a new generation. As adults, such teens presumably go on to find things that are *really* scary – like Pia Zadora.

The Lonely Lady
(1983, Director: Peter Sasdy)

One of us, who shall remain nameless, wanted to watch *The Lonely Lady* after seeing it nominated on an America Online message board as the worst film of all time. The other one of us, named Scott, thought this was a really bad idea. Nevertheless, we pressed onward, little knowing the doom fate held for us.

The Lonely Lady breaks all the rules of good filmmaking. It's based on a novel by Harold Robbins, it stars Pia Zadora, and it's about the lives of Hollywood creative types. These three elements, in combination, have been known to kill small dogs. Utterly predictable and painful, this is a film to inflict on your children as punishment.

We had a friend over the night we watched *The Lonely Lady*. Afterwards, she turned to us and said, "You know, I thought I knew what a bad film was, but this . . . I didn't know movies like this could exist!" We enjoy teaching our friends new things, but never so much as when those mental breakthroughs come after ninety minutes of non-stop exposure to Pia Zadora.

In essence, *The Lonely Lady* is the film upon which the infamously atrocious *Showgirls* was based, except that it shows more of the leading lady's life, both before and after the essential material presented in *Showgirls*.

Pia Zadora (the mind reels at the casting choices in this movie) plays Jerilee Randall, a simple schoolgirl living in San Fernando. She dreams of becoming a famous writer. While at a party, she meets the son of Walter Thornton, her favorite screenwriter. The young man invites her over to his house; she accepts, hoping to get a glimpse of her hero's home and working environment. They drive away with some other kids from the party, and that night she is assaulted by one of the son's friends, using what he finds easily at hand on the lawn. The "friend," played by Ray Liotta, is interrupted in his assault by the elder Thornton (played by Lloyd Bochner), who arrives in time to save her from an even more disgusting fate.

Walter's rescue of Jerilee begins a friendship between the two, and before you know it, the two fall in love. (All together now: *ewwwww!*) They marry. Their marriage falls apart when Jerilee's script rewrites actually improve one of Walter's screenplays and he feels belittled. Jerilee then goes through affair after sordid affair in her attempt to write her own screenplay and get it produced.

It is a very telling thing that copies of the novel *The Lonely Lady* published after the film's release do *not* use stills from the film on the cover to promote the book. Many other books do this: *Silence of the Lambs*, and *Jurassic Park*, for example. The difference is that *Silence of the Lambs* and *Jurassic Park* were two of the most successful book-to-film adaptations in history. *The Lonely Lady* is a film which most of its participants would probably like to forget. We wonder: if Ray Liotta were given a lifetime achievement award, would its presenters have the nerve to begin his film montage with a scene in which he molests Pia Zadora with a garden hose nozzle? Thoughts like these send us into mad fits of giggles, usually at the most inappropriate of times.

Despite her Golden Globe award for "Best New Actress" in the movie *Butterfly* (see sidebar for more), Pia's thespian talents are taxed beyond credibility here. As a matter of fact, the actress she reminds us of most is Kathy Ireland, whom the boys on *Mystery Science Theater 3000* described as being able to portray one emotion: dull surprise. Well, Pia was Kathy before Kathy. As Jerilee, Zadora gives dull surprise a workout you would not believe. The actor who got Jerilee pregnant refuses to have anything to do with her? Dull surprise. A weird Euro-trash couple proposition her sexually in exchange for producing her script? Dull surprise. A producer compares her script to her aborted pregnancy? *Dull surprise.*

On to the real pain this movie dishes out: skanky sex scenes. Tons of 'em. A plethora. A googol of them. It doesn't help that Jerilee seems to sleep with everyone in Hollywood, or that she's played by Pia Zadora. Or that she is supposed to be less than twenty years old. Every time she bumps uglies with some guy, something bad happens, as in the case of the producer who forces her to take drugs during the act. You would think she'd learn. (Actually, you would think *we* would learn to stop picking films like this, but we digress.)

This movie was made with so little art, it almost made us cry. The actors stink. Scenes that are unpleasant in ways we can't describe are thrown on the screen for us to . . . what? Enjoy? Why was this film made? Why did we rent it? At one point during the screening, we were rendered physically unable to speak, let alone operate a remote control in order to turn the damn thing off. Trust us: Jerilee Randall is a lady who *deserves* to be lonely.

Although our practice thus far has been to include movies with actors who have a few good movies under their belts, we've singled Pia Zadora out as a paragon of bad acting. None of her other credits in a starring role have been worth the film they were printed on, despite the additional presence of supposedly credible actors. Pia's putrid freshman effort as an adult (in which she was joined by Orson Welles!), *Butterfly*, netted her a Golden Globe for Best New Star, thereby tarnishing the reputation of the Globes for more than a decade.

After *Butterfly* came *The Lonely Lady*, which won her more awards: a record ten "Razzie" awards, which are given the night of the Oscars for scurrilous cinematic achievements. The record was subsequently broken by *Showgirls*, which earned its eleventh Razzie for being the "Worst Remake" – of *The Lonely Lady!*

Also hot on *Butterfly*'s heels was *Fake Out*, in which Zadora plays a Vegas showgirl who rats out her mobster boyfriend and falls under the protection of Telly Savalas and Desi Arnaz, Jr. This sucker nailed shut the coffin of Arnaz's cinematic career, but Pia went on to make *Pajama Tops* (a sex farce stage play on videotape) and *Voyage of the Rock Aliens* (an allegedly comedic rock musical) before her movie jobs dwindled to cameos and musical appearances.

To be fair, Zadora relaunched her singing career rather successfully, but she still found time to appear in movies like John Waters' *Hairspray* (undoubtedly her best work as the Beatnik Chick), *Naked Gun 33 1/3* (a memorable cameo in which she falls into a tuba), and *Troop Beverly Hills*, a frightening Shelley Long flick in which Pia appears as herself in a fashion show. Today, Zadora has forsaken a life in front of the camera for a life with her children, bringing her life around into a sort of full circle. Her very first movie role was at ten years old in the children's "classic" *Santa Claus Conquers the Martians*.

Are You in the House Alone?
(1978, Director: Walter Grauman)

A warning right up front: Such is our disgust at this movie that we are going to spoil its only plot twist. So if you don't want to know, or if you're really offended by spoilers, skip to the next review.

We picked up *Are You in the House Alone?* in the horror section of a local video store. That classification turned out to be false advertising, because *Are You in the House Alone?* is not really a horror film. It plays more like a twisted ABC after-school special with a really disgusting moral.

Are You in the House Alone? was made for TV in 1978, which is pretty amazing considering the subject matter. The movie opens as young Gail (Kathleen Beller) is wheeled out of a house on a gurney. She has been raped, but she will not identify her attacker. "No! No one will believe me," she protests.

The movie then flashes back to the months before the rape, and we are made to see how this ugly scene came about. While trying to make it through the trials of everyday life as a high school student, Gail finds a threatening note stuck in her locker door. Up to this point it could be a slasher flick: a high school student stalked by a psycho. The movie follows standard protocol by introducing a round of suspects. Is it the swarthy, Harvey Keitel-ish ex-boyfriend who dumped Gail because she wouldn't sleep with him? Is it Steve (Scott Colomby), her new boyfriend? By far the creepiest candidate is Gail's photography teacher, who tells Gail that she needs to look "sexier" when she models for her self-portraits.

Meanwhile, Gail's home life is falling apart. Her mother (Blythe Danner) wants to return to her old job as a real estate agent, but dad argues vehemently against it. This plot thread is later magically resolved without the inclusion of the audience. Then dad loses *his* job and spends his days boozing at a bar across the street from his office, without telling Gail. Why are we subjected to this? Apparently to pad the movie, because none of what happens at home has anything to do with what happens at school until the film finishes its flashbacks and we return to the present and learn the rapist's true identity.

Here comes that spoiler. The rapist turns out to be Phil, the well-to-do boyfriend of Gail's best friend, as played by Dennis Quaid. Quaid is appropriately revolting, so much so that we were amazed that of all the young actors here, he is the only one who went on to a successful career. What is it with teenaged actors who make their screen debuts as rapists? (If you've been skipping around the book, turn back to read about Ray Liotta and *The Lonely Lady*.)

The fact that Phil is Gail's best friend's boyfriend, of course, leads to all kinds of juicy character conflict. Gail has labeled Phil, the most eligible bachelor on campus and the son of a wealthy family, as a rapist. Here's where the movie starts to get really frustrating. Phil doesn't even try to deny he had sex with Gail. He claims it was consensual. Everyone believes him, apparently because Gail is known to have had sex with her boyfriend, Steve. So the moral is, "Don't have premarital sex, because if you're raped by a psycho, even one who leaves lots of evidence behind, beats you so badly you end up in the hospital, and even admits to having sex with you, no one will believe it was really rape because obviously you asked for it." The movie spends a little while drumming this moral into us, and then backs away from it by saying the real reason Phil won't be arrested is because his father is friends with a judge. So what, is this movie now trying to be a scathing indictment of the justice system? Or is it actually embarrased by its own crudity?

In the real world, Phil would have denied any contact had ever happened and gotten himself a decent lawyer. In this TV movie, however, he provides Gail with ample opportunity to gather evidence that he is indeed a rapist. When Gail discovers that another girl in school is beginning to get the same notes, she sets up a trap using a Previously Mentioned Plot Device: her talent as a photographer. Using a timed shutter and rolls and rolls of film, Gail catches Phil in the act of leaving a note in the girl's locker. He then discovers

Gail's trap and proceeds to attack her, allowing plenty of time for the eyewitnesses to arrive. Roll credits.

The thing that most disgusted us about this film is the way the movie lingers over Gail's trauma, especially during the rape scene. We are spared nothing within the limits of television censorship, and the resulting emotional distress, while perhaps an accurate portrayal of the feelings of a rape victim, is stomach-turning to watch. Perhaps it hits a little too close to the mark, as if the director simply turned on the camera and said, "Okay, Dennis, now go *rape* her." Some things are better left off camera, especially since this scene brings nothing to the film but some tawdry shock value.

Our final complaint about *Are You In The House Alone?* is its billing as a horror film. Certainly, it uses horrific elements, but from the opening moments of the movie it is clear this is a rape drama, not a horror movie. For horror fans, especially those who would be treated to John Carpenter's *Halloween* that same year, it's like ordering a steak and being served tuna casserole.

One of the tricks of the horror and suspense movie trade is to attempt to creep out prospective viewers with the title alone. Thus have a number of films been saddled with titles that may or may not pertain to their content, but which include questions or oblique statements, usually posed by the killer/monster/villain to his/her/its victims.

Examples? You bet we got examples!

I Know What You Did Last Summer (and its sequel, *I Still Know…*)
What Ever Happened to Baby Jane?
What's the Matter with Helen?
Don't Go to Sleep
Don't Answer the Phone
Don't Be Afraid of the Dark
God Told Me To
Kill, Baby, Kill
Don't Go in the House
Tails You Live, Heads You're Dead
There's Nothing Out There
Don't Mess with My Sister!
Sorry, Wrong Number
Faster, Pussycat! Kill! Kill!
Let's Scare Jessica to Death

Tammy and the T-Rex
(1994, Director: Stewart Raffill)

We have heard that Denise Richards won't talk about *Tammy and the T-Rex*, her debut as a leading lady in a motion picture. Why won't she talk about it? It may have something to do with the fact that her character falls in love with a dinosaur – but don't worry, she loves him for his mind.

Denise plays high school cheerleader Tammy, which allows for an opening scene set during cheerleading practice, which in turn gives her a chance to display her acting assets. Tammy is in love with a football player named Michael (Paul Walker), though her gang-leading ex-boyfriend Billy (George Pilgrim) still stalks her. Tammy also has a male best friend, Byron (Theo Forsett), who is both black and gay – that's right folks, he's two, two, *two* stereotypes in one!

When Billy catches Michael and Tammy together, he does what any surly, jealous ex-boyfriend would do: he drags Michael off to the wild animal park and strands him in the vicinity of some hungry lions, where he is mauled, but not quite fatally. Hurriedly slapping on her sluttiest outfit, Tammy rushes to Michael's hospital bed, only to be greeted by a mad scientist, Dr. Wachenstein (Terry Kiser). Unbeknownst to Tammy, Wachenstein is experimenting with robot bodies and has decided that he wants to transplant Michael's brain into his newest experiment – a robot dinosaur. The next thing she knows, she's slapping on her second sluttiest outfit to rush to Michael's funeral.

Michael wakes up in his new body and, as would only be natural for someone in his position, he goes on a killing spree. This culminates in a party scene in which Michael goes to town on Billy's gang. Soon the killing grows old, so Michael kidnaps Tammy. Once Tammy figures out Michael has undergone the Godzilla treatment, the race is on to find Michael a new body so his brain can reside in a receptacle more suited to loving Tammy in the way she needs to be loved. The balance of the film comprises many scenes in which Tammy and her T-Rex run from the evil doctor and/or the town's lone lawman. Incidentally, Sheriff Black happens to be Byron's father, thereby adding another stereotype to Byron's repertoire: the misunderstood son of the sheriff.

Tammy and the T-Rex is supposed to be madcap comedy, but the absence of drollery disqualifies it from the category. We're supposed to laugh at the shallowest stereotypes (Byron is effeminate and cowardly, Wachenstein is German and constantly exchanges double entendres with his assistant Helga) and low-rent pratfalls. Of course, the concept that Tammy might be sleeping with a dinosaur carries most of the "humor" during the film's last act. The only thing that's really funny is watching the film with the knowledge that Denise Richards would go on to be a star. The absurd ending carries no irony, and we suspect the film's original script had a different conclusion in mind for our star-cross'd lovers.

The movie is extremely low budget, so don't expect much in the way of dinosaur effects. The T-Rex is played by a full-sized prop most of the time, but it isn't a movie prop. It's one of those animatronic dinosaurs that show up periodically at science centers. As such, the T-Rex can't do much more than move its head a little. In that way, it's a lot like George Clooney playing Batman. In order to make the otherwise static dinosaur interact with the actors, some very unconvincing T-Rex gloves and boots are also used. It's a good thing, too – without those gloves, Mike's stubby little T-Rex arms would be too short to reach the telephone he uses shortly after his escape. Dinosaur lovers (who have already been spoiled by the glut of dino movies in recent years) will either sob in despair at the mistakes or have a great time picking the details apart.

Let's face it: the only reason anyone would watch this movie is because Denise Richards is in it. How does she acquit herself under these trying circumstances? Well, let's just say comedy has never been her *forte*. To make up for her lack of wit, the producers dress Richards up in some pretty funny outfits. Tammy can't afford to shop at Tramps-R-Us, so she goes to Sluts-B-Used. If this film were made in the '80s, we could at least understand the sub-Madonna look, but this film was made in the '90s. People knew better by then. Didn't they?

> Although this is far from the only black mark on Richards' cinematic resume (*Wild Things* and her unspectacular turn as a Bond girl in *The World Is Not Enough* come to mind), *Tammy and the T-Rex* inducts our young star into a more exclusive (if not quite honorable) club: people who made crappy dinosaur movies. Too many Hollywood personalities have made the mistake of thinking that the inclusion of dinosaurs will automatically make a movie a hot property.
>
> Dinos have long been an attractor of small children, but Steven Spielberg upped the ante in 1993 with the release of *Jurassic Park*, a monolithic hit which has since spawned its own sequels, including the sub-par *The Lost World: Jurassic Park* and the more tolerable *Jurassic Park III*. Following the release of the initial movie, however, legions of adults suddenly recalled their own youthful infatuations with prehistoric monsters and studios scrambled to capitalize on the market.
>
> Roger Corman's New Horizons company claimed to beat Spielberg to the punch by releasing *Carnosaur* two weeks earlier than *Jurassic Park*, but we're guessing the sting was somewhat alleviated by the fact that *JP* made 200 times as much money at the box office as did *Carnosaur*. Nonetheless, *Carnosaur* hatched two sequels of its own which aped better sci-fi movies (notably *Aliens*) and went straight to video.
>
> Whoopi Goldberg stepped into the ring with the execrable "comedy" *Theodore Rex* (backed up by such notables as Juliet Landau, Carole Kane, and Bud Cort), and the sickly-sweet *Land Before Time* animated franchise got a kick in the tail with seven insipid sequels and counting – which is only appropriate, since they were made by Amblin Entertainment, one of Spielberg's pet film studios. Full Moon Entertainment insulted the world's intelligence with the *Prehysteria!* films, and of course no one can dispute the influence of *JP*'s velociraptors when watching the 1998 Hollywood incarnation of the biggest, baddest irradiated dinosaur of all: *Godzilla*.
>
> Lest you think Spielberg began the dinosaur craze, however, let us point out the numerous dinosaur movies prior to 1993, including the original *King Kong* (remember the dinos in the jungle?) and a number of enjoyable Harryhausen flicks like *The Valley of Gwangi*. Here again, moviemakers repeatedly mistook the success of dinosaur stars as licenses to churn out crap, a statement quickly borne out by such catastrophes as *Baby (1985)*, *Dinosaurus!* (1960), *King Dinosaur* (1955) and *The Lost Continent* (1951). Call it Tyrannosaurus Blecch.

Cyborg 2
(1993, Director: Michael Schroeder)

We wonder how we will explain to future generations the nearly decade-long obsession America had with post-apocalyptic cyborg films. Does it really make sense to have cyborgs running around after the apocalypse? In most of these movies, running automobiles are rare. What are the chances that cyborgs could continue to operate under conditions that would destroy cars?

Cyborg 2 begins with the obligatory title crawl (borrowed from *Blade Runner*, another 'bot-centered flick) which explains the futuristic world to us, freeing us from actual exposition within the movie. Our ears are assaulted with obtuse expository conversations anyway, because it's cheaper to have characters talk about events than it is to actually show them. In any case, the title crawl (read aloud by Jack Palance) informs us that this is a future in which corporations are paramount and "cyborgs have replaced humans in every respect, from the soldier in the field to the prostitute in the brothel." Because this is a b-movie, however, we know we are only going to see soldiers and prostitutes. Post-apocalyptic cyborg movies rarely feature people from other professions in significant roles.

The movie then moves to a board meeting at Pinwheel Robotics, a top supplier of cyborgs, right after Spacely Sprockets and Cogswell's Cogs. The executives watch a man and woman have sex and, at the height of passion, the woman explodes. Beyond being the screenwriter's fantasy, this is supposed to be a demonstration of "glass shadow," a liquid explosive that can be injected into a cyborg then detonated at any time. The head of Pinwheel, Martin Dunn (Allen Garfield), plans on sending just such an explosive surprise to a rival company, disguised as an executive call girl. Frankly, this plan is about as over-complicated as the script could make it, but then there is also some sort of underlying conspiracy between Dunn and a distinctly non-Asian cyborg named Chen (Karen Sheperd). We couldn't be bothered to keep it all straight, and frankly, it didn't matter.

The glass shadow is injected into a pretty young cyborg named Cash, played by Angelina Jolie in her first adult role (her first role as an adult, as opposed to the kind of adult role we'd like to see from Jolie). Cash is allegedly the first cyborg with completely human emotions, but it's obvious that Jolie was hired for her looks, not her ability to portray human emotions. "Don't worry about it," we can hear the casting director intone. "If her emotions seem lacking, we'll just say she's playing a robot!"

Cash decides to make a run for Mombasa, the only place where cyborgs can live free to eat scrap metal and dream of electric sheep. (Once again, we began making up better movies in our heads as this one began to fail us.) Accompanying her is Colt (Elias Koteas, the *other* Robert DeNiro), so named because actual character names are too long and hard to remember. Colt's only motivation for breaking corporate law and aiding Cash's escape is that he wants to have sex with her. Actually, that gives *Cyborg 2* an honesty unlike that of other movies of its type, so we'll let that one slide. Colt falls in love with the winsome robot by the end of the film, typically ruining that honesty.

Cash and Colt are pushed and prodded along by Mercy (Palance), a seemingly omniscient cyborg who uses random TV sets as communication devices. Does it matter that TVs don't have built-in cameras, or that they're not plugged in? Not to Mercy, who makes mysterious pronouncements from every nearby screen with the camera pulled in close on his lips and teeth. If you thought watching Jack Palance in a movie was scary, try spending an hour with just his mouth.

On the run, our main characters helpfully explain where they plan to go. Following budget restrictions, they of course plan to go to cheap places like the "warehouse district" (couldn't it have at least been something futuristic like the "warehouse zone" or the "warehouse sector?") and the "old city museum." They are chased by Chen and a blade runner . . . er, *bounty hunter* named Bench (Billy Drago) who specializes in capturing cyborgs. The resulting chase/fight scenes make up the balance of the film, and they're all dark and confusing. We are treated to another eight variations of the final fight from

Blade Runner, though you could be excused for thinking the important part of *Blade Runner* was that it was shot in buildings that drip. The finale of *Cyborg 2* is a fight between Colt and Bench underneath the whirring propellers of an abandoned, dry-docked freighter. This sounds a lot more exciting than it is on film, because the propellers are about the size of dinner plates.

Cyborg 2 is a dark, unpleasant movie with little to distinguish it from any other films of the genre. If you must see it, look forward to the quiet scene between Colt and Bench that could very well be the two actors gossiping between takes, and of course, the first of many nude scenes Angelina Jolie has done during her career. Now there's an obsession we *won't* have to explain.

Of course, most of these post-apocalyptic cyborg films were inspired by *The Terminator* and *Mad Max*. Immediately following those two hits was *Cyborg*, starring Jean-Claude Van Damme. If you didn't guess it was a bad movie from the words "Jean-Claude Van Damme," we can assume you have never seen a movie with Jean-Claude Van Damme. *Cyborg* was directed by Albert Pyun, another name not usually associated with quality pictures, in the same way that internal bleeding is not usually associated with good health. Pyun has actually made no fewer than nine films dealing with some variation on post-apocalyptic cyborgs: *Cyborg, Knights, Nemesis, Nemesis 2: Nebula, Nemesis 3: Prey Harder, Nemesis 4: Death Angel, Heatseeker,* and *Omega Doom*. Somehow he missed making the sequel to his own magnum opus (designated as such because *Cyborg* is one of the very few Pyun films that played in theaters instead of going straight to video), but it's not as if the sequel's director has done bold new things with the franchise.

Cyborg films are a favorite of low budget action movie makers because they are so cost-effective. They allow the filmmaker to include the trappings of a sci-fi action movie (a robot) while allowing that robot to be as cheap as hiring an actor, and usually not a good actor, just a large actor. The illusion that the actor is a robot can be created in any number of cheap ways, including some cheesy *Terminator*-esque make-up, sound effects whenever the cyborg moves, or most commonly by letting the other characters *tell us* that someone is a cyborg. The cyborgs on the video covers for films like *CyberTracker* and *Cyborg 2* were more robotic-looking than anything seen in the actual movies. When robots do eventually take over the world, we hope they go after these moviemakers first.

Hercules Goes Bananas
(1970, Director: Arthur Allan Seidelman)

Arnold Schwarzenegger is often touted as a man of humble beginnings. The child of poor parents, Schwarzenegger even joined the Austrian Army as a way of adding more fresh meat to his diet while bulking up for the Mr. Universe competition. Those who have seen *Hercules Goes Bananas* (with the imaginative alternate title of *Hercules in New York*) can attest that Arnie's film career is no exception to the pattern of lowly starts.

In 1970, the Austrian Adonis was cast as Hercules. It's not difficult to guess why: Steve Reeves, a Mr. Universe twenty years before Schwarzenegger, proved to be the ideal Hercules in looks if not in acting prowess. Reeves' affable smile (and adequate command of the English language) carried him through the acting rough spots so well that he appeared in a dozen or so Hercules-like roles. Schwarzenegger, on the other hand, could barely string a sentence together in the language of Hollywood, so a voice actor dubbed over his lines, and his polysyllabic name was Americanized to "Arnold Strong."

Not that any of these attempts to make this bodybuilder more palatable to U.S. audiences could have helped this film, in part because they masked the very individuality that made Schwarzenegger appealing in later movies. The end product is a lukewarm comedy with the most rudimentary of jokes and a chop-suey plot that commits criminal offenses against Roman mythology, all backed by an incessantly annoying *bouzouki* score.

It's a nice day on Mt. Olympus, which is to say you can barely hear the traffic from nearby 5th Avenue. In this movie, the home of the gods has rather obviously been simulated in the middle of New York's Central Park. Hercules (Ah-nuld) complains to his father Zeus (Err . . . don't they mean Jupiter?) that other Roman gods like Mars are allowed to go to Earth, but he isn't. Eventually Zeus gets so annoyed with Hercules that he zaps his son to Earth as a punishment. We're sure there was some logic in there somewhere.

Hercules falls into the sea and is rescued by a passing ship. The ship takes Herc to New York City, where the real comedy can begin. Sadly, the comedy does no such thing. After a few misunderstandings involving Hercules' ignorance of what we mortals call "money," Hercules hooks up with a pretzel vendor named (what else?) Pretzi, played by Arnold Stang. Stang is a gifted voice actor who brought Top Cat and other cartoon characters to life. Here he's more of a Sad Sack, desperately clinging to Hercules for validation.

Now that he has a sidekick to guide him through the modern world, the comedy can start. Too bad the comedy has a previous engagement in a movie starring John Cleese. Instead, Hercules runs across some college athletes and humbles them. He also meets Helen (Deborah Loomis), daughter of a college professor. After some allegedly hilarious misunderstandings, they go on a date and love blooms. The two go on a horseback ride through Mt. Olympus . . . er, Central Park, and Hercules saves her from a bear that escaped from the zoo, or at least a guy in a cheap bear suit. This makes Hercules famous, and he becomes a professional wrestler.

At last, the comedy can work its magic, except it got lost on the way to the set. Hercules becomes involved with some mobsters, and then Juno (okay, they got her name right) decides to goad Zeus into sending Nemesis, the goddess of retribution, after Hercules.

Hercules Goes Bananas is a perfect testament to the fact that eight year-old boys shouldn't be allowed to write movies. We have no actual proof that screenwriter Aubrey Wisberg relied on his grandson for plot inspiration, but it's the only way we can explain the fact that Samson and Atlas come to Herc's aid in the final climactic battle against Nemesis and the mobsters. Correct us if we're wrong, but we're pretty sure that Samson is from a different set of stories altogether, and if Atlas exists, shouldn't he be holding the planet on his shoulders? Come to think of it, if the human race and the deities who watch over it are as depicted in *Hercules Goes Bananas*, Earth could probably do with a good bump.

The idea of dubbed voices in the movies usually calls to mind foreign films aimed at juvenile audiences, or Asian action movies that have been dubbed into English to relieve viewers of the awful burden of reading. We often wonder what stand-up comedians would do if they didn't have badly dubbed Godzilla and kung fu films to reference for easy laughs.

However, even "serious" films have dubbed actors for various reasons. One of the most obvious reasons is to cover the fact that an actor can't sing if the role requires it. Natalie Wood was covered by Marni Nixon in *West Side Story*, and even though Julia Roberts and Woody Allen sang their own songs in *Everyone Says I Love You*, Drew Barrymore's voice was a counterfeit.

In rare cases someone's voice has to be dubbed for health reasons, or because the onscreen actor died before the soundtrack could be properly finished. David Niven's voice was provided by Rich Little in *Curse of the Pink Panther*, which might be considered Mr. Little's only real contribution to entertainment – if only *Curse* weren't such a wretched film.

In Tim Burton's *Ed Wood*, Vincent D'Onofrio may have been a great stand-in for the young Orson Welles, but to complete the illusion his voice was actually provided by voice actor Maurice LaMarche. This illusion would have been more convincing if LaMarche didn't use the exact same voice to play a lab mouse bent on world domination in the cartoon *Pinky and the Brain*.

There are two embarrassing episodes of dubbing, however, that we should not neglect to mention in this book.

When the post-apocalyptic thriller *Mad Max* was released in the U.S., its star Mel Gibson was dubbed, apparently because it was thought that his Australian accent was too strong. That three *Crocodile Dundee* movies and a Yahoo Serious pic have been released in the U.S. unmolested really has to make you wonder.

Andie MacDowell's voice was dubbed by Glenn Close in *Greystoke: The Legend of Tarzan*, presumably because Andie's Southern drawl was too strong for the role of Jane. If only Close had dubbed all of MacDowell's subsequent performances – or if we're going to dream, let's go for broke and wish away MacDowell's entire screen career.

Critters 3

(1991, Director: Kristine Peterson)

As modern horror films acquire numbers in their titles, they are driven to find new ways to make the same monsters interesting in more than one movie. The easiest way to do this is to change the setting. This strategy has worked well for bogeymen including Jason, Leatherface, and the Leprechaun. The search for new places in which to conduct horror stories has become so ridiculous that it has become a modern cliché to set an installment in space. But for *Critters 3*, it wasn't yet necessary to look that far afield. *Critters* and *Critters 2* were set in the rural town of Grover's Bend, and *Critters 3* moves the ravenous puffballs to the city.

As the Sawyer family (father Clifford, son Johnny and daughter Annie) travels home from vacation, their truck gets a flat and they stop at a rest stop near Grover's Bend. While there, Johnny and Annie meet Josh, played by a very young Leonardo DiCaprio. All three of them in turn meet the half-crazed Charlie (Don Opper), the human who became a Critter bounty hunter in the previous installments. Charlie warns the kids about Critters. It's a good thing, because it so happens that a Critter has laid a bunch of Critter eggs in the undercarriage of the family's truck. Before his heart can go on, Josh is taken away by his own family, hopefully not to be seen again.

The Sawyers drive home to an apartment building filled with all those broad stereotypes that populated sitcoms and allegedly funny movies in the '80s. There's the tough and sassy blue-collar woman, the sharp-tongued fat lady, the good-hearted old couple. There are no other hyphenated residents of the apartment building, however, because Frank the maintenance man is actively trying to drive the tenants out so he can sell it to an evil developer.

Needless to say, the Critters hatch and invade the building. Things start slowly enough: Frank is the first to die in the building's laundry room. Soon after the comical fat lady is attacked, and everybody holes up in the attic to try and fight off the hairy menaces. Think *Die Hard* crossed with *Gremlins*, filmed by the creative minds behind *Beverly Hills Bodysnatchers* and *Assault of the Killer Bimbos*.

It bears mentioning that the monsters rarely do anything far from the edge of a horizontal surface. Money must have been tight and it's so much less expensive to operate a hand puppet from just behind a washing machine than it is to create a prop with an opening in the middle. Henson's Creature Shop these folks ain't. We wouldn't have minded this quite so much if there had been an actual story to distract us from the shoddy puppetry, but there wasn't.

Speaking of the plot, the situation in the apartment building is further complicated when Mr. Briggs, who wants to buy the building and put up a mini-mall, shows up and cuts the power and telephone, effectively trapping everyone in the building. Oh, and this Mr. Briggs just happens to be Josh's stepfather, who has brought Josh along to "teach him about business." Apparently this apartment building is on the corner of Coincidence Street and Plot Convenience Avenue. Mr. Briggs is killed and everyone else tries to get out of the building, which turns out to be very hard to leave.

The selling point of the original *Critters* film was its humor, but inspiration has become a little thin by this third installment. The biggest laughs are supposed to come from the juxtaposition of TV broadcasts with the action (Julia Child natters on while the Critters eat Mr. Briggs, women's bowling appears as Annie sends an ashcan bouncing down the stairs), watching the Critters drink dishwashing liquid, and Don Opper's Tarzan impression. We found it more amusing to watch how infrequently the background used in the rooftop set matches the exterior locations they actually filmed. When the characters are on the roof it looks like the apartment is located in the business district of L.A., but the real building appears to be in the suburbs.

Also providing some unintentional humor is Leonardo DiCaprio, who must still have been suffering through *Teenage Mutant Ninja Turtles* jokes at this point. A good four years away from his career breakthrough in *What's Eating Gilbert Grape?*, DiCaprio nonetheless spends an inordinate amount of time preening on screen with his trademark eye rolling. Our "special edition" of *Critters 3* would include new footage of the Critters feasting on the pre-teen hero while *Titanic* plays on a nearby television. Alas, our best ideas rarely make it to the screen.

Leonardo DiCaprio has the signal honor of starring in the most profitable movie to date: *Titanic*. But given the so-so performance of some of his films and the pure box-office gold of others, we began to wonder: what aspect of his successful pictures helped them rake in the cash, or at least some critical favor? Could it be that, in his better films, Leo's characters end up dead? Our analysis suggests that when Leo's character kicks the oxygen habit, the film is bound to do well. Sure, the female half of the audience is perfectly happy to ooh and ahh over DiCaprio's boyish looks, but you have to give the men in the audience something too – and we want to see him *die*.

Other heartthrobs have flirted with improving their films by removing themselves: Look at Chris O'Donnell's hugely satisfying death scene at the beginning of *Fried Green Tomatoes*. He got run over by a train! If only that had happened to him in *Batman & Robin*, someone might have liked that film – but let's not get carried away.

But in DiCaprio's case, history clearly shows that his films do best when he takes a dirt nap. He had a supporting role in the cult western *The Quick and the Dead*, and he got shot by Gene Hackman. Go Gene, go! Not a huge success, but a fairly well regarded film today. Leo attained star status in *Romeo + Juliet*, where as Romeo he was taken in by a priest's plot to fake Juliet's death. Is it just us, or were all the priests in Shakespeare's plays trained by the Legion of Doom? It always seems like their first instinct is to deal with a problem by spinning an elaborate web of lies. In any case, Leo went on to die his famous icy death in *Titanic* a year later. But after that he insisted on living through the much-hyped *The Beach*, only to see it limp to a box office total that was a mere fifteen percent of his greatest success.

Where should DiCaprio go from here? May we suggest he star in bio-pics based on the lives of Clyde Barrow, Edgar Allan Poe, and General Custer? If they make a movie about the USS *Indianapolis* he should leap at the chance, especially considering his track record with boats. And if he wants to stand on some train tracks, we wouldn't mind.

If DiCaprio's next few films also go the way of *The Beach* and he gets desperate enough, he could star in some future zombie epic. (*Romeo + Juliet 2: Back from the Grave*?) That would give him the opportunity to die *twice*, and that would make twice as much money, right?

Texas Chainsaw Massacre: The Next Generation
(1994, Director: Kim Henkel)

Horror movie franchises are known for degenerating as they go on, but this third sequel to *The Texas Chain Saw Massacre* is truly ridiculous. It does not continue the story in any meaningful fashion, but rather tries to remake the original film. Sadly for viewers, the only way it improves on the original is in the spelling of the title and the quality of the film stock.

Texas Chainsaw Massacre: The Next Generation opens with the last group of people (outside of a horror movie) who would ever get involved with a remote family of cannibalistic hillbillies: four high school juniors on prom night. After an opening card that mimics the first installment's claims to be a documentary, we are introduced to our main characters. Jenny, Sean, Heather, and Barry leave the prom early, all the while bickering endlessly to give us some insight into their characters. Barry (Tyler Cone) is a jerk who is cheating on Heather (Lisa Marie Newmyer) because she won't have sex with him. Sean (John Harrison) is a friend of Barry's who hangs out with Jenny, to whom Barry constantly refers as "a dog." At this point we should mention that Jenny is played by Renee Zellweger, who is about as far from being a dog as Pia Zadora is from winning an Oscar.

The four take a wrong turn and end up on a desolate stretch of dirt road in the middle of the woods, where they are involved in a collision with another car. No one seems to be hurt, but the teenaged driver of the other vehicle passes out. Despite Heather's claims that "something bad is going to happen," our heroes make the last decision real people would make in this situation: they split up.

Leaving Sean to wait with the car, Jenny, Barry, and Heather walk down the road until they find a real estate office staffed by Darla (Tonie Perensky). Darla seems to be obsessed with her own fake breasts, but she does call her redneck boyfriend Vilmer (Matthew McConaughey) to come help the kids out. Vilmer, who is the worst nightmare of every person who has ever called for road assistance, arrives at the scene of the wreck and snaps the other driver's neck. Then he chases Sean around the woods with his tow truck! Sean, unable to outrun one of Detroit's finest creations, dies beneath Vilmer's wheels. Vilmer, determined to do the job right, runs over the body eight or ten times.

Meanwhile, Jenny, Barry, and Heather follow horror flick protocol by separating while trying to relocate the site of the wreck. When they all happen upon a familiar-looking home, they decide to split up yet again, this time to check out the house. With the victims now separated into their single-serving portions, various members of the clan that lives in the house are free to hunt the teenagers down.

If you've seen the original *Texas Chain Saw Massacre*, you've seen this, but in a much scarier fashion. All the highlights of the earlier film are here: Leatherface impales Heather on a hook. Barry wanders around the house until he gets brained. Leatherface chases Jenny around the house and surrounding woods until she takes refuge in Darla's office, only to find out Darla is part of the cannibalistic clan. In the original film this scene was a big gotcha, but here it's a pointless revelation because Darla's connection to Vilmer (the new head of the clan) has already been established.

There are just two innovations to the story: Jenny, as the character who is taken hostage and forced to sit at the family's dinner table, *almost* fights back rather than remaining a passive victim. We say almost because the plot requires her to stay in the house, so she isn't allowed to fight back very much. In addition, this clan doesn't really seem to be cannibalistic. Instead, they are part of some kind of conspiracy to scare people, or something. Late in the film, the family is visited by Rothman (James Gale), a well-dressed Englishman who berates Vilmer for not making the "experience" terrifying enough. Rothman, we surmise, represents the ticket-holding audience.

This movie was so badly botched, even the people who made it refused to release it. It sat on the shelf for two years, hurting no one. But then this evil was released to the public by the source of so much evil in today's world: *Jerry Maguire*.

Jerry Maguire, of course, is the hit film that co-starred Zellweger, which explains why she looked so familiar in *TCM:TNG*, and why she kept telling Leatherface, "You had me at *hello*." When Zellweger and McConaughey became big stars in 1997, the release of this film – to video at least – became inevitable.

You can't expect much from the other actors (and you won't get it), but how do the future stars perform in this freshman effort? Zellweger acts like a frightened kitten all the way through, which is about the most we can expect with this script. She should also get points for putting up with people who constantly make fun of her looks. McConaughey, on the other hand, overacts to an extent that would make Jack Nicholson raise his eyebrows approvingly. Whether he's slapping himself in the forehead repeatedly or screaming, "Get her, Leather, we got some more fun today!" Matthew's intent seems to be give a performance so embarrassing (not only to himself but to the film and the profession of acting) that the movie would never be released. We thank him for the attempt.

Rothman, working tirelessly on the behalf of the audience, delivers a final message from the film's creators: "It's been an abomination. You really must accept my sincere apologies . . . I can't tell you how disappointed I am." Buddy, we're right there with you.

Mazes & Monsters
(1982, Director: Steven Hilliard Stern)

Tom Hanks is arguably the most respected actor working in Hollywood today. Fortunately for those of us writing books like this one, he wasn't always the acting/producing juggernaut we know and love. Practically everyone over the age of 30 remembers Hanks' early star turn as a cross-dressing yuppie in the sitcom *Bosom Buddies*. Hell, we always thought Peter Scolari was going to be the one to go on to stardom from that show, but what did we know? Hanks' first starring role in a "serious" movie, however, was *Mazes and Monsters*, a psychodrama that has not aged well.

Mazes and Monsters was based on a novel by Rona Jaffe, which was in turn based on the real life case of Dallas Egbert III, a sixteen year-old sophomore at Michigan State University. One day in August 1979, Egbert disappeared, taking none of his possessions with him. Egbert's family hired a private investigator, William Dear, to find the young man. At his first press conference Dear advanced a bizarre theory that Egbert had been obsessed with the fantasy role-playing game Dungeons & Dragons – so obsessed that he took a sword and went hunting for monsters in the university's steam tunnels until he had a fatal accident.

There were a few little problems with this theory, mostly involving the fact that there was no evidence that Egbert played Dungeons & Dragons with anyone on campus, but the image of a loner nerd pretending to be a medieval warrior caught on with the media. Egbert was found a month later and his disappearance turned out to have everything to do with his drug use and confused sexuality and nothing to do with Dungeons & Dragons (as Dear later explained in his book *The Dungeon Master*), but the more exotic image had stuck.

In *Mazes and Monsters*, Tom Hanks plays the Egbert character, Robbie Wheeling. Wheeling has just enrolled in college, and his parents remind him of the "trouble" he had with Mazes and Monsters, a game that is a mere alliteration away from D&D. But Robbie isn't at school long before he falls in with a group of M&M players, and we don't mean people who enjoy little colored candies. Robbie becomes the fourth player for the group, which includes "Maze Controller" Jay Jay Brockway (Chris Makepeace, his bodyguard nowhere to be seen), Daniel (David Wallace), and Kate (Wendy Crewson). A good portion of the first act follows Robbie and Kate as they fall in love in typical '80s TV movie style – in other words, happy times montages and sappy love songs.

Before you can say "commercial break," things go wrong. Robbie begins to take his M&M character, a cleric, too seriously. Then Jay Jay comes up with the bright idea of playing M&M in the forbidden Piquot Caverns near campus. This involves dressing up in costumes rejected by the local Renaissance festival and wandering around pretending to be scared by props that Jay Jay has littered about the abandonded mine. Unfortunately, Robbie has a hallucinatory encounter with a monster that leads to bizarre dreams and soon his cleric character has taken over his life.

One of the first things that struck us nerds is how little Mazes and Monsters resembles any real role-playing game. Obviously the filmmakers never bothered to do any research. M&M is played with no dice, and we never see the mess of papers that is associated with every role-playing game we've ever witnessed. Essentially, the players tell Jay Jay what their characters want to do, and Jay Jay tells them if they're dead or not. No hit points, no saving throws, no rolls against charisma to see if the serving wench sleeps with you. It's pretty damn boring. Also, the idea that you could play a role-playing game like this in real time in a dark cavern is pretty ridiculous. You'd be as likely to find a bridge tournament as a role-playing game under conditions like that.

The largest suspension of disbelief this movie asks of us is that the main thing driving Robbie crazy is his obsession with the game. Other than that, his life seems fine. Hell, he's even getting laid on a regular basis, which is more than what 99.9% of all Dungeons & Dragon players could claim in 1982. The idea that a role-playing game could take over someone's life so totally that it could drive a sane person insane seems to be widespread (though these days this belief has been transferred to computer games of various sorts), but has no basis in reality. If games like D&D really had such power, the nerd population of the world would be a lot smaller.

Eventually Robbie goes so bonkers that he leaves campus and starts wandering New York City. At this point the movie becomes the Tom Hanks *tour de force* for which we've been waiting. Watch Tom sweat and stumble through subway tunnels. Watch him mumble *faux* Old English platitudes to homeless people. Watch him fight a mugger to protect his little leather pouch of magic spells. If we could keep a straight face while doing so, we might even suggest that this material served him when, twenty years later, he played a marooned man in *Cast Away*. In this movie Tom Hanks is to acting as vinegar is to chocolate milk. Mixing the two will turn your stomach.

If Hanks were the only disappointment in the movie, we might have ended the review there. But no: Makepeace and the other teenaged idiots in front of the camera contribute to our pain by reciting phony dialogue and frowning in mock concern. Imagine an adolescent version of "Mary Worth," set in the '80s, and you just might get a feeling for the sort of universe in which Robbie Wheeling lives. If we had to deal with these petulant blockheads on a daily basis, we might take to wandering the streets of Manhattan ourselves. Add Robbie's wheedling mother and belligerent dad (Lloyd Bochner, the monarch of abusive movie fathers) and you begin to wonder why it took an hour of movie time for Robbie to flip his lid, and why the movie remains focused on the ill effects of the game. Sure, some lip service is paid to Robbie's missing brother and his unhappy family life, but the message is clear: get mixed up in medieval fantasy, and you'll end up a loonie Just Like Robbie.

Considering that loonies like Robbie go on to marry beautiful women, make twenty million dollars for three months of work, and win two Academy Awards despite extreme goofiness and bad hair, we're thinking hard about digging out those old D&D manuals from our parents' attics.

Graduation Day
(1981, Director: Herb Freed)

A quick look around the horror section of any decent video store will reveal many films like *Graduation Day*. They're high school horror/revenge flicks, inspired by their dishonorable predecessors like *Prom Night*. Why exactly anyone thought audiences wanted to watch the same story over and over again is beyond guessing, but that didn't stop studios from turning out the same movie dozens of times with different (and usually school-event related) themes and titles.

Graduation Day distinguishes itself from its celluloid colleagues by never actually showing the event in question. Although the events in the movie take place around a high school graduation day (parties, rehearsals, last minute exams, last-minute school pranks), we never see anyone graduate. No diplomas, no "Pomp and Circumstance," no grimacing principal in front of an audience – just a lot of silly music video scenes and a crazed killer bent on eliminating the members of the school track team.

Our story begins with the accidental death of a young track star, Laura, during a race. Her coach pushes her to the finish line, where a blood clot in her brain leaves her face down on the track. Flash forward to the last days before graduation, when Laura's sister Anne returns to town from her Navy assignment. Coincidentally, this is also the period of time when the other members of the track team begin to go missing, one by one.

Anne is in town to attend the graduation to pick up some posthumous honors on Laura's behalf. The weird thing is that she's the closest thing to a main character the film has, yet she disappears from the movie for more than forty minutes. The middle part of the film is devoted to the murderer's rampage, as the various kids are stalked by Steadicam™ shots and then dispatched. Every movie killer has their preferred killing method, and this one seems to like spikes.

The center section of the movie also sets up a bewildering array of suspects for the identity of the killer, including the coach, Laura's ex-boyfriend Kevin, the school's principal, and a crazy campus cop. Probably the most noteworthy thing about this part of the movie is that it includes a young Vanna White playing one of the school's students. Yes, folks, before she was turning letters on *Wheel of Fortune*, she was turning in lousy performances as a screaming teenager.

The most excruciatingly painful thing about the movie has to be the nearly eight-minute long musical number by a band named Felony. As near as we could tell the name of the song they play is "Gangster Rock," and it goes on forever. Because Felony is playing at a high school function in the '80s, the students roller-skate around the band as they play. And because Felony is a band in the '80s, all the members wear heavy female make-up even though they're all guys. At least we hope they were all guys. Felony reminds us of Duran Duran, only less talented. Yes, *less* talented than Duran Duran.

So students get killed for a while, and then Anne, after a long absence from the film, confronts the killer. Now if you remember the beginning of the flick, Anne is a Navy officer, so she should have *some* training in self-defense, right? Well, Anne displays some lame karate chops, but besides that, she displays all the attributes of the final female victim of any horror film. She stumbles and falls for no reason, she mysteriously avoids the safety of other people, and she studiously ignores the weapons that fall out of the killer's hands. So much for the fighting precision of our trained Navy personnel.

Fortunately, *Graduation Day* did provide us with two of the important staples of teen horror flicks: copious nudity and improbably complicated death sequences. Providing us with some of that nudity is Linnea Quigley, who practically made a career out of exposing herself in such films. Here she seduces a music teacher into giving her a passing grade. Imagine what she had to do for the *math* teacher! As to improbably complicated deaths, since it's the track team that's going down, the deaths all involve athletic equipment. Man, we knew pole vaulting was dangerous, but this is just darn silly.

Zombie High
(1987, Director: Ron Link)

Our initial hope upon seeing the title of this film was for a movie featuring mind-altering chemicals and reanimated corpses. You know, kind of a *Dazed and Confused* meets *Night of the Living Dead* sorta thing. That might have been funny, especially since stoners and zombies are both desperately in need of the same thing: brains. We would call such a movie *The Grateful Undead*. Instead, we ended up with boarding-school brats threatened with experimental brain surgery that converts them into Young Republicans. Think of it as *The Undead Poets Society*.

When Andrea (a twenty-four year-old Virginia Madsen) arrives at Ettinger High on an unexpected scholarship, her initial thoughts are of schoolwork, roommates (including super-hottie Sherilyn Fenn), and her boyfriend Barry, who still attends public school a lengthy drive away. Soon though, she becomes concerned about the doings of the faculty. It seems that normal, fun-loving American kids are turning into cold, success-oriented robots, which usually doesn't happen until their early thirties. Andrea soon gets wind that a medical operation is involved in this process, and is horrified when one of her friends dies on the operating table.

So what's a girl to do? Why, start a romantic relationship with her history teacher, of course! The teacher, Dr. Philo (vaunted TV and film actor Richard Cox), whose on-campus apartment resembles a leftover set from *Miami Vice*, begins to court Andrea despite their age difference. Andrea finds herself attracted to the older man, especially after he introduces her to the mysteries of the pin screen – a sure sign that this film was made in the late '80s. She realizes, however, that Philo is part of the sinister plot to deprive the Ettinger students of a crucial part of their brains so that the faculty might live forever. And in an amazing coincidence it just happens that after the school's surgeons remove that vital bit of brain they can replace it with a crystal which allows the school faculty to control the newly zombified students via radio waves. To paraphrase one of the policemen in the film, it's the craziest damn thing we ever heard. Will Andrea escape the clutches of Philo and the evil Dr. Eisner? Or will she be subjected to the operation and thus buy a minivan and begin reading *Woman's Day* years before her time?

About a half-hour into *Zombie High*, we realized two things. First, this movie hates closeups. Dozens of scenes go by without a single camera angle nearer than a medium-close shot. This makes it difficult to get a good look at Andrea or any of her friends, which would facilitate the process of telling one from the other. Sherilyn Fenn (later a star of *Twin Peaks*) had been on screen for five minutes before Chris realized it was her, and that's really saying something.

The other thing we realized is that the screenwriters watched a lot of other, better movies and tv shows while they were writing the script for *Zombie High*. Not only do they rip off a Woody Allen joke in the first twenty minutes, but later scenes put us in mind of *Coma*, *The Stepford Wives*, *The Dukes of Hazzard*, and *The Streets of San Francisco*, just to name the ones we wrote down in our notes. The plot was also suspiciously like that of the second Night Stalker movie, *The Night Strangler*. *Zombie High* features people from the Civil War era gaining functional immortality by consuming brain chemicals, which is pretty much the plot of *The Night Strangler*, and in both films the protagonists discover what's going on by stumbling upon a painting. It's one thing to steal a premise, but individual plot elements?

Just as we were prepared to suffer meaninglessly for another forty minutes or so, the strangest thing happened to *Zombie High*. It became mildly funny. It's almost as if the filmmakers sensed the true movie badness for which they were headed, and decided to go for self-parody after an hour of deadly-serious screen time. Scenes like the school dance, in which the zombie kids all boogie in step, actually relieved the sheer boredom that plagued the beginning of the movie. But hey, let's not kid ourselves. It's still a crappy little flick.

King Kong
(1976, Director: John Guillermin)

When watching *King Kong* (1976), it's tough to not think of *Godzilla* (1998). Both were modern remakes of monster classics. Both had lame scripts and a suspicious lack of big name stars despite big budget pedigrees. Most crucially, both used different special effects techniques than their predecessors to bring the monster to life.

Where the two films differ is that *Godzilla* (1998) tried to be its own movie. *King Kong* '76 follows the plot of the original quite closely, with only a few changes. What's amazing is that every one of those changes is for the worse. This isn't just a matter of updating. It's a matter of rendering the film silly and boring at every turn. Despite the thrill that monster-movie lovers might feel at the prospect of an update of their favorite giant ape, there are scenes in this movie that will reduce them to the level of despondent two-year olds, standing alone on a cold street corner rubbing the tears from their eyes.

The original *King Kong* followed a movie crew looking for nature-themed thrills. That, at least, explained what a beautiful American woman was doing on a Pacific Island. *King Kong* '76 follows an expedition by the Petrox Company to find oil on a hidden Island. Years of watching '50s science fiction films has taught us that women can't do real science, so we weren't surprised to see that none are present on the expedition. Instead they have to find a woman along the way, namely the castaway Dwan. No, that isn't a typo, that's her name, and she's played by Jessica Lange. She also just happens to be an actress. She was on a friend's yacht when it exploded, but because she was on deck, she was able to get to a life raft. It seems she didn't like the movie playing below deck. She explains:

```
Did you ever meet anyone before whose life was
saved by Deep Throat?
```

We assume she's some kind of *X-Files* fan.

You will notice that much of the added material dates the film horribly. Sure, today it seems a little quaint in *King Kong* (1933) that Carl Denham could achieve fame by making nature documentaries, but we can roll with it. *King Kong* '76, on the other hand, hits us over the head with its '70s setting at every turn. There are many references to "the energy crisis," and while a movie crew has a timeless glamour, the adventures of an oil prospecting crew don't exactly stir the blood.

Meanwhile, the film is so desperate for a hero that one has to stow away on the ship. That hero is Jack Prescott, played by Jeff Bridges. (Because it's the '70s, Jeff is even shaggier than Kong.) Jack works as a primate paleontologist, and he wants to go to the hidden island for which the Petrox ship is bound.

Once our characters get to the island, things go as you'd expect. The expedition, with Dwan (snicker) in tow, finds a giant wall and some suspiciously African-looking natives living on the Pacific island. The islanders want to sacrifice Dwan to Kong, their local god. They kidnap her from the ship in the dead of night and lash her to a ceremonial platform just outside the gates. Then Kong comes through the jungle, knocking over trees left and right. If the islanders do this often enough to justify building a platform, wouldn't it seem likely that Kong would have already knocked over all the nearby trees?

The plot holds no surprises. Dwan is taken prisoner by Kong, who taunts her for having such a stupid name. Although she comes to understand and even be fond of Kong, Dwan is nonetheless grateful to see Jack, who rescues her from Kong's clutches. Since the island is woefully devoid of oil, the expedition's leader, Fred Wilson (Charles Grodin), decides not to go back empty-handed and devises a way to capture Kong. Once on the island of Manhattan, Kong escapes and does some predictably stupid things.

We would like to be able to say that this movie might have gone over better if its makers had waited another twenty years for better special effects technology. Given the story and acting on display here, however, the goofy (but plentiful) special effects are the least of this movie's worries. Rick Baker's effects and performance as Kong vary from laughable to breathtaking. There are moments in which Kong is more alive and believable than his human co-stars, but occasionally a badly matted shot or a cut to the stiff, mechanical full-size version will ruin the illusion. It would have been nice to see Kong act a bit more like an ape (there's very little knuckle-walking going on here, further reinforcing the idea that it's just a guy in a costume), but so long as he's wetting down the already half-naked Jessica Lange in a waterfall and then blowing her dry with his monkey breath, we find it difficult to complain at any length about Kong himself.

To be fair, not all of the actors are chewing the scenery. A bit of slack-jawed wonder and earnest staring is expected from Jeff Bridges; he is backed up by Rene Auberjonois (one of the most underrated actors of all time) and a very steady Jack O'Halloran, whom you may remember from *Superman II*. Their good work is hampered, however, by the vapid camera lovemaking from Jessica Lange and over-the-top show from Charles Grodin. This was Lange's film debut, and it's no wonder that her career took a three-year vacation afterwards. Sadly, the same cannot be said for Charles Grodin, who was working again in no time.

The script offers no assistance; it is full of bad jokes, including a plethora of wink-at-the-camera humor. Grodin's character exists merely to be proven wrong five seconds after he says anything, and when he's not being stupid, he's acting dumb. "Let's not get eaten alive on this island!" he yells. "Bring the mosquito spray!" Just when we think his character couldn't be any flatter, a well-placed step from Kong helpfully shows us just how two-dimensional the guy can be.

The high-handedness of Prescott's dialogue irked us a bit as well. When someone remarks that the island's natives will be glad to be rid of Kong, Jack expresses the opposite opinion: "They'll miss him a lot. He was the terror, the mystery of their lives. And the magic. A year from now that will be an island full of burnt out drunks." Amazing, huh? Because usually you'd think that the presence of a 50-foot tall man-eating gorilla in the immediate vicinity would *cause* people to drink, not prevent it. But then we're not primate paleontologists like Jack Prescott. We were also a bit suspicious when this animal rights booster picks up an abandoned chinchilla coat for Dwan, and then compliments her on how she looks in it.

The worst insult, however, is the complete removal of dinosaurs from the story. When they looked at the original movie for inspiration for their remake, did the filmmakers somehow miss that the dinosaurs were the best part? The only other wildlife we see on the island is a very large and very immobile snake puppet that King Kong wrestles to a very gory end. Ugh.

Despite the bloody helicopter attack on Kong at the climax and the movie's inevitable failure at the box office, this movie had a happy ending for nearly everyone involved. Jessica Lange got positively vicious notices for her work here, some of which intimated that she should stick to her original line of study: mime. She later went on to win two Oscars for her acting. Rene Auberjonois got a role on *Star Trek: Deep Space Nine* and the lifetime income that comes with it. Rick Baker went on to win six Oscars for his work in cinema makeup, including the first-ever Oscar for makeup design. Charles Grodin has a cable talk show. Jeff Bridges is one of the most respected actors of his generation. And, God help us, producer Dino De Laurentis got a lifetime achievement award from the Academy of Motion Picture Arts and Sciences. Just in case you weren't sure the universe was a cold, unfeeling place, proof comes along.

PART TWO

I Need A New Agent!

"I Need A New Agent!"

As we saw in our first chapter, finding a dignified way to start out in the movie biz can be a challenge. Holding on to dignity can be even harder.

Hollywood careers would be easy if a good start guaranteed good results, but managing film projects can be like an Oprah Winfrey diet. Look at Sean Connery – he hit the big time as the embodiment of James Bond on the silver screen and became the envy of every man, the fantasy of every woman. There was no reason for him to make a bad movie, but we see him front and center in films like *Meteor* and *Highlander*. Good lord, he followed up an Academy Award for *The Untouchables* by starring in *Highlander II: The Quickening* just four years later! (Don't worry – we'll get to his biggest blunder, *Zardoz*, in a later chapter.)

We see the same pattern over and over again. Gene Hackman won an Oscar for the *French Connection* in 1972, and again for *Unforgiven* in 1993. In between, however, he made the ill-advised *Superman IV: The Quest for Peace*. Raquel Welch made a great impression in fantasy classics like *Fantastic Voyage* and *One Million Years B.C.*, but after that she wallowed in movies like *Fathom* and *Myra Breckinridge*.

Sadly, there is no sign that more modern actors have learned from these cautionary examples. Cuba Gooding, Jr. won an Oscar in 1997, but after that it was Pepsi commercials and the worst *Speed* rip-off of them all, *Chill Factor*. Claire Danes was supposed to be the next big thing after *Romeo + Juliet*, but what happened after that? *The Mod Squad*. Let us also ask the question on the minds of *Swingers* fans everywhere: why did Vince Vaughn think a remake of *Psycho* was a good idea?

A large part of this "sophomore slump" syndrome is the fact that while actors may be wonderful at acting, they are not necessarily the best judges of script quality. Once a star has risen to the point where she may choose her own projects, she may not find herself in the company of the same kinds of filmmakers who picked her out of an audition line. This certainly explains the case of Madonna, whose fame came from her music, not her acting. By dint of celebrity cross-breeding logic, she was able to choose her own acting projects from the start, and thus she made regrettable films like *Who's That Girl?* from the outset.

Unfortunately, it's not easy to tell an actor, ego newly inflated by public adoration, that his idea of a good movie is skewed. So much easier to blame the public for not "getting it," or the studio for promoting the film improperly, or his agent for steering him in the wrong direction. While it's true that many actors eventually get their bearings and find the films that suit them best, we're sure that an immeasuarable number of talent agents have suffered the wrath of callow movie stars who floundered after that first big break.

Getting In
(1994, Director: Doug Liman)

Aspiring directors looking to break in to show business are often called upon to make low-budget films which go straight to video. Poorly funded, written by the producer's friend or relative, and acted with little inspiration, these movies take up space on the video shelves of the civilized world, just waiting to be rented by some schmoe who sees a familiar face on the cover. These directors call it "paying your dues." We call it "making crap."

So when we went to see a talk by Doug Liman, director of the indie film hit *Swingers* and the pop flick *Go*, our ears perked up when he mentioned the film with which he "paid his dues." Liman was proud of the opening sequence, which he filmed for $500 of his own money. (The producers had no money left for the title sequence Liman wanted, so he was forced, for the sake of his art, to come up with the cash himself.) During those few minutes of film, we got a look at the people acting in this crappy video: Andrew McCarthy, Christine Baranski, Matthew Perry, Kristy Swanson, Dave Chapelle, and Calista Flockhart. That's when we knew we were destined to review *Getting In*.

To be fair, those opening minutes are quite good, especially for that kind of money. Liman had some great stories about the rat scurrying around the halls of the college psychology lab, and the cat who refused to chase it. (Instead, Liman says, the rat chased the cat and they edited the film to make it look otherwise.) Because rats refuse to move on cue, in one scene we see the rat dragged after the camera with some fishing line. Apparently the ASPCA wasn't on the set that day, and Liman excuses it by explaining that the rats were intended for consumption by snakes anyway. But beyond this inspired piece of guerilla filmmaking, *Getting In* is fairly representative of these tired "college hijinks" films that pass for comedy.

Gabriel Higgs (Stephen Mailer) is the most recent son in a long line of Higgs men, all of whom have attended The Johns Hopkins University since its very first class. Despite his love of botany, Gabe submits to his family tradition and applies to Johns Hopkins. Unfortunately, a mistake on his MCAT test places him on the waiting list, and rather than tell his parents about it, Gabe decides to try and convince the five candidates ahead of him to withdraw from the list. He begins with a girl upon whom he has a crush, Kirby Watts (Swanson, who is a long way from even the mediocre *Buffy the Vampire Slayer*). But in the typical "overcome by her beauty" mix-up, his attempt to convince her to drop off the list is misinterpreted as a come-on, and he ends up with a date instead.

Gabe next meets with Rupert Grimm (Andrew McCarthy), a morose type who gladly drops off the waiting list. Gabriel then breaks his date with Kirby, because he needs to go to New Hampshire to see Randall Burns (Matthew Perry, who is on some TV show these days, we hear). Randall turns out to be an idiotic frat-boy, and Gabe has to fall back on his backup plan, bribery. But Randall wants more money than Gabe can provide, and Randall threatens to reveal Gabe's scheme if he doesn't get the money he wants.

At this point something must have been cut from the film, because Gabe and Kirby magically fall in love. Then Gabe breaks into his parents' house to steal a valuable painting in order to get the money to bribe Randall, but he later finds this unnecessary, because Randall is dead! It seems that after Gabe visited him, Randall died in a bizarre lab accident. (Check out stomptokyo.com for pictures!) As Gabe and Kirby's romance progresses, all the other people on the list die soon after Gabe contacts them.

After Mr. Perry, the most noteworthy victim is Amanda Morel, played by Calista Flockhart. She dies after eating a poisoned pizza. That's right: we see Calista Flockhart *eat!* Some folks might want to watch *Getting In* for this feature alone, but we warn you—it takes place in a long shot. She might just take the bite and chew. We have no way of knowing if she actually swallowed.

The humor in *Getting In* is constantly undercut by the fact that the jokes are all punch line and no set up. The worst offender is Dave Chappelle as a computer nerd named Ron. Ron is supposed to have extreme agoraphobia, and towards the end of the movie this fact, plus the reason for it, come into play. However, the initial mention of his fear is either non-existent or so brief that we missed it while blinking.

Apart from a few interesting camera setups and Swanson in some revealing clothing, *Getting In* is a waste of time for its viewers, its cast, and certainly its director. While it may have helped certain folks involved in its production get into the film industry, we advise that you keep it out of your video player.

Matthew Perry will forever hold our enmity for being closer to Salma Hayek than we shall ever be while filming *Fools Rush In*. But the film that should have contained his finest hour, *The Whole Nine Yards*, was a debacle. This movie attempted to launch Perry as a comedic leading man, with his shaggy dog ways and some lame Kramer-esque physical slapstick. Why then was Perry cast as a dentist, one of the least likable of professions? And then they made him a *Canadian* dentist, which didn't help matters at all – even if it *was* intended as a joke. Maybe it's for the best that the only thing anybody remembers about that movie is Amanda Peet's sudden departure from her blouse.

If we've learned anything from the sitcoms gone by (*M*A*S*H*, *Cheers*), it's that TV success does not necessarily translate to movie success. Perry is hardly the only "Friend" with a checkered film past.

Jennifer Aniston's appearance in *Leprechaun* not only showcases her less-than-stellar acting abilities, but also her original nose. Let's just say the nose has improved.

Matt LeBlanc? Three words: *Lost in Space*. Before that, LeBlanc allowed himself to be upstaged by a chimp in *Ed*. He was pretty convincing in *Charlie's Angels*, but he *was* playing a bad actor.

David Schwimmer, despite his status as (arguably) the most annoying member of the *Friends* cast, actually ranks pretty high when it comes to movie roles. About the worst we can say is that he was "Cop #2" in *Wolf*. Still, he has yet to break from the long-faced sensitive-guy character we see in *Six Days, Seven Nights* and *The Pallbearer*.

Lisa Kudrow has the most varied track record, with cult hits like *Clockwatchers* to her credit, but also flops like *Lucky Numbers*. We're split on *Romy and Michele's High School Reunion* – is it genius or junk?

Courteney Cox - Hardly anything embarrassing since hitting it big, except not showing the sense to jump off the *Scream* franchise after the second film. Before *Friends*, however, she was the female lead in *Masters of the Universe*. Some things we simply can't forgive.

Amityville 3-D

(1983, Director: Richard Fleischer)

The scariest thing about *Amityville 3-D* is that you could get the mistaken impression that it was preceded by six films: *The Amityville Horror, Amityville II, Amityville 3, Amityville 3-A, Amityville 3-B,* and *Amityville 3-C. Star Trek* fans make this mistake a lot. No, the 3-D in the title refers to a short-lived three-dimensional movie craze, which ruled genre films in 1982 and 1983. Moviegoers attending these films were given a pair of cardboard glasses, and once the audience put them on it would result in an amazing effect, namely that the audience would look extremely silly.

Actually, it was supposed to make the movies' images seem to have depth. But that hardly matters, because you're only going to see *Amityville 3-D* on tape, and it's not presented in 3-D. No cardboard glasses are available to help raise the entertainment value on this one.

John Baxter (Tony Roberts, the *other* Ron Perlman) is a reporter with a decidedly skeptical outlook. In an amusing first scene, Baxter and his spunky photographer Melanie (Candy Clark) expose some con artists who use the mystique of the Amityville house to run a "contact your dead relatives" séance scam. Baxter then strikes up a conversation with the real estate agent who handles the house, and pretty soon Baxter has bought the joint for a deep discount.

Baxter is sure that the whole curse thing is bunk, despite the presence of a bottomless Hell pit, home of Ultimate Evil, in the basement. He announces to his ex-wife Nancy (Tess Harper, who is scary in any dimension) and his daughter Susan (Lori Loughlin) that he's going to move in. Susan even picks the room with the creepy eye-like windows as her own when she visits dear old dad. But darn it all, wouldn't you know it, weird things start happening.

Because this movie was filmed in 3-D, the one thing you can be sure of is that when anyone dies, they will probably do so with one extremity reaching directly into the camera. Our first victim is the real estate agent, who is attacked by flies (Ultimate Evil loves flies!) and dies of a heart attack on the stairs. Then Melanie is killed in a fiery car wreck, and in the aftermath her charred skeleton lurches towards the camera. The accident takes place nowhere near the house, and it's unclear why her charred skeleton would be mobile at all, but what do we know? We're not Ultimate Evil.

One of the film's greatest pleasures is the discovery that Susan's best friend Lisa is played by a teenaged Meg Ryan, the perpetual star of Nora Ephron romantic comedies. We divine that Lisa is a rebellious, adventuresome teenager because she wears a jeans jacket. Susan, being a good girl, wears a sweater. Weren't the '80s grand?

Lisa is intrigued by the house's legend, and spends about ten minutes playing "Exposition Girl" for newcomers who don't know the history of the place, which involves multiple murders and supposedly paranormal goings-on. She is so absorbed in the legend that she organizes her own séance with Susan, a couple of boys, and a homemade Ouija board in attendance. The house answers Lisa's question ("Will one of us die in the next year?") with a definite yes before ending the game by tossing the pointer (a drinking glass) into the wall. Deprived of their supernatural entertainment, the group of kids decide to go boating.

Yes, boating – because *that's* what you want to do right after being told by the Amityville house that one of you will die in the next year. Whose boat it is or why they steal it from a nearby dock isn't explained, but shortly thereafter one of the kids drowns, so Baxter and his parapsychologist buddy, Eliott West (Robert Joy) must rescue the teenager's soul from the demon who inhabits the basement Hell pit.

Amityville 3-D is by far the most entertaining entry in the Amityville series (but that's not saying much). This is mostly because it has a fairly straightforward plot and doesn't waste a lot of time. Roberts is always fun to watch, especially with his history as a Woody Allen regular, and the "before they were stars" factor (Loughlin later went on to play John Stamos' wife on the TV series *Full House*) really amps up the amusement value for audiences today. Also keeping things lively is the fact that all of those extended shots of objects thrust into the foreground (flashlights, boom mikes, even a fly – because Ultimate Evil loves flies!) make it apparent that the producers of the movie felt the film's success was riding on the 3-D process. Perhaps they were right: without it, this is just another goofy horror flick that happens to have some future big-name talent.

> 3-D films are often thought of as a fad from the '50s, and it does seem like the technology had its heyday about that time. Titles like *Creature from the Black Lagoon*, *It Came from Outer Space*, and *Cat-Women of the Moon* were fairly popular, but ubiquitous pictures of scrubbed-clean teenagers in '50s fashions wearing goofy cardboard glasses have probably done more to cement the association of 3-D movies and that particular decade in the popular consciousness.
>
> In truth, the 3-D gimmick has been trotted out regularly, especially in horror, science fiction, and other genre films. The need for ever-scarier and more fantastic sights eventually drives movie producers to whatever gimmicks are at hand, and 3-D is quite a gimmick.
>
> In the '60s, that meant the producers of "go-go" flicks got their chance to titillate audiences with the benefit of 3-D technology. Titles like *Mr. Peek-A-Boo's Playmates* and *The Playgirls and the Bellboy* were appropriately descriptive, but promotional tag lines could fill in admirably: the poster for *The Stewardesses* claimed that the film went "From 3-D to XXX."
>
> The '70s had its share of adult films in 3-D (including the follow-up *International Stewardesses*), but more interesting were the arty horror films like *Flesh for Frankenstein* and the Korean giant gorilla flick, *A*P*E*. You can find many of these pics in their "flat" versions on video today, but sadly the opportunities to see them in their 3-D glory are rare.
>
> The '80s saw something of a renaissance for big-budget 3-D movies, particularly in third installments of popular franchises. *Jaws 3-D*, *Friday the 13th 3-D*, and of course *Amityville 3-D* were released, alongside sci-fi tales like *Spacehunter: Adventures in the Forbidden Zone* (with Molly Ringwald) and the bizarre Michael Jackson musical short, *Captain Eo*.
>
> In recent years, 3-D movies have been relegated to theme parks and IMAX features; apparently the process is now deemed too hokey to take seriously. This is likely to remain the case until a truly talented filmmaker discovers how to take advantage of the concept without thrusting long, thin objects directly into the camera.
>
> …Will you *please* get your mind out of the gutter?

Trancers
(1985, Director: Charles Band)

Charles Band had a dream. He wanted to make a big, gritty futurisitic cop movie like *Blade Runner*. Though the mind was willing, the wallet was weak. So Band, director/producer/perpetrator of such classics as *Dungeonmaster* (1985) and *Crash and Burn* (1990), settled for what he could get: Helen Hunt (cheaper than a real actor) and Tim Thomerson (cheaper than most performing chimps) in a *Blade Runner* rip-off that cuts corners whenever possible.

Trancers tells the story of Jack Deth (Thomerson), who lives in Angel City around the year 2247. Luckily for Band, Angel City consists of a diner, a council chamber from an Elks Lodge, a time travel lab, and a beach with a matte painting in the backround. Fashions seem to have changed little, unless you count the fact that the clothes are all two sizes too big for the people who wear them.

Deth has "singed" his archenemy Whistler with his trusty laser gun, and has been amusing himself by going after Whistler's psychically controlled minions, called trancers. He has just retired when he hears from "The Council" that Whistler is still alive, and has traveled back in time. Whistler is attempting to destroy the benevolent Council by killing their ancestors in 1985.

Deth agrees to go back in time to "singe" Whistler again, just to be sure. In this movie, time travel is achieved through the use of a drug that transfers your memory into the body of one of your ancestors, which is on one hand a clever reference to *La Jetee*, and on the other hand much cheaper for Charles Band to film than an expensive time machine prop.

Deth travels back into the body of his ancestor – an ancestor who has just finished a one-night stand with Lena, played by Helen Hunt. The rest of the movie takes place in Los Angeles, mainly so Band doesn't have to spend a whole lot of money transporting his crew. After much exposition and fish-out-of-water "comedy," Jack and

Lena team up to stop Whistler, who is now in the body of a police inspector. Whistler has already started turning people into trancers, so their work is cut out for them.

Before long, a Yuletide theme emerges from this cinematic mess. Naturally, it's almost Christmas in the past/present (depending on how you look at it), and Lena has a job working as an elf at the mall. When Santa turns out to be a trancer, hell-bent on Jack's destruction, our favorite line is uttered: "Security – we've got trouble at the North Pole." There's trouble in this seventy-six-minute long video as well (short running times cut down on those pesky reproduction costs), with a sad punk rock version of "Jingle Bells" and several other lame Christmas jokes rounding out the holiday theme.

Hunt, whose teeth and acting have both improved since *Trancers*, probably had the most fun while making this film. After all, she got to drive the Thunderbird, wear the skimpy little elf dress, and drive her motor scooter through a window. Okay, it only *looked* like she drove the scooter through the window, but at least she got to take credit for it, asking the window owner to open the door on the other side of the apartment and then wishing him a Merry Christmas.

Our favorite Thomerson/Hunt dialogue exchange:

```
Deth (watching an old cop show): What kind of a
name is Peter Gunn?

Lena: What kind of a name is Jack Deth?
```

While we're at it, what kind of a name is Helen Hunt?

Thomerson, on the other hand, was given the painful assignment of playing Jack Deth, hair greased back, trench coat donned, K-Mart plastic ray gun at the ready. He is forced to talk incessantly about "squids," those people too weak to resist Whistler's mind control powers, and also must endure such blows to his ego as being forced to ride around on a Honda scooter instead of a real vehicle. ("Yessir, Mr. Band, renting scooters for the film will only cost half as much as those Harleys the writers wanted.")

In the end, however, *Trancers* is surprisingly watchable. We first realized that we actually liked this film when we began making excuses for the plot holes.

Scott: If they can send a gun and a watch back in time, why do they have to send Jack Deth back into the body of an ancestor?

Chris: Maybe physical time travel doesn't work on living beings.

Scott: You would think they would explain that.

Chris: Maybe they did and we missed it while you were complaining about *Blade Runner* parallels.

Scott: Maybe.

This actually continued for some time: every time something silly happened, we went out of our way to explain it for them. So we must have liked this film. We must have. And really, about the only thing we couldn't explain was the boom mike hanging down from top left during the scooter chase. ("No sir, Mr. Band, we don't need to reshoot that take. The audience will never notice! Besides, why buy more film?")

Trancers is either a mediocre science fiction film or the pilot to a fairly good sci-fi TV series. Given that *Trancers 5* is available and *Trancers 6* is probably in the works, the phenomenon has lasted longer than most sci-fi TV series anyway. The plot, while not watertight, is easy to follow and has a good number of action sequences. Helen Hunt is certainly easy on the eyes, and Thomerson is at the best we've seen him so far. We weren't bored, and it wasn't too painful. So, in the Christmas spirit, we're going to include it as the only decent film in this book as a preface to its execrable sequels.

Merry Christmas, Jack Deth. Merry Christmas, Charles Band. Merry Christmas, everybody.

Trancers II

(1991, Director: Charles Band)

Some of you may be wondering why we even started reviewing *Trancers* movies. The quick answer is, we saw that there were five of them (five!), and that they must have been pretty good in order for there to be so many of them.

Boy were we wrong!

This *Trancers* travesty follows six years after the original *Trancers*, with Jack Deth, cop from the future, trapped in 1991, and he's married to Helen Hunt, returning as Lena. Boy, his life's hell. Apparently, he's also doing well enough in the money department that he got Lena some much needed oral surgery.

Somehow, the trancers are back. In this film, we have even less of an idea what a trancer is than we did in the first one, and the script does not feel the need to let us in on the secret. Further sequels only introduced more conflicting information about trancers and their origins, so eventually we stopped trying to figure it out.

Anyhoo, it seems The Council (from the future) has sent Jack Deth's dead first wife, Alice, back in time (from just before her death, natch!) to 1991, where she appears in the body of a mental patient, thereby making it impossible for her to trigger the beacon for the TCL chamber, a device that will take Jack back to the future.

Luckily for plot expediency, the mental asylum in which Alice Stilwell (Megan Ward) is incarcerated just happens to be owned by Dr. E.D. Wardo, an eco-nutcase who also just happens to be the brother of Whistler, the villain in the original *Trancers*.

Much is made of the fact that Jack, played again by the inimitable Tim Thomerson, now has two wives. This gives Helen Hunt a rare opportunity to display her comedic skills, as she catches Jack kissing Alice, not once, but twice! Hilarious!

When you watch *Trancers II*, play this little game: Whenever Jack Deth kisses anyone but his wife, Lena, say the words "Cue

Helen Hunt." Then bask in the admiring glow emanating from your friends, who will be stunned to discover that you can actually control the images on the TV.

We would say something here about Megan Ward's acting, but she doesn't do any. To be fair, though, she's in the majority. None of the actors seem to be making an effort at anything besides collecting a paycheck.

Instead let's talk about the only thing really worth watching in this movie disaster: the one-liners. Let's face it, they're the closest thing that *Trancers II* can claim as a *raison d'être*.

For example, what other movie could possibly bring you a line such as the following?

```
"So help me Hap, the next time someone hands you an
exploding ham, I'm going to pass the mustard."
```

That's right! There *is* no other movie that could get away with that line! And no other actor but Tim Thomerson could deliver it straight-faced. Of course, that's not the only witty rejoinder in this film. There is another one. But on the advice of our lawyer, we now have to tell you that you're going to have to rent *Trancers II* yourself in order to find out what it is.

While you have that videotape in your house, be sure to watch the *Full Moon Video Zone* magazine-documentary-wrap party-thingy after the credits. Not only do you get to watch an interview with Thomerson, Hunt, and their co-stars, but you also get the coveted "*Trancers II* Bloopers" clips! Incredible! This is quite a bit more entertaining then the actual movie. Amongst the things we learned (we are not making these up):

• Tim Thomerson does one hell of a Mae West impersonation.
• Martin Scorsese and Ron Howard only cast their immediate family in their films. Charles Band takes nepotism to the next level.
• Tim Thomerson's next role is going to be a "different kind of character for him." In *Dollman* he will play a wise-cracking cop from the future who is thirteen inches tall. As opposed to his role in *Trancers*,

where he plays a wise-cracking cop from the future who is of normal size.

• Albert Pyun, a director and a regular member of the Full Moon stable, seems to be a really nice guy. Unfortunately, we know that he has directed such detestable films as *Alien from L.A.* and *Captain America*. This is the cinematic equivalent of saying that Jeffrey Dahmer seemed to be a nice guy, but you wouldn't go to his house for dinner.

• Various cast and crew members have a lot of deep things to say about *Trancers II*, apparently mistaking it for a good movie. In truth, our friend Amy hit the ol' nail right on the head when she said that *Trancers II* was probably "excreted from an orifice unknown to the sun." The last film Amy watched with us was *The Lonely Lady*. Her opinion of our movie choices is sinking rapidly.

Once we became familiar with Tim Thomerson's face through the *Trancers* movies, suddenly we began seeing him *everywhere*. His filmography spans more than thirty-five years, over eighty films, and dozens of TV guest appearances. Despite his popularity as a character actor, however, he rarely lands regular acting gigs or serious starring roles.

Thomerson's first film role was in 1976's *Car Wash*. This was followed by movie after movie in which he played bit parts like "tour guide," or someone's brother or boyfriend. Most often he was a detective or sheriff, as in *Fade to Black*, *Honkytonk Man*, and *The Osterman Weekend*. Later, Tim would go on to some fairly high-profile appearances, swapping lines with the likes of Tom Hanks and Mel Gibson in films like *Volunteers* and *Air America*. His TV guest appearances read like a hit list for shows in every decade: *Laverne & Shirley*, *Starsky and Hutch*, *Hill Street Blues*, *St. Elsewhere*, *Moonlighting*, *Baywatch*, *Xena: Warrior Princess*, and *Ally McBeal*, just to name a few.

Thomerson's true calling, however, was the genre film, and his career kicked into gear when he played Charles Band's answer to Han Solo in *Metalstorm: The Destruction of Jared-Syn*. Thereafter, Tim became a fixture in Band's new production company, Full Moon Entertainment, and not only starred in the *Trancers* films but also played the lead in the *Dollman* movies and countless other low-budget sci-fi flicks.

Today, the man who brought Jack Deth to life continues to work in TV and (mostly independent) film, although our hopes remain that he will someday gain the recognition he deserves.

Trancers III: Deth Lives
(1992, Director: C. Courtney Joyner)

Trancers III is subtitled "Deth Lives." It should have been subtitled "The Sinking Ship," because at this point you can see the good actors abandon the series while you watch the plot descend into the murky depths of confusion. Let us show you what we mean.

In 1991, Jack Deth (the irrepressible and gruesomely fascinating Tim Thomerson) is fighting for his marriage with Lena (Helen Hunt). His obsession with his detective work has led to the demise of their love life, and it looks like tonight might be the last chance he has to patch things up. So of course, an ugly android from the future named Shark kidnaps him back to his original time, many years after our own. There he is shown the dark future that awaits the human race if he fails his next mission: (everybody chime in here) Destroy the Trancers being created in the past!

To do so, Deth is transported back to 2005, when the trancers first start to appear. Lena has moved on with her life and become a successful journalist who is exposing the military's secret plot to create a new breed of trancer soldiers. In a weirdly prescient and metaphorical plot twist, Lena tells Deth that she wants nothing more to do with him, and sends him on his way with a defector from the military trancer camp to help complete his mission. Bidding him farewell, she leaves his presence and moves on to a happier life.

As we all know, Hunt herself left the world of b-movies and went on to star in a successful sitcom (*Mad About You*) and a summer blockbuster (*Twister*) before winning a Best Actress Oscar for snogging with Jack Nicholson in *As Good As it Gets*. We'd call that moving on to a happier life. Thomerson, on the other hand, stayed with the sinking ship and went on to play Jack Deth in two more goofy *Trancers* movies and a host of other b-movie projects (although, to his credit, he continues to work even after cutting his ties to Full Moon Productions).

"I Need A New Agent!"

Similarly, Art LaFleur turned down the chance to reprise his role as Deth's boss McNulty in *Trancers III*, instead moving on to perhaps no more meritorious but certainly higher-profile projects such as *Forever Young*, *Jack the Bear*, and *First Kid*.

A movie like this makes you philosophical. What is a trancer? In the first movie, it was a zombie created by Whistler through his psychic powers. In *Trancers III*, it's a soldier taking a special drug. And in *Trancers 4*, trancers are vampires. Why do we have this sneaking suspicion that if there were a Tim Thomerson fan club, we'd join? And why do none of the *Trancers* subtitles make any sense? *Deth Lives? Jack of Swords?* What will be the next?

Our suggestions:

- *Trancers 6: Deth Takes a Holiday*
- *Trancers 7: Deth's Back (What about his back?)*
- *Trancers 8: Deth Wish*
- *Trancers 9: Deth and the Maiden*
- *Trancers 10: Deth Be Not So Kind*
- *Trancers 11: The Quickening*
- *Trancers 12: Deth Becomes Her (Deth played by Helen Hunt in this movie)*
- *Trancers 13: Deth By Boredom*
- *Trancers 14: Deth On The Nile*
- *Trancers 15: Deth Valley Days*
- *Trancers 16: Lena On Me*
- *Trancers 17: Squid Pro Quo*
- *Trancers 18: Singe You Left Me*
- *Trancers 19: Jack of All Trades, Trancer of None*
- *Trancers 20: Deth Race 2000*

We could go on forever, but then we'd never finish this review.

Credible performances were turned in by the principal actors. Andy Robinson (better known to some of you as Garak the Cardassian tailor/spy from *Star Trek: Deep Space Nine*) was a wonderfully maniacal Col. Muthuh, the new mastermind of the trancers. He gets to combine two great genre characters into one role – the mad scientist and the mad military officer. We saw Robinson speak once, and when asked about this film, he described it as a "dead dog of a movie." Obviously, morale was high on the set. Melanie Smith, as

R.J., the defecting trancer, didn't make us puke, and that's about all we can ask. Tim Thomerson was, well, Jack Deth. Deth is a one-note role: singe them trancers, woo them babes, be hostile towards everyone else. He acts like a gorilla bucking for Alpha Male.

The other trancers, however, were pretty awful, and how could they be any less with the script they were handed? For instance, how often do you think the Pentagon puts top secret military training facilities under strip clubs? And how often do you figure they do their recruiting in those strip clubs? Well, that's exactly what happens in *Trancers III*. No wonder R.J. wants to defect. These guys went to the Charles Band school of project funding.

Suffice it to say that if you're into the *Trancers* movies because of the science-fiction aspects, this is the last one you're going to want to watch. Not only does the next film move on to a goofy medieval setting, but by the time we catch up with them, the trancers are a completely different set of monsters. Ah well. We can't say we expected much.

Viva la Deth!

After *Trancers III: Deth Lives* there were two more *Trancers* films, *Trancers 4: Jack of Swords* and *Trancers 5: Sudden Deth*. We're not going to cover those in detail in this book because Charles Band wasn't able to trick any famous people into starring in them. It didn't stop the two films (produced at the same time in Romania, so they feature all the same cast and crew) from being a waste of talent.

The movies were directed by David Nutter, who would later make a name for himself helming some of the best episodes of *The X-Files*, *Millennium*, and *Dark Angel*, all TV shows on the Fox network.

Trancers 4 and *5* were written by Peter David, a writer best known for scripting several comic book series, including *The Incredible Hulk*, *Aquaman*, and the most recent incarnations of *Supergirl* and *Captain Marvel*. David is renowned for his ability to bring a new spin to stale characters, but his scripts for these two movies move Jack Deth to a medieval fantasy world, and it doesn't really work.

If you find yourself fascinated with the *Trancers* franchise, however, both movies are worth renting for Thomerson's trademark surliness, an occasional witty one-liner from Peter David, and the *Video Zone* magazine featurette with behind-the-scenes tomfoolery.

Anaconda

(1997, Director: Luis Llosa)

When a movie wants to get on our bad side, all it has to do is kill off our favorite character in the first scene. It happened in *Robin Hood: Prince of Thieves*, when Brian Blessed picked up a big sword to fight the bad guys, and was seen later only as a hanging corpse. It happened again in *Congo* when Bruce Campbell was killed by a POV shot mere minutes after the trailers ended. Now we have *Anaconda*, which teases us with the presence of Danny Trejo, one of Hollywood's most entertaining character actors. Sadly, Danny's character puts a gun to his own head before anybody else in the cast even shows up. Danny was probably trying to tell us something, but we were too stupid to figure it out until way, way too late.

If this had been a movie about Danny Trejo fighting a giant snake, we probably would have liked it a lot more. Instead, *Anaconda* pits the snakes against an ethnically diverse group of documentary filmmakers. On the Amazon, and looking to make a film about the Blair Witch, our filmmakers include Jennifer Lopez as director Terri Flores, Ice Cube as cameraman Danny Rich, and Jonathan Hyde as narrator Warren Westridge. There are a couple of other people along too, mainly so there will plenty of victims around for the snakes.

As they chug down the river on their rickety hired boat, they pick up a shady character named Paul Sarone, played by Jon Voight. Voight seems to base his performance on the captain of the *Rita* in *Creature from the Black Lagoon*. You remember him, he claimed that the catfish in the river were "keelers." As a matter of fact, all the creatures of the Amazon were "keelers" according to him. Paul's equivalent statement is that the "river has a thousand ways to kill you." He, of course, is the film's villain, an avaricious snake hunter who has manipulated the unknowing filmmakers into becoming the bait for his next set of slithery targets. Voight obviously has more fun than anyone else in the cast (save, perhaps, Eric Stoltz, whose character is mercifully comatose for the the last half of the film), strutting about with an evil leer on his face and a machete in his hand.

As entertaining as Voight might seem, the rest of the cast and the stupid plot crush the life out of *Anaconda* more effectively than could any snake. This is the dumbest bunch of documentary filmmakers ever to exist, certainly dumber than should have been allowed to take a trip down the Amazon. Several of the characters are even supposed to be experts in this sort of adventuring, but in general they end up just as dead as the city folk, victims to the snakes and their Amazing Yo-Yo Snake Action™. Not that this was much of a disappointment, since the actors on screen are turning in half-hearted performances at best. Kari Wuhrer seems to be trying to shed her T&A film image, but sadly, not her clothing. Hyde's largest contribution was the laugh we had when we saw the rest of his filmography. Jennifer Lopez had better line delivery as a Fly Girl.

Why is Lopez in this film, anyway? For most of *Anaconda*'s running time, it seemed to us that Lopez and Voight were engaged in a steel cage match to see who could damage their career more. Lopez has to be the winner, just because her career is still ahead of her. Voight (whose roles of late have run the gamut from Hispanic sleazes to Caucasian sleazes to Native American sleazes) has already had his career, and can now afford to be in bad movies and have fun doing it. The fact that Lopez went on to be in *Out of Sight*, on the other hand, should be considered a miracle.

Perhaps the only thing besides Voight that didn't disappoint us was the film's liberal use of the snakes themselves. Too frequently, the monster effect in a monster film is too expensive or too hokey to show regularly during the course of the movie. Not so with the anacondas, who spend the final third of the film terrorizing the remaining members of the crew. These animatronic and computerized reptiles have been rendered well, and we get some nice good looks at them. The problem is that we don't think anacondas actually move like that – do they really zip around so quickly, and can they really defy gravity by coiling around nothing? We weren't kidding when we called it Amazing Yo-Yo Snake Action™. Note to Hollywood:

even super-strong creatures need some leverage with which to work. *Anaconda* also informs us up front that anacondas sometimes spit up what they eat, just so they can eat it again. This isn't true, and even if it were, we doubt that snakes would projectile-vomit entire monkeys or people around for dramatic effect.

We would love to suggest another, better giant snake movie, but we couldn't think of one. So if you really need to see a movie that delivers on the giant snakes, *Anaconda* is for you. Anyone else will want to avoid it like a projectile-vomited monkey carcass.

There may be no better way for an actor to embarrass himself than to appear in a giant snake film. After the surprise success of *Anaconda* (coming soon – *Anaconda 2!*) giant reptile movies seemed like a good idea. Now, video rental stores all over the country are lousy with giant reptile movies, like *Crocodile*, *Blood Surf*, and *Komodo*.

Before *Anaconda*, there was *Curse II: The Bite*, a sequel in name only to the Lovecraft-inspired *The Curse*. A radioactive snake bites a teenager, who subsequently decides to fight crime as Snake-Man! No, we're joking. The teenager slowly mutates into a horrible monster for ninety minutes, and his hand turns into a snake head. The only thing in the movie scarier than the transformation is Jamie Farr.

Dirk Benedict undergoes a similar change in *SSSSSSS*. His character, the assistant of a scientist obsessed with the survival capabilities of snakes, is given "venom treatments" which produce some rather startling dermatological (or should that be herpetological?) results. Still, it was better than most *A-Team* episodes.

Shortly after *Anaconda* came *King Cobra*, a staggeringly incompetent film directed by Hillenbrand brothers David and Scott. Pat Morita and Erik Estrada put in time on this stinker about a genetically engineered cobra. Sadly, the combined might of Officer Ponch and Mr. Miyagi can do little to save this bastard creation.

In 2001, Hollywood hatched *Python*, wherein a giant, acid-spitting snake terrorizes a small town. Robert Englund (now taking any part he can get since the death of the *Nightmare on Elm Street* franchise) plays yet another snake-loving scientist, but in an epochally bad performance as a commando leader, pretty boy Casper Van Dien steals the show. Or rather, Van Dien's unrecognizable accent distracts viewers even from a monstrous reptile.

66 *Reel Shame*

The Tower
(1993, Director: Richard Kletter)

The first time we saw *The Tower*, it was on the Sci-Fi Channel, which is actually the only place you can see it these days, because it hasn't found its way to video yet. Now, before you start complaining about a review of something you can't rent, rest assured that the Sci-Fi Channel plays this movie a lot. It will be on again, and all you have to do is figure out when and then find a friend who subscribes to that cable channel.

The Tower caught our attention because it stars Paul Reiser, who starred in the TV sitcom *Mad About You* with Helen Hunt, one of our favorite whipping-girls in the b-movie world. When we looked in the *TV Guide* to learn the name of the movie, we discovered that Reiser was billed under the name "Ray Palsley." Ray Palsley? Hooo boy, when the shameless Paul Reiser changes his name for a flick, you know it's gonna be crap of the highest (or should that be lowest?) order! Since then, the credits appear to have been changed back to Paul Reiser, but we'll never forget the hilarity of that afternoon.

We don't know if Reiser has kept this movie from getting out on video, but if we were the ones in this stinker, we'd do all we could to keep it off the market, too. But when *The Tower* appeared on Sci-Fi again, we caught it on tape and decided to give it a review.

To be fair, *The Tower* has reasonably high production values, given that it was made for TV. It's a fairly standard iteration of the "killer-android-on-the-loose" subgenre known as the "killer building." Reiser's character gets stuck in the building after hours and must survive its attempts to kill him in the name of security. The main problems are a plot with little swiss-cheese holes all through it, and that the film is trying to be really annoying.

Problem #1: Reiser's character, Tony Minot (pronounced "my-not," but constantly mispronounced as "mee-noh"), can't seem to figure out that he's one of the most cursed individuals on the planet. Not only does he have a silly phonetic palindrome for a name, but he's also just gotten a job in the most depressing office building in the country. And when his boss gets trapped in an overheating sauna, he diddles with the computer system in a vain attempt to turn the heat off rather than simply shooting the lock off the door with the boss' gun. This guy doesn't triumph over the odds – he pulls bonehead moves and gets phenomenally lucky (despite being such a cursed individual, as previously mentioned).

Problem #2: All of the characters have the John Fogerty tune "Bad Moon Rising" on the brain. No wonder the building wants to kill them: they're annoying! We hear this tune in so many variations throughout the movie that Fogerty's net worth probably doubled in value from the royalties.

Problem #3: The relationship between Paul Reiser and the other main character, Linda, is never defined. They appear to be old friends at times. In other scenes, Linda states that she hardly knows Tony. The entire situation is cloaked in a haze of mystery that we never penetrated. Or maybe we just didn't care. Yeah, that was it.

Problem #4: At one point, Tony is trapped on a floor that is on fire, and the building has started to pump away the oxygen to kill the fire as well as Tony and Linda. Amazingly, the only heavy object Tony can find is a bowling ball, which he attempts to bowl through a window, rather than the more sensible strategy of using it like a bludgeon. Speaking of which, wouldn't *Bowling for Oxygen* make a neat game show? When the window breaks, there should have been an enormous fiery backdraft as the oxygen-rich air hit the fire, but the writers of the film obviously didn't spare much thought to the physics of the situation.

Our real beef with this film, however, is the building itself. What kind of architect gives his building the ability to use deadly force in the name of security? Who ever heard of elevator doors that can close with great enough force to kill someone? And who the heck equips an office building with a self-destruct mechanism? "Toilets will explode in ten . . . nine . . ."

The offices themselves are darn depressing. Everything is cast in dark, metallic tones. We hope the office windows automatically lock – we wanted to toss ourselves out of one after about ten minutes, and all we had to do was watch a movie that was set there. Pity the poor schmucks who might spend forty hours a week in such a place.

The darkest moment of our lives – we mean, of the film – is when Linda and Tony get trapped in an elevator, and decide to tough it out by doing what all people in the movies trapped in elevators do: they sing. And what do they sing? That's right, "Bad Moon Rising!" If one could chart Paul Reiser's career, this one scene would be the absolute nadir. And since we're talking about Paul Reiser, that's really saying something.

The Tower is *Die Hard* without any bad guys. One lone yutz runs around an office building, breaking things. The boredom made *us* want to break things, like Reiser's nose. If you'd like the opportunity to point at Paul Reiser and laugh at him, not with him, this is the movie for you.

No Way Back
(1996, Director: Frank Cappello)

We're pretty sure that the title *No Way Back* refers to the career of its principal actor, Russell Crowe. By this time Crowe had been sucked into the Hollywood movie machine and was making mass-market pap like *Virtuosity*, and there was certainly no way back to his early days of indie Australian films like *The Crossing*. Fortunately he already had the energetic Sam Raimi western *The Quick and the Dead* to his name, and Crowe's performance in *L.A. Confidential* would soon put him on the map as a serious actor. But the experience of shooting a stinker like *No Way Back* must have filled the New Zealander (by way of Australia) with some doubt, especially when he met his co-star: Helen Slater.

Slater, who established her schlock-movie cred in the big-budget flop known as *Supergirl*, had since clawed her way up in acting respectability with movies like *Ruthless People* and *The Legend of Billie Jean*. Unfortunately, she found her way back to *Supergirl* level with a string of TV movies and this very confused little film.

We say "confused" because it's difficult to divine the flick's intent. Is it an action film? Well, sort of – there *is* a lot of shooting. Is it a spoof of action films? In that case, wouldn't it be funnier? Is it a cop film? If so, why does it spend so much time busting on cops?

In the pre-credit sequence, we see a Japanese man beaten to death by a racist skinhead gang. See what we mean about not being funny? But after the credits, things get weird. The FBI is trying to bug the apartment of that same gang's leader, who is the son of a rich, important man. The head of the operation is Zack Grant, played by Crowe, who has apparently stolen Antonio Banderas' hair. Grant's plan is to send in a rookie agent (Kelly Hu, who was on the TV series *Martial Law*) undercover as a prostitute. She is supposed to go up, let down her hair and drop a bugged hairpin, then retire to the bathroom before anything can happen. There she's supposed to take a pill to induce vomiting, because as Grant says, "No man is going to want you around if he thinks you're going to throw up during orgasm." We can think of some people in Internet chat rooms who might dispute this claim, but it seems to give the rookie some solace as she enters the building.

Once up in the apartment, the rookie, Seiko, drops the hairpin down the toilet, grabs a gun, and does a *La Femme Nikita* on everybody in the apartment. Alerted by the sound of gunfire, Grant enters the apartment, gun drawn, and finds Seiko standing by a window. When Grant asks her what happened, she jumps backwards through the window and lands directly on top of the rental truck Grant's team was using for surveillance. If her name had been Timex, she might have survived that fall. But as it is she dies, and with her dying breath she drops the live grenade(!) she was holding, which in turn rolls *under* the truck, blowing it up really good.

The skinhead's father, a mobster named Frank Serlano (played by Michael Lerner, wearing a mustache way funnier than anything in *The Beautician and the Beast*), attends his son's autopsy before vowing revenge. Zack has determined that Seiko may be connected to a Yakuza gun dealer in New York named Yuji Kobayashi (Etsushi Toyokawa, who was in *Angel Dust*). Going undercover with a Japanese partner, Zack arranges to meet with the Yakuza. The rendezvous is held in a Manhattan warehouse where motorcycles are hung from the rafters, straddled by beautiful women, and sold to the highest bidder. Say what you will about the Yakuza: they know marketing.

In any case, that Zack Grant magic is still working and the auction turns into a bloodbath. This is partly because the Yakuza try to kill Grant and his partner, partly because Serlano's skinhead goons have followed Grant to the meeting. Nearly everyone ends up dead, although Grant somehow captures Yuji alive. Wasting not a moment of grief or even a single word on the fact that his tactical planning has led to the death of another FBI agent, Grant drives Yuji to the nearest airport and proceeds to take his prisoner back to Los Angeles on a civilian flight with no back-up. By now you will have figured out that Zack Grant is the Dudley Do-Right of FBI agents.

Enter Helen Slater as the ditsy flight attendant. We imagine her screen directions went something like this:

Director: Ever see the movie *Airplane*? Well, we couldn't get Julie Hagerty, so we want you to duplicate her character as much as you can.

Slater: Okey-dokey!

Slater's character, Mary, exchanges some verbal barbs with the acerbic Grant, foreshadowing the fact that they'll be spending the rest of the film together. Sure enough, Serlano has smuggled a goon with a plastic gun onto the plane. Mayhem ensues, and the plane lands rather clumsily in the middle of nowhere. Yuji escapes in the confusion and takes Mary hostage. Grant pursues and thus begins an exhausting moronic series of situational flip-flops as Grant and Yuji each gain the upper hand over the other.

To call this film stupid would do a disservice to the word "stupid." We could make up stories about the film's auteur, insinuating that somehow a Hollywood movie set carpenter got his pet project greenlighted, but we don't have to: the truth is that a movie set *greenskeeper* got his pet project greenlighted. Yes, somewhere between acting as construction foreman on *Independence Day* and doing time as the head greensman on *Dr. Dolittle*, Frank Cappello's dream of writing and directing his own film came true. We have no problems with working one's way up the Hollywood ladder, but Frank: was this *really* the script on which you wanted to spend your big chance?

Shakes the Clown
(1996, Director: Bob Goldthwait)

Here's a situation we've all been in: You want to rent a movie about alcoholic clowns. But when it comes to alcoholic clown movies, how can you tell the good ones from the bad ones? What is the yardstick by which we judge alcoholic clown movies? Luckily, we have an answer for you. According to the Boston Globe, *Shakes the Clown* is "the *Citizen Kane* of alcoholic clown movies." Well there you go! Rent this movie! What more do you need to know?

What you need to know is that there's a moment in this film when Stenchy the Clown slams his head down into the bar and cries, "Who made this planet?!" Our immediate response was to yell "Goldthwait! Bob Goldthwait!" in the hopes that Stenchy might then do something amusing, like beat the hell out of Goldthwait's character, Shakes. He certainly deserves something of that sort for writing and directing *Shakes the Clown*.

The movie starts, naturally, with Goldthwait throwing up. Actually, it starts with a dog eating pizza, but the vomit scene is mere seconds after that. Funny stuff, huh? Yeah, we thought so too. The general thrust of the picture is that Shakes is an alcoholic and, despite the fact that he's a pretty good clown, the booze affects his work. He is passed up for host of the local kids' TV show, much to the disappointment of his pals Stenchy (Blake Clark) and Dink (Adam Sandler – yes, *that* Adam Sandler), both clowns who expected to be included in the show when Shakes got the job.

The clown who does get the hosting job is Binky (Tom Kenny), a self-proclaimed jerk who doesn't get much respect from the other clowns. With his lackeys, Boots and HoHo, Binky not only takes Shakes' job, but also frames Shakes for the murder of the local clown talent agent, Owen Cheese (Paul Dooley). So Shakes' job is this: clear his name, kick the hooch habit, and find true love with Judy (Julie Brown), a waitress at the clown bar named the Twisted Balloon. Gee, so far this sounds like a Tolkien novel.

If you're one of those people who is scared of clowns to begin with, *Shakes* won't do anything to convince you otherwise. In fact, if you generally appreciate clowns, this movie may change your mind. The clowns presented here are some of the scariest people we've seen in a long time. The comments from the barflies at the Twisted Balloon made us squirm uncomfortably in our seats. For most of the film, Shakes himself is a frightening apparition with a beer-soaked wig and drool-stained makeup. It's not a pretty picture.

One of the only things we liked about *Shakes the Clown* is its depiction of the different castes of clown society. Whether these castes exist or not, we don't know, but they're darn funny to think about. Mimes, of course, form the lowest class of clown, at least in the eyes of the "party clowns" like Shakes. Then there are the horrific rodeo clowns, who terrorize the party clowns and brag of being kicked in the head by bulls. We really wish Goldthwait had done a little more with this idea than simply mime-bash, but it did make us smile when he thrust a cardboard container over a mime's head and said, "Get outta *this* box!"

If the story and characters are bad, then the acting is reprehensible. Although Goldthwait is completely believable as Shakes, keep in mind that he's playing a drunken slob who can't do anything right. It's not exactly a hard role to play. Julie Brown spends the entire movie talking like Elmer Fudd, slurring her R's and L's, which is weawwy – uh, *really* – annoying. It makes you want to bweak her widdle neck. Amazingly enough, the best performance came from Adam Sandler as Dink. Dink was the only person on screen for whom we felt any affection at all.

At this point you're probably saying, "Well at least no one more 'talented' than Adam Sandler got roped into this outhouse of a movie." Oh, how wrong you'd be! Robin Williams actually appears in this mess. True, he's billed in the credits as "Marty Fromage," but he's here, playing a high-strung mime instructor. He's not just a mime, he's a mime on the edge! This sounds a lot funnier than it actually is, but you could say that about lots of things in this movie.

Perhaps the most amazing thing about *Shakes*, after all is said and done, is that Bobcat Goldthwait has been talking about making another *Shakes the Clown* movie. What makes him think anyone would want to watch more of this unamusing and even repulsive shtick?

PART THREE

Sex Sells

"Sex Sells"

If we thought this old adage were literally true, we would have pictures of our own naked butts on the cover of this book. We doubt it would sell more copies, though. As sex symbols go, we make pretty good authors.

It can not be denied, however, that celebrity sex sells, especially when it comes to beautiful celebrities who take off their clothes for a movie camera. It seems like there is no end to the number of young women who will take off their clothes to "further their careers." As a matter of fact, many video stores devote entire sections to these women and their movies, under the misleading subject of "Mystery." The only real mystery involved in these sections is whether any given film will feature young starlets taking their clothes off, over-the-hill stars taking their clothes off, a serial killer taunting the police, Jeff Fahey, or – more often than you might think – all four. Only a few of the starlets involved in such "erotic thrillers" go on to substantial Hollywood careers.

Some young female stars reach a point in their careers where they try to shed a pre-teen or teen image of wholesomeness by appearing in a "grown-up" film. The results are rarely included in annual movie top ten lists. Elizabeth Berkeley didn't exactly go from *Showgirls* to Oscar acceptance speeches. In this chapter we will cover the on-screen maturations of Shannen Doherty, Alyssa Milano, and Drew Barrymore.

Sometimes an actress can be convinced to do nudity if it's "important," especially if it's the only way they can get work. We were as surprised as everyone else to find out Gillian Anderson did a sex scene in the obscure film *The Turning*. So we have a review here. We were even more surprised to hear rumors that Dame Judi Dench appeared nude in a late '60s version of *A Midsummer Night's* don't have a review because we want people to buy our book.

This book is aimed primarily at those people who are most interested in film, and we have to face the fact that the majority of those people will be heterosexual males. But for the rest of you reading out there, possibly because you found this book sitting on a bus seat and have nothing else to read, we have included coverage of the *lack* of coverage of Johnny Depp's ass early in his career. We also have reviews of some early films by other male stars in which they don't actually get naked, but women get naked near them. Which, so long as movies are made primarily by and for men, is probably the most for which you can hope.

The Turning
(1992, Director: L.A. Puopolo)

There is only one conceivable reason for watching *The Turning*, and that's the same reason the film was released on video: it features, however briefly, the unclad mammaries of Gillian Anderson. Anderson, otherwise known as Agent Dana Scully from TV's incredibly popular *X-Files*, did her early dues-paying as a young actress in this goofy and depressing small-town drama.

The Turning is based on a play called *Home Fires Burning*, and it's obvious that the source material was meant to be presented on stage: there are lots of scenes in which characters do nothing in particular besides sit around and talk. Contrast this to other movies in which characters sit around and talk, but do it in interesting locales or while doing something that doesn't look silly on stage, like driving a car.

The story focuses on Clifford Harnish (Michael Dolan), a young man who returns to his home town of Pocahontas, Virginia, after an absence of four years. Cliff has apparently been hanging out with Neo-Nazis, because his new mission in life is to rebuild his family while wearing swastikas. Unfortunately, his arrival coincides with the day his parents' divorce is made final. When he observes his mother, Martha (Tess Harper), sinking into an alcoholic depression, and discovers his father's new life with a different woman (Karen Allen), Cliff decides to take matters into his own hands.

Believing Dad's new girlfriend Glory to be the cause of the divorce, Cliff decides to terrorize her into leaving his father, Mark (Raymond J. Barry). Cliff arrives at her house and slips in under false pretenses. He warns her to stay away from Mark, and tells her to show up at the lake the next morning, where Mark and Cliff will be fishing, to break off the relationship in Cliff's presence.

Instead, Glory decides to expose Cliff in Mark's presence (a decision no one in real life would make, considering she had ample opportunity to talk to Mark before the fishing trip), and Mark must then decide how to reconcile his love for his son with his repulsion for the psychotic hate-monger that Cliff has become. Many dramatic speeches result, including one scene in which everyone seems to be holding everyone else at gun point – with only one gun in the room.

We know that our discerning readers really don't care about the psycho plot of this sick coming-home drama; they want to read about Gillian Anderson and what does or doesn't appear on screen. The owners of the film's distribution company must have been thrilled to see Anderson's rise to stardom, because they were in possession of the only film in which she makes a nude appearance. The cover proudly declares that *The Turning* features Gillian Anderson of *X-Files* fame, complete with logo. The box art prominently features Ms. Anderson, to the exclusion of any other actors who were in the film, and shows her unbuttoning the top button of her dress. (This is a classic bit of misdirection, since the scene pictured is actually one in which she is buttoning the dress up.)

So, what part does she play in the movie? You may have noticed that she was not mentioned in our plot synopsis above. This was apparently her first movie work, as she is listed in the credits as "And Introducing Gillian Anderson." She plays April, a waitress at a local diner. We would estimate her screen time at less than ten minutes. It turns out she was Cliff's girlfriend before he left town years before, and, in the only scene most of you reading this care about, she and Cliff have sex on a kitchen floor.

The question then becomes: is watching this movie worth a glimpse of Scully's secondary sexual characteristics? Alas, not by a long shot. The movie was shot in a real town, and the production looks very authentic, which is why the pretentious and circuitous dialogue stands out. No one who was really in this situation would act like these characters, or say the things these characters say, so even the supposedly sultry sex scene lacks conviction. They haven't seen each other in years – they can't wait two minutes to walk back to the bedroom? If you must rent *The Turning*, watch it in fast-forward mode until you see red hair. You might as well get what you paid for with a minimum of unnecessary pain.

Caligula

(1980, Director: Tinto Brass)

Caligula has a wonderfully tainted reputation as an experiment gone awry. Borne into the world by Bob *"Penthouse"* Guccione and American novelist/playwright Gore Vidal, with help from some of the more respected acting talents of the day and a gaggle of Penthouse Pets, it is not what any one of its creators had hoped it would be. "Adult entertainment" purveyor Guccione never gained widespread or critical acceptance, and Vidal and others found the seamier aspects of the industry undermining what could have been a credible drama – although with the story and acting the way they are, such credibility is likely out of reach, as an R-rated version of the film clearly demonstrates.

Malcolm McDowell plays the Roman emperor Caligula, who assumes the throne rather violently when he learns that his grandfather Tiberius (Peter O'Toole) plans to kill his heir rather than see his line live on. After dispatching with the aged Tiberius, Caligula uses his power in attempts to shock "an unshockable society." Considered mad by most historians, Caligula systematically did his best to offend or kill the more powerful members of Rome while maintaining popularity by giving away his wealth.

Very little of the political intrigue comes through in this version, but Caligula's madness is rarely in doubt. The film is a cavalcade of violence, sex (some of it even watchable), and other depravity, although explicit acts are rarely performed by the principal members of the cast. One of the more transparent attempts to introduce more sex into the film is the hardcore scene between two Penthouse Pets who are ostensibly spying on Caligula from the next room. To include this scene in the film, Guccione sneaked on to the set at night to film these sequences and smuggled the negative out of Italy to thwart the country's laws giving the director authority over a movie's final cut.

The end result? Two and a half hours of badly edited and occasionally intelligible dialogue punctuated by random acts of violence, sex, and a lot of background nudity. Also, a lot of hurt feelings and lawsuits as the people associated with the film tried to back out. Vidal withdrew his name from the film, although he is still credited as writer of the screenplay from which the film is "adapted," and Tinto Brass, who directed most of the film, is touted as the principal photographer. The actors have since reacted to the film by trying to distance themselves from it, accepting it with good humor (John Gielgud announced that, at 75, he had just finished his first pornographic film), or defending their performances, whatever the finished film may have looked like. It can hardly be denied that Helen Mirren spends the film trying to bring some dignity to the proceedings, no matter what silly thing she is given to do.

If curiosity drives you to see *Caligula*, we suggest you pick up the unrated DVD edition. It includes a "making of" documentary, which was itself made during the film's production. The evidence of this is the presence of both Tinto Brass and Gore Vidal, who, while they had their differences during the making of *Caligula*, would later come to agree that they no longer wished to be identified with the movie. The featurette, almost an hour long, is full of wonderful quotes from the likes of Guccione ("this isn't pornography, it's paganography") and Helen Mirren: "[*Caligula*] has an irresistable mixture of art and genitals in it." While quite dry in some spots (such as the bit where Gore Vidal expostulates from his comfy armchair, pointing out pictures of himself with Billy Wilder and Charlton Heston on the set of *Ben Hur*), the documentary about *Caligula* can be more entertaining than the movie itself.

Embrace of the Vampire
(1994, Director: Anne Goursaud)

Embrace of the Vampire made it into our pile of videos one weekend for two reasons: we heard it was chock-full-o-skin, mostly Alyssa "*Who's the Boss*" Milano's, and it had an insanely high rating (8.0 out of 10) in the Internet Movie Database. Unfortunately, the former seems to be the main cause for the latter.

This is not to say that *Embrace of the Vampire* is all bad, but neither do we think it should be ranked with the likes of *Sunset Boulevard*, *Modern Times*, *Raging Bull*, and *Annie Hall*. Ah well. On to the plot.

The highly-watchable Alyssa Milano plays Charlotte, a beautiful yet virginal college student. As the movie begins, her biggest worries are dealing with the undeserved holier-than-thou image she has with her peers, and whether she should sleep with her current boyfriend, Chris. Things become worse when a vampire (Martin Kemp) comes upon the scene.

You see, this vampire (known throughout the film only as "the vampire") knows that Charlotte is actually his beloved princess from ages long ago, reincarnated in the modern world. As he was transformed into a vampire before he could marry the princess, he now plans to make Charlotte into a vampire and regain his lost love. Darn those vampires looking to regain their reincarnated lost loves! Apparently, he must do this while she is still a virgin, and still under eighteen years old (unsurprisingly, that birthday is just three days away).

In order to make Charlotte more receptive to his advances, the vampire gives her dreams that will undermine her confidence in her relationship with Chris. Not only that, but the vampire gives Chris dreams, too, so that their love will be broken and our undead villain will be able to put the moves on Charlotte.

So of course it happens that over the course of these three days, Charlotte participates in a nudie photo session, is nearly seduced by the lesbian photographer, and gets ecstasy slipped in her drink – all of which is completely unrelated to the vampire plot. Yup, that sounds like freshman year to us! It's fairly obvious that Milano chose this role for the same reason that other former child actresses do *Playboy* spreads or play rape victims: to divorce themselves from their childhood spectres and establish themselves as adults. Fortunately for Milano, *Embrace of the Vampire*'s adult situations play seriously enough to achieve the desired result (there can be no doubt that our star is all growed up) without seeming overly pretentious. It's a vampire movie, she doffs her top, and she can now move on to other adult roles. Considering the way Drew Barrymore handled the same situation (bouts with alcoholism and drug abuse, a *Playboy* shoot, *and* a torrid movie in which she plays a young sexpot), we think Milano did pretty well.

Of course, our synopsis of the plot thus far is much simpler than the way the events are portrayed in the movie. For some reason, the vampire will die if he doesn't seduce Charlotte, and sometimes it's not clear whether he wants to merely drink her blood or actually make her a vampire. It's also not clear why Charlotte's birthday is significant – what's the deadline for? Is the vampire's time limit merely coincidental to her eighteenth birthday, or does the birthday itself impose restrictions? And what does being a virgin have to do with any of this?

Fortunately, one of the things we were looking for in this film was plentiful. Milano, clothed and unclothed, does a fairly good job transforming herself from misunderstood good girl to vampire-influenced bitch. If only the same could be said for her romantic partner (Harrison Pruett), who was pretty limp throughout the whole film, even in the scenes he shared with Jennifer Tilly.

Probably the best character actor in the movie was Jordan Ladd, who played the resident Bad Girl, Eliza. Still, she did remind us of a cheap *Heathers* ripoff, especially when she was drugging Charlotte's wine. Another semi-honorable mention goes to Rachel True, who played Charlotte's best friend Nicole. Unfortunately, the vampire attacks Nicole halfway through the film and she disappears from the story completely. None of her friends miss her, and frankly, neither did we.

We would guess the reason this movie was made was to capitalize on the then total lack of movies based on Anne Rice novels. The movie contains all of the alleged sensualism of a Rice novel, along with the obscure symbolism, such as an ankh being instrumental to someone's conversion to vampirism. As a matter of fact, you sort of have to assume that the vampire is from a Rice novel, or else his apparent resistance to sunlight and bisexual shapechanging would be even more confusing than they are already.

At other times, *Embrace of the Vampire* carts out the most annoying cliche of modern horror movies: None of the characters act like real people would in the same situation. To give just one example, Charlotte loses the cross she used to wear, and can't find it. So Nicole puts the ankh around her neck, the same mysterious ankh Charlotte was grasping when she was found unconscious outside her dorm wearing nothing but her nightgown. Who would do such a thing? What were they thinking? If *we* were found unconscious holding an ankh, we would throw it into the nearest convenient ocean. Or maybe take it to an antique store and see what we could get for it. But wear it? Never!

Then there's the end of the movie, where a special effect is actually used, but it is so brief and pointless (the Vampire sort of zaps Chris with a bolt from his hand), one wonders why it was included at all. When the vampire dies, rather than dissolving or doing anything else entertaining, he sort of rolls over onto his back and shrivels up like a cockroach. This is entertaining in its own way, but not for the reasons the filmmakers intended. We just can't help thinking there was a big can of Garlic Raid just off camera.

While it's a good source of some schlocky fun, *Embrace of the Vampire* doesn't achieve any more than that. The film certainly has more entertainment value than most vampire movies – unfortunately, not saying much.

Blindfold: Acts of Obsession
(1994, Director: Lawrence L. Simeone)

9-0-2-1-NAKED!

Like so many of the films that deserve to be included in this chapter, we first picked up *Blindfold: Acts of Obsession* because we heard its lead actress, Shannen "Brenda from *Beverly Hills 90210*" Doherty, gets naked in the film. While this is not the noblest of reasons to watch a movie, it is at least a common and honest one.

In the case of Ms. Doherty and *Blindfold: AoO*, we were not to be disappointed: the rumor that she dispenses with her clothing turns out to be true. True every few minutes, or so it seems. Actually, her breasts appear so often they should have been given separate billing. The weird thing is, they rarely appear in the same shot as Shannen's face, almost as if they *are* separate characters. (Despite that fact, we don't think Shannen uses a body double). It's enough to distract you from the fact that the actress' face occasionally gives the impression that it belongs on the wall of a Cubist art gallery.

Doherty plays Madeleine Dalton, a woman who is drawn to bad boys – or at least she was at one time. Now she's married to the rather boring Mike Dalton (Michael Woods), who is a real estate broker with a *Glengarry Glen Ross* sort of thing going on. It shouldn't be all that surprising that he has trouble getting it up in bed.

Under the advice of her creepy psychiatrist Dr. Jennings (Judd Nelson), Madeleine decides to spice up her sex life with Mike by playing games. For the benefit of our younger readers, let's pretend that the games they play are Parcheesi, Chinese Checkers, and Candy Land. Oh, and Snakes and Ladders. But these games create only momentary marital bliss.

9-0-2-1-MURDER!

Meanwhile, in a what seems like a totally unrelated plot, women around Santa Monica are blindfolded, handcuffed, and then knifed to death. Because this is a bad movie, the police take only a cursory interest in solving the murders.

Take, for instance, the scene in which the police respond to a report that a blindfolded, handcuffed woman was seen being dragged into a building. The first cop who responds actually brags to his superior that he "took a quick look around" and found the building "clean." So who will actually make the half-hearted attempt required to find the body that almost certainly has to be there? Why, the androgynously named Chris Madigan (Kristian Alfonso), who also happens to be Madeleine's sister. (Her maiden name was *Madeleine Madigan?* It's a terrible thing when parents hate their children.) Chris finds the body after an excruciatingly long and pointless "looking around the basement" scene.

It turns out that Dr. Jennings has some sort of connection to a presumed-dead killer with an identical *modus operandi*. The police files on the previous killer's case are repeatedly described as being "vague," mainly because they would have to be for the plot to work. When the killer is revealed at the end, you can't help but wonder: what sort of police department would put together a file on a psychopathic multiple murderer and not include a single picture of him?

9-0-2-1-BORED!

Much of the fault for this movie's failure should be laid on Doherty's shoulders. As the plot progresses, Madeleine becomes more and more obsessed with the games she plays (for you kids, she's playing Sorry!) - so obsessed that she can't tell the difference between pain and pleasure, blah blah blah. Doherty should make us believe that's she's consumed by all of this game-playing, but she doesn't even come close. As a matter of fact, she seems pretty bored with everything that's going on. It's as if the actress told the director, "Hey, you got my breasts on camera! You don't need me to act, too!"

Not all of the film's problems lie with its well-endowed leading lady, however. Somewhere along the line, Judd Nelson either convinced someone he could act, or came into possession of some very compelling blackmail material. In this vehicle, Nelson slaughters his lines neatly and efficiently, boring us within seconds of his appearance. Alfonso, bless her heart, is trying her best, but it's just not enough. She's a long way from her *MacGyver* guest apperances in this made-for-cable stinker. Her worst moment comes when she faces the psychotic killer. She has a gun and he doesn't – and as with so many other bad movies, she inexplicably *doesn't* shoot him, despite the fact that she is an allegedly seasoned cop.

9-0-2-1-WHY?

One could wonder why Doherty would make a movie like this. It was obviously doomed from the start. Shannen couldn't (or wouldn't) put the effort into the role that was needed. The part isn't exactly great, especially considering she doesn't do anything but scream and stumble around during the film's climax. Plus, there are rather obvious script and editing problems, like the rather clumsy contrivances to put the main characters in the same place at the same time.

Throughout her career, Shannen Doherty has shown one consistent trait (other than the bizarre construction of her facial features): the ability to jump ship in the middle of a project. She did it with *Beverly Hills 90210*, she did it with *Charmed*, and she certainly stopped contributing somewhere in the course of making this movie.

From this review and other comments in this book, one might get the impression that we're not fond of Shannen Doherty. In truth, we have great respect for the woman and her work. *Heathers* is one of our favorite *teen noir* flicks, in large part due to Doherty's performance. She was the perfect foil for Jason Lee in Kevin Smith's *Mallrats*, and we even have to give her credit for a remarkable career resuscitation with her contribution to the WB TV series, *Charmed*. Plus, how could we hate someone who helped remake *Satan's School for Girls*?

As to her admittedly unusual looks (upon which we have harped perhaps a bit too much), we should say that they do not detract from her beauty so much as they distract from her work. The slight angle at which her eyes are set is the sort of thing that you may notice but never *un*-notice, no matter how hard you try. After that, it's difficult to become absorbed in a performance when you're busy noticing how Doherty is tilting her head, or the angle at which the director is shooting her closeups to mask the irregularity. We hear you can do amazing things with CGI these days....

Private Resort
(1985, Director: George Bowers)

Those puerile-but-profitable nuggets of joy known as "teen sex comedies" come to theaters in waves. *American Pie* may be a huge hit now, and it may have inspired a series of not-so-interesting imitators (*Road Trip*, *Get Over It!*), but it certainly isn't the first. Back in 1981 there was a film called *Porky's*, which spawned an interminable stream of horny guy comedies – interminable, that is, until they terminabled around 1986. It was a pretty good run, though, and that example only goes back one generation of the ever-renewing, amoeba-like teen movie organism.

Private Resort is a typical example of the genre, made notable because it stars Johnny Depp (*Ed Wood*, *Donnie Brasco*) and Rob Morrow (*Northern Exposure*, *Quiz Show*). Like most stars of teen comedies, *Resort's* principal actors are well out of their teens – 22 and 23, respectively. In this case their advanced years may be forgiven, however, because they play horny college guys who hang out at a private resort in Florida, looking for love – or at least some cheap gratification.

The resort features more well-toned women in bikinis per square yard than you're going to find anywhere outside of Hugh Hefner's bedroom, and of course that is really the point. *Private Resort* exists to display as many examples of a certain popular part of the female anatomy as possible. In the Stomp Tokyo editorial bullpen we call these popular parts "maguppies," and we use the term maguppies because in these sorts of movies they exist, unlike actual women's breasts, as entities separate from any human being. The ladies who provide their maguppies to be shown in the movie usually don't have any lines of dialogue, unless by dialogue you mean the surprised cries the women emit when their maguppies are "accidentally" revealed. Further separating maguppies from humanity is the fact that the women who portray the "true love" partners of our principal characters rarely show their own maguppies.

Ben (Morrow) and Jack (Depp) are standard-issue characters for what *Mallrats* director Kevin Smith called "Le Cinema de Tit." They are horn-dogs and will grope any cooperative girl indiscriminately, but they are capable of being tamed by that one special woman. Ben is the sensitive one (though compared to the sensitive guy he played in *Northern Exposure*, Morrow is a Neanderthal in this movie), and Jack is the instigator who continually implores his friend to relax and have fun. Almost as soon as they get to the resort they run afoul of Reeves (Tony Azito), the tight-ass house detective who doesn't understand that young people deserve to have fun.

We can only assume that the screenwriter felt guilty at the prospect of accepting money for repeatedly typing "and then a girl loses her top," because he introduces what might be considered a plot. It involves a jewel thief who calls himself The Maestro (Hector Elizondo), and who stays at the resort to steal an expensive diamond necklace from the widow Rawlings (Dody Goodman) With both *Grease* and *Grease 2* under her belt, Goodman is no stranger to youth "comedy." Jack and Ben enter this plot by way of some particularly unpleasant misunderstandings. Not only does Jack misinterpret a woman's reactions to his advances, but that woman turns out to be the Maestro's wife, Bobbie Sue. You may recognize Bobbie Sue as the splendiferously over-endowed Leslie Easterbrook, who did her own crap comedy time in six out of the seven *Police Academy* films. When the Maestro returns to his hotel room unexpectedly, Ben is forced to cover for Jack by masquerading as the hotel barber. The resulting haircut is of course disastrous, and Ben spends the rest of the film fleeing from the Maestro, often without the benefit of clothing.

Other plot bits (they rarely last more than a couple of scenes) include Reeves' embarrassing encounters with a woman clad in a really small bikini (a major source of maguppies, naturally), Ben's blind date with a young spiritualist who unexpectedly offers her maguppies to the audience, and the puzzling antics of a pair of sumo wrestlers who show up for no reason. It's all completely inane, and without the presence of two well-known actors there would be no reason to watch. We suppose that for movie buffs it might be a vaguely interesting time capsule of what was considered funny in the mid-'80s – Andrew Dice Clay makes an appearance as a boorish, over-cocky boyfriend – but that's about as far as it goes. Our sensitive comedy detectors actually warned us of dangerous deposits of *anti*-comedy in *Private Resort*, so we suggest you handle it carefully.

We expect a good amount of female nudity from pictures like this one. *Private Resort* doesn't disappoint, but it also provides us with more than enough bare skin from our male stars. We're sure that many of our female readers will scowl when we say that we eventually asked God to put some pants on Rob Morrow. Those same readers, however, will probably grin delightedly at the sight of Depp's derriere, which also makes an appearance. Little Johnny? Sorry ladies – the only privates in this movie are in the title.

By the '90s the teen sex comedy had devolved into the skin flicks that choke the shelves at nearly every video store. They are pretty easy to pick out, because about half of them have the word "bikini" in the title. Let's face it, on this kind of movie you don't want your marketing to be too subtle. If your audience can't pick out your movie while drunk, there is a good chance it will never get rented.

The originator of the form was probably *Malibu Bikini Shop* (1985), but they didn't really begin until *Bikini Summer* and its sequels came along in 1991. The plot of nearly all these movies is as follows:

A young person runs , or more usually inherits, a small business. But though the young person tries his best, the business is failing. Mean members of the establishment want to get their hands on the business or property, so the business must become profitable quickly. Someone comes up with the smart idea of having the people who work at the business wear bikinis, and presto, things turn around. And just to keep viewers at home from getting too bored, the bikinis come off pretty often.

Among the businesses that have been given the bikini treatment are car washes, bistros, drive-in theaters, hotels, and even a Native American burial ground!

For the purposes of this book, however, these movies don't have much value. The actors in these movies never go on to great things. The women are chosen for chest size and willingness to display that size to the camera, and the men are chosen for having the courage to deal with the very real danger of spending a lot of time in the company of naked women.

Zapped!
(1982, Director: Robert J. Rosenthal)

As we covered in our review of *Private Resort*, the '80s brought us a great many "teen titty films." In such films, a typically overaged cast of wannabe movie stars played horny teenaged boys and at-first-quite-Puritan-but-then-suspiciously-easy teenaged girls. Viewed as a kind of Holy Grail by then-adolescent boys, these movies usually featured underdog everyday Joes oppressed by dumb-jock overlord bullies. The heroes are usually unsuccessful at getting girls or exacting revenge upon the bullies until some coincidence, invention, or well-crafted plan (but usually coincidence) allows them to do so.

All of these things are secondary, however, to the promise of a flash of breast or the hastily-revealed derriere of one (or more) of the girls in the flick. Entries in this sub-genre include the innumerable and execrable *Porky's* films, *Fast Times at Ridgemont High*, *My Tutor*, and the movie under discussion here: *Zapped!* We are sorry to report that, despite the highly-touted (by classmate Joey in the seventh grade) finale during which an entire prom loses its clothing, this movie is too dull to keep viewers awake until they can reach that titillating final scene.

The underdog heroes in *Zapped!* are Barney Springboro and Peyton Nichols, played by those eternal on-screen partners-in-crime, Scott Baio and Willie Aames. Apparently the acting chemistry between these two actors was so great in *Zapped!* that shortly thereafter they were paired together in the TV series *Charles in Charge*, which lasted until 1990. In that great decade known as the '80s, Scott and Willie were not just an acting team – they were an institution.

Baio's nerdy Barney character spends all of his time in the school science lab, experimenting with chemicals and mice. Our introduction to Barney involves drunken scuba diving mice, an idea which surely sent the screenwriter into hysterics, but loses a lot in the execution. At Peyton's behest, Barney is testing his super-grow plant formula on a batch of marijuana plants, which are conveniently hidden behind the school principal's prize orchids. At our high schools, the nerdy science kids went home after school to watch *Robotech*. In the world of *Zapped!*, nerdy science kids experiment freely with mind-altering drugs.

In a fashion similar to that which produced Cary Grant's youth formula in *Monkey Business*, some of Barney's chemicals (and some of Peyton's cheap beer) are combined to produce a potion that provides telekinetic abilities to its consumer. (Regrettably, there are no chimpanzees present to provide entertainment as in *Monkey Business*. Marilyn Monroe is also woefully absent.) Although the potion's effects are initially unnoticed by Barney (who has only fed the formula to a mouse), he is soon enveloped in a cloud of the stuff and begins to notice the fact that he can now move things around just by screwing his face into an uncomfortable position.

What does Barney do with these new powers? Mostly, he tries to impress Bernadette (Felice Schachter), an intellectual but cute fellow student. Barney also uses his new powers to fulfill certain adolescent fantasies, such as hitting a winning home run, and exposing Heather Thomas' bra.

Unfortunately, the screenwriters couldn't come up with enough stuff for Barney to do to fill an entire movie. Geez, how could they? Movies are *sooooo* long. We're pretty sure *Zapped!* was eight hours long, at least. So there are numerous, annoying sub-plots that boost the film up to feature length and beyond. Peyton lusts after Jane (Heather Thomas), who resists his charms because her college-age boyfriend has promised her a trip to Hawaii for graduation. Scatman Crothers plays the school's gym coach who, at the film's absolute nadir, becomes high from the second-hand smoke of supergrown Mary Jane and has a dream about Einstein and salami. An entire five minutes of screen time is wasted on a *Star Trek* fantasy during which Barney levitates a model spaceship around his bedroom. Finally, there's the budding romance between the school's principal and a teacher (Sue Ann Langdon). This last one is not so much a subplot as a running gag – as in you will gag and run every time it appears.

Nothing comes together in the film's climatic prom scene, which exists only to inject some last shots of female nudity into the proceedings. It's easy to imagine how this scene came into being. The writers got together and said, "You know what would be really cool? *Porky's* meets *Carrie!*" And so we are treated to a prom scene in which Barney rips the clothes off of most of the females present, though the nudity is of the coy, peeking kind. When breasts do show up in *Zapped!* they tend to appear in close-up, independent of any woman they might be attached to. We guess that makes it easier to body-double actresses with pesky no-nudity clauses.

Boring, boring, boring. As we slogged through this dreck, we begged, pleaded and threatened the film constantly in the hope that we could somehow warp reality into making this movie funnier. Instead we got Scott Baio telekinetically dousing his father with prune juice. *Next!*

The problem with "magical" sex comedies is that they are aimed at the sort of people who might actually find that sort of thing amusing – teenagers. In order to reach that audience, the filmmakers must satisfy the requirements of the Motion Picture Association of America, and so, in a film that should be all about the racy things that people would do with magical powers, nothing really racy ever happens.

The worst offender in this sub-genre is *Weird Science*, the movie in which two teenaged geniuses (Anthony Michael Hall, Ilan Mitchell-Smith) create the perfect woman (Kelly LeBrock). These pubescent Einsteins are then too stupid to do anything *with* this woman, besides use her as their ticket into popularity. In the one nod to teenaged lecherousness, the boys shower with their creation, but do so fully clothed and while cowering in a corner. What did we expect from John Hughes, the patron saint of whitebread teen angst?

Love Potion No. 9 hits a bit closer to the mark. This time, two twenty-something lovelorn geniuses (Tate Donovan and Sandra Bullock) happen upon a chemical formula that imbues the consumer's vocal chords with aphrodisiacal powers. Naturally, the awkward pair decide to further their own romantic lives in the name of science. This "ideal" scenario is later ruined by the dramatic structure, which requires them to fall in love with each other.

Fully exploring the perverted depths of magical sex comedies is *School Spirit*, which features a frat boy-turned-ghost (Tom Nolan) who evades heavenly induction for the sake of one last score. Devotees of sexually immature behavior take note: *that's* dedication.

Sizzle Beach U.S.A.
(1974, Director: Richard Brander)

Kevin Costner's billing as a "special guest star" in *Sizzle Beach U.S.A.* proves that one needn't be a writer of textbooks to revise history. In this case, you only need to be Lloyd Kaufman, the brain behind Troma Studios. Kaufman bought the picture in 1986, about ten years after its initial release as *Malibu Hot Summer*. Coincidentally, this was also about the time that Kevin Costner became a household name. Kaufman promptly released the film with the sexier title *Sizzle Beach U.S.A.*, slapped a new copyright date on it, and proceeded to squeeze every last dollar he could from Costner's newfound stardom with his "new" film.

Costner's special billing status isn't the only thing of interest in the opening credits of *Sizzle Beach U.S.A.* For example, there is a blonde doing calisthenics on a beach. We were pretty sure this would be a metaphor for one of the movie's themes, but we're darned if we could figure out which theme. The titles also helpfully inform us that Craig Kusaba wrote the film's "original screenplay." This means that the story wasn't adapted from another work, as opposed to all the bikini movies based on the works of Henry James.

Our top-billed heroines (if they can be called heroines in this film without conflict) meet in a California coffee shop when the folk-singing Janice (Terry Congie) is accidentally locked in the women's restroom by a faulty doorknob. To her rescue come Dit (Leslie Brander, the director's wife) and Cheryl (Roselyn Royce), two ladies who fell victim to the same trap mere minutes earlier. Because of their temporary imprisonment, they missed their bus to Malibu, but Janice offers them a ride to their destination. Their friendship thus afixed by the common bond of lavatory confinement, the girls drive to the beach for a summer of love, laughs, and self-exploration.

They stay in a beach house that belongs to Dit's cousin Steve (Robert Acey), whom we meet in the arms of a buxom, bikini-clad brunette. Our first clue to the fact that this film was actually made in the '70s was the line Steve's date uses to lure him up to his own bedroom: "I'd like to go up and see your John Travolta poster." Forgoing the point that Steve would either have to be gay or twelve years old to display a John Travolta poster in his bedroom, by 1986 Travolta's popularity with women, gay men, and twelve year-old boys had dwindled considerably. This gratuitous "Barbarino" reference, the harvest gold kitchen appliances, and a number of horrible silicone breast implants give away the movie's '70s origins.

Cousin Steve is only too happy to harbor an extra pair of nubile women in his home, and soon the cast is sitting in the living room, listening to Janice croon her latest folk epic:

worlds of creation die of cancer
a tender rose hides a storm
breasts of destiny hold no answer
against feelings of scorn

what to do when streets are sleepy?
when dreams are done where to go?
going somewhere can be the answer
getting there can be the war

Irretrievable minutes go by as the girls begin their new lives: Janice falls in love with Steve and prepares to enter a singing competition. Cheryl meets a successful businessman on the beach but, to prove her independence, follows her dream of becoming a high school gym teacher. And Dit? Well, Dit takes acting classes and goes horseback riding at the ranch of a certain John Logan, played by – you guessed it – Kevin Costner.

Costner's character is ostensibly a very rich man, who owns ranches in multiple states. How a twenty-two year-old baby-faced yokel like Costner got to be a wealthy landowner is unexplained but it does make for a few amusing moments as Dit "figures out" that he owns the stables and that he conceals his wealth in order to meet women who will like him for his personality. In real life, of course, he would be required to *show* a personality, but in a b-movie he gets the girl without one.

The film wanders through these little plots aimlessly, looking for something with which to drag itself forward. Eventually the movie settles on the big singing and songwriting competition, which allows for a kind of climax. But before we can get there we get a look at the seamy side of the recording industry as envisioned by low budget filmmakers. The song competition, put on by a club owner, is actually rigged so Janice can't win despite her obviously superior singing/songwriting talents. Luckily it turns out that John employs a midget named Pete. Initially this results in the following conversation:

```
Pete: I really like tall women.
Dit:  I'm only five-one!
Pete: Baby, to me that's tall!
```

You see? It's funny because he's a *midget!* Get it? Proving that he has his ear to the ground (he's not the only one who can make dumb "short" jokes), Pete learns that the singing competition is rigged, thus leaving Janice with no hope of fulfilling her dream. John decides to prove his love to Dit by helping Janice. He does this by teaming up with Pete to prevent the "winning" singer's arrival at the contest. Never mind that a man of Logan's wealth could set Janice up in her own studio; according to these filmmakers, it's much more interesting to watch Kevin Costner and a midget run a frightened couple of bad actors off the road and force them to strip at gunpoint.

The meandering plot of *Sizzle Beach U.S.A.* is explained by its producer Eric Luzell, who describes it as a "no concept" film. In the commentary provided on Troma's DVD, Luzell explains that each day of shooting began with an impromptu scripting session, followed by an afternoon of unlicensed guerilla filming on the beach or another location. This accounts for the sudden disappearance of cousin Steve (his relationship with Janice dissolved in an off-screen fight) and Janice's new-found love affair with Gary, a character who is introduced in the film's final twenty minutes. Gary, it turns out, was the actress' real-life boyfriend, with whom she was willing to make the movie's final – and steamiest – love scene.

Costner's part in the film is short, but embarrassing. His acting isn't the film's worst, but it is wooden enough that Pete would have upstaged him even without the intrinsic entertainment qualities of a midget. Costner's apperance is not as embarrassing, perhaps, as subsequent performances in *Waterworld* and *The Postman*, but it's still bad enough that he tried to buy the rights to the film to bury it forever. Fortunately for us, Lloyd Kaufman got there first.

> Even the casual observer of Hollywood trends knows that Kevin Costner is no stranger to stinky movies. Early successes like *Bull Durham* and *The Untouchables* gave his career enough steam to overcome the accompanying stumbles, and justifiably so. In 1990, however, the Academy of Motion Picture Arts and Sciences awarded Costner with three nominations and two Oscars for his work on the early American historical epic *Dances With Wolves*. In one night, the Academy created a Frankensteinian monster that would haunt moviegoers for years.
>
> With his new-found freedom, Costner immediately punished his adoring public with the shadowy, depressing *Robin Hood: Prince of Thieves*. His portrayal of Jim Garrison in *JFK* was acceptable, but it was quickly followed up by an utterly vapid role in *The Bodyguard*. Film after slipshod film arrived, alternating between self-indulgent attempted-epics like *Waterworld*, and half-hearted returns to formula like *Tin Cup*. In the most egregious example of the epic disasters, Costner cast himself as the title character in the post-apocalyptic science fiction drama *The Postman*. Hoping to recapture the common-man aura that proved so successful in *Bull Durham* and *Field of Dreams*, the man voted the "most erotic male" by the readers of the German magazine *Amica* threw himself into another baseball film. Not even the directorial powers of Sam Raimi, however, could save the movie from the fact that the forty-four year-old Costner made an unconvincing pro baseball player and an even less convincing romantic lead.
>
> Any mention of Sam "Army of Darkness" Raimi brings actor Bruce Campbell immediately to mind. In the mental comparison between Costner and Campbell, we find ourselves wondering why Costner is the one who got the lion's share of the fame. After all, Campbell is relentless in his attempts to serve audiences instead of himself, affable where Costner is taciturn, and extremely gracious when dealing with fans. We've never bumped into Costner so we don't know how he deals with his public, but somehow we doubt he's quite as eager to please as the man who has taken endless zombie sucker-punches for our amusement.

Poison Ivy
(1992, Director: Katt Shea)

Drew Barrymore – how do we love thee? Let us count the ways! We love thee for thy sassy-little-girl cutseyness in *E.T.: The Extraterrestrial*. We love thee for growing up to be a total hottie. We love thee for thy *Playboy* photo shoot. We love thee for thy gutsy breakthrough in *Scream*, and thy subsequent string of entertaining movies like *Everyone Says I Love You*, *The Wedding Singer*, and *Charlie's Angels*. (O most especially *Charlie's Angels!*)

And yes, we love thee for thy trampy little b-movie, *Poison Ivy*.

The most obvious indicators of Barrymore's career at the time of *Poison Ivy* are her co-stars. Sara Gilbert was doing her best to move on from her years-long role as Darlene on the sitcom *Roseanne*. Leading man Tom Skerritt was well into his unending stretch of doctor and cop roles. Cheryl Ladd was (and apparently still is) supporting the Lifetime Channel single-handedly with TV movies told from the perspectives of fretful mothers, angered girlfriends, and battered wives. Solid actors, all, with some good movies to their credit, but not the sort of material to which one wants to hitch one's star. Unfortunately, Barrymore was seventeen and still pulling herself out of an alcoholic haze and the resulting career slump. After roles like "Vampire Victim" in *Waxwork II: Lost in Time*, the lead in *Poison Ivy* probably seemed like a good opportunity.

Ivy (Barrymore) meets Sylvie Cooper (Gilbert) during detention at the private school they both attend. Ivy is "one of those scholarship kids" at the posh academy, who lives with her inattentive aunt in a trailer. As the two girls get to know each other, the movie plays like a coming of age drama, with lots of angst-ridden monologues from Sylvie: "I always seem to be looking at life from the wrong side of the window." After they become friends, Ivy hangs out at the Cooper mansion and insinuates herself into Sylvie's family.

Darryl Cooper (Skerrit) is the general manager of a local TV station, where he is known for blistering on-air editorials against teenaged irresponsibility. This proves to be particularly ill-advised when his own teenaged daughter enjoys calling bomb threats into the school office. Meanwhile, Cooper's wife Georgie (Ladd) lies in bed at their palatial estate, dying of emphysema.

Before too long the inevitable happens. (Inevitable, at least, in a movie found in the "Mystery" section of the video store.) Ivy and Mr. Cooper start with some flirtatious banter, then make eyes at each other, then stick their tongues down each other's throats, then – well, you get the idea.

Poison Ivy's creators don't even play at subtlety. Ivy becomes the center of the household, playing comforter to Georgie, best friend to Sylvie, and of course mistress to Darryl. While it's easy to see Ivy as a symbol of Darryl's long-gone youth and the wife he is losing to disease, it's not so easy to see Barrymore as the manipulator she portrays. She's still too darn cuddly for words – a necessary quality in an actress trying to project neediness, as she does, but an undesirable trait for someone who must also perform Ivy's more maleficent acts.

Sara Gilbert, on the other hand, takes to her role instantly, if inexpertly. Sylvie is a tight knot of self-conscious, apprehensive neuroses. Her parents ignore her, but she loves them too much to truly act out for their attention. Ivy's bad-girl ways and too-blunt honesty (it is one of the movie's few strokes of wit when Ivy takes mercy on an accident-mangled dog by bludgeoning it to death) attract Sylvie, but this bookish rich girl playing at Gothic despair lacks the contempt necessary to duplicate Ivy's attitude. Gilbert, whom we are used to seeing as the wiseass sitcom daughter of a white trash comedienne, shows enough helplessness to pull the character off. As smart as Sylvie is supposed to be, she doesn't understand Ivy's desperation and gives her the benefit of the doubt too often.

The analysis above is probably more than *Poison Ivy* deserves. This film shouldn't be likened to serious drama any more than a kindergartner's stick-figure crayon drawing should be compared to a portrait by Renoir. For example, the big showdown between Ivy and Sylvie boils down to a competition for the loyalty of the family dog

(Ivy comes prepared with a pocketful of pungent dog treats). This might have had more dramatic punch if it hadn't immediately been followed by the removal of Barrymore's skirt.

Barrymore followed up her role in *Poison Ivy* with a TV movie that deals with a similar subject. *Beyond Control: The Amy Fisher Story* is based on the life of a real-life teenaged manipulator who made headlines in the early '90s with a poster boy for idiocy named Joey Buttafuoco. As ham-fisted as Fisher was in manipulating her lover and attempting to murder his wife, we can't help but feel that she was probably out of Ivy's league.

Although Barrymore did not return to the role of Ivy, *Poison Ivy* was so successful (on video, naturally) that a sequel was pumped out to keep the money flowing. This time Alyssa Milano was tapped as the main character, Lily. She was reunited with Anne Goursaud, the director of *Embrace of the Vampire* (discussed earlier in this chapter). The result of their work was a dismal little movie in which Milano treats us to comparatively little nudity.

The law of diminishing returns held true in the third installment, *Poison Ivy: The New Seduction*, which starred an even less famous actress, Jaime Pressly. Legend has it that Pressly got the role in the third movie because she had been Barrymore's body double for the nude scenes in the first. Given that Pressly was fifteen years old when *Poison Ivy* was made, we find that difficult to believe. More crucial to Pressly's casting, we'd wager, was her experience as a model – and the willingness to pour a bottle of champagne over her bare chest.

Zandalee

(1991, Director: Sam Pillsbury)

As you've learned by now, every famous, respected Hollywood Actor has a skeleton in his or her closet. Jennifer Aniston has *Leprechaun*. Sylvester Stallone has *The Party at Kitty and Stud's*. When it comes to Nicholas Cage, the closet sometimes resembles an *Evil Dead* film. Perhaps the worst of the lot is *Zandalee*, a silly erotic drama that shows us a hell of a lot more of Judge Reinhold's butt than we ever needed to see.

We first meet Zandalee (Erika Anderson) dancing naked around a bedroom. From there, the film goes way downhill, mainly because of the introduction of Judge Reinhold (alumnus of the Burt Reynolds Dinner Theatre), playing Zandalee's husband, a poet named Thierry. Just so there are no misunderstandings, we don't see Judge Reinhold's naked butt in the first scene. *Zandalee* saves that particular pleasure for later in the film.

In the years that Zan and Thierry have been married, Thierry's poetry has gone to hell, along with his relationship with his wife. You know, this film was made in the '90s. By this time, any movie that equates creative impotence with sexual impotence had better darn well come up with something new to say about the subject. Instead, *Zandalee* unfolds in exactly the way you would expect. Except for showing us Judge Reinhold's butt, which we would *never* expect.

Enter Johnny, played by Nick Cage. He's a painter and childhood friend of Thierry's who begins hitting on Zandalee in a most blatant fashion when Thierry introduces them. Boy, when you need someone to act really wacked out, call on Nick Cage. Johnny was actually in jail for a while, and this allows the introduction of Steve Buscemi (credited only as "OPP Man") as a jailhouse acquaintance of Johnny's who drifts in and out of the plot for no good reason.

As if the blatant nudity of the film's first few minutes didn't tip you off (almost always a sign of bad things to come), Johnny and Zandalee begin a torrid and graphic sex affair. Not *love* affair mind you, because in between each tryst, the two characters can barely stand to be in one another's company. We're supposed to believe that Zandalee is attracted to Johnny because he can still paint and has the passion that goes with active creativity, but the truth is that the artist line is a load of crap. Thierry has neglected her so badly that she'd probably hop in the sack with just about anyone.

Eventually, Thierry catches on to the affair, and the usual rounds of jealousy and recriminations begin. Zandalee must choose between her married life with a self-proclaimed "paraplegic of the soul" and sweaty sex with the grody painter whose most profound statement is: "If I can't paint, everything just turns to s---." Choices, choices.

Other than gratuitous nudity, there is nothing particularly erotic in *Zandalee*, and it certainly isn't thrilling. So we can't really say that *Zandalee* is one of the myriad Erotic Thrillers that flood video store shelves every month. However, the director of the movie, Sam Pillsbury, seems to have had quite a career making made-for-tv thrillers with names like *Sins of Silence* and *Shadows of Desire*. Pillsbury also made *Free Willy 3*, which in retrospect may not be the film we thought it was.

Zandalee also acts as a primer to anybody out there who wants to become a loan shark. It teaches the following lesson: If you try to kill someone who is in arrears to you, and you kill someone standing next to him instead, do not, repeat, *do not* yell your catchphrase at the top of your lungs as you make your getaway. This is because the person who you tried to kill owes you a lot of money, and knows who you are, and can now put you in jail pretty easily.

Final words about *Zandalee*: The people who make these lousy skin flicks know that we're only tuning in to see some gratuitous nudity – why do they insist on foisting a lousy story upon the viewing public as part of the deal? *Zandalee* might have made a great *Playboy* video, but as a love story about art, passion, and betrayal, it's an utter disappointment. We longed for Cage to appear in full Elvis regalia, parachuting into the scene from above – anything to break the monotony.

The Temp
(1993, Director: Tom Holland)

Awful *femme fatale* movies had something of a mini-renaissance in the early '90s, including such noxious titles as *Basic Instinct*, *The Crush*, *The Babysitter*, *Poison Ivy* . . . oh, the list goes on and on. They all feature, in one form or another, a conniving woman who is initially attractive on many fronts but eventually reveals her true colors and is nearly responsible for the downfall of all who put their trust in her. We wish we could say that *The Temp* is the worst example of this sub-genre, but the truth is, most of them are easily as painful as this movie. However, don't let that deceive you: *The Temp* is very, very bad indeed.

Peter Derns (Timothy Hutton) works as a marketing executive for the Mrs. Appleby cookie company. The environment is highly competitive, especially since Appleby was recently acquired by another company, constantly referred to as "the boys in New York." When Peter's regular assistant takes leave to be with his wife during childbirth, Kris Bolin (*Twin Peaks* alum Lara Flynn Boyle, also familiar to fans of TV series *The Practice*) arrives to save the day. Not only does she finish the all-important report due by noon, but she also reorganizes Peter's entire life in the space of a week.

Kris decides she likes working for Peter so much that when the regular assistant returns to work, she arranges an "accident" involving a paper shredder. Personally, we're the types to check the power eight times before sticking our hands into something with that much destructive potential, but there it is. A whirring sound, a spray of blood, an agonized cry, and Kris is sitting pretty in Peter's office again. She even sends the poor cad a sympathy card.

Unfortunately for Peter, Kris doesn't stop there. She has found that she likes being upwardly mobile, and so the company undergoes a colossal series of accidents and firings as Kris works her way to the top, trying to seduce Peter along the way. Peter, who is just exiting therapy for acute paranoia, doesn't know whether he imagines that Kris is engineering these events, or if she's really responsible. What he does know is that she's not making it any easier for him to reach a reconciliation with his estranged wife.

From here, *The Temp* spirals downward into absurdity. Not only are we led to believe that Kris can get away with murder (repeatedly), but she can also hack the company e-mail system, engineer a batch of cookies that cause test market volunteers to cough up blood, and a number of other highly unlikely activities that are usually outside the scope of your average temporary office employee. We began to think that Kris might actually be innocent, because her tally of crimes became too massive to believe.

The script is not completely to blame for *The Temp*'s hemorrhage-inducing awfulness; the cast does its part to lower the film's quality even further. Boyle should have gotten some sort of shame award for her overacting as Bolin. Faye Dunaway (as Derns' boss, Charlene) *did* get a shame award for hers – the Golden Raspberry for Worst Supporting Actress that year. Hutton chose to go the other route, becoming the most relentlessly boring screen personality we've seen since Jeff Muldovan in *Trancers 4*. Rounding out this roll call of shame is Dwight Schultz, who should really stick to those oddball characters on TV. His dull executive role in this movie made us pine for the wacky adventures of "Howling Mad" Murdoch on *The A-Team*.

When we see films like this, we often wonder what could have inspired a movie studio to make a film this wretched. Was the script re-written on the set? Were all the people involved suffering some mass hallucination that they were making a good movie? Perhaps the flick itself offers a clue: maybe somewhere, in an office in Hollywood, a vengeful temp is secretly greenlighting projects just like this one. Now *that's* scary.

Barb Wire
(1996, Director: David Hogan)

If you're going to go to the trouble of making a movie centered around a pair of breasts, we say: set your sights high! That's exactly what the makers of *Barb Wire* have done. Not only have they constructed a film showcasing Pamela Anderson, she of the once-grossly-enhanced mammaries and limited acting ability, but they've done it as a remake of *Casablanca*.

When we first heard that *Barb Wire* stole its story from one of Hollywood's greatest films, we figured the rip-off could only extend so far. We were right, but it extends a lot further than we dared expect. The film takes place in the "last free zone" of the United States, recently taken over by a Nazi-like congressional regime. There, Barb (Pamela Anderson Lee, in the, uh, titular role) runs a nightclub and engages in an occasional round of bounty-hunting to support her employees. Dutifully, a romantic figure from her past arrives with a new love, and that new love must be smuggled out of the country. Barb, of course, accidentally acquires exactly what they need to escape, and then must weigh her own interests against those of "the resistance."

Throw in a weaselly little guy (the dependable Clint Howard), a big fat guy, a corrupt-but-goodhearted cop, some trustworthy employees/friends, some resistance members, and a goose-stepping, screaming commandant with his goose-stepping, Nazi-uniformed goons, and you've got a movie that reminds you so much of *Casablanca* it's impossible to think of anything else. Then, the movie takes a turn to the silly and we're back in comfortable territory again.

Even though you would be hard-pressed to tell this from anything in the movie, Barb Wire is a character who originally appeared in a short-lived series of books from Dark Horse Comics, who scored a major hit when their character The Mask was translated to the big screen. *Barb Wire* is a good example of a comic book that has no real reason to be made into a movie, and of a comic book movie with no particular connection to the book that spawned it. We wish that movie producers would stop making comic books into movies on the strength of having an interested star and a finished script; the star should be able to act and the script should be good.

Rumor has it that Pamela Anderson Lee Anderson turned down the lead role in a film called *Hello, She Lied* (later titled *Miami Hustle*) because she didn't want to do such gratuitous sex and nudity. *Miami Hustle* was later made with Kathy Ireland in the lead. Not only was *Hustle* a better film than this one, but none of the sex or nudity involved Ireland! When it comes to picking roles, we're thinking that Pamela Anderson Lee Anderson Lee is a fork or two shy of a place setting. Suffice it to say that even in the rated version of *Barb Wire*, Pamela Anderson Lee Anderson Lee Anderson's über-boobs could probably have been given a screen credit of their own. In fact, they were nominated as the Worst Screen Couple in that year's Razzie Awards.

About the only thing to recommend this film, other than the limited thrill of seeing the exposed body of a Barbie doll made flesh, are the action sequences. If nothing else, these filmmakers really know how to bust stuff up and make it look impressive. But even here the film is bankrupt for inspiration, as the climactic fight on top of a piece of construction equipment hoisted into the air by a large crane is lifted whole from *The Protector*, one of Jackie Chan's early American efforts.

Films like this always give us hope that one day we might see one of our screenplays produced. We've got this great treatment for a remake of *Citizen Kane*, and we envision Arnold Schwarzenegger as the tycoon who also happens to go in for kinky S&M games. We call it *Citizen Pain*. Any Hollywood producers reading should e-mail us at guys@stomptokyo.com.

Cruel Intentions 2

(2000, Director: Roger Kumble)

Cruel Intentions 2 took a long and tortuous path to home video shelves, but that didn't stop it from being an utter piece of crap. As aficianados of Hollywood's less savory fare, we shudder to think how close we came to missing out on this film entirely.

Cruel Intentions, of course, was the trashy prep school tale based on *Dangerous Liaisons*. It starred up-and-coming stars like Sarah Michelle "Buffy" Gellar, Reese Witherspoon, and Ryan Phillippe. The film was mostly noteworthy for those stars, and a couple of leeringly erotic scenes, like the one in which Gellar kisses another girl.

Perhaps inspired by the successful translation of *Buffy the Vampire Slayer* from big to small screen, someone thought that *Cruel Intentions* would make a good TV series. The resulting project, entitled *Manchester Prep*, was intended to air on the Fox network, but despite airing some perfunctory publicity for it, Fox decided to withdraw the show because of problems with its quality.

Let us repeat that, because it bears repeating. Fox decided that *Manchester Prep* wasn't *good enough* for their network. This is the same network that has inflicted *Cops*, *When Good Pets Go Bad*, and *Temptation Island* on America. Any series unworthy of Fox should turn up its toes and die... or consider moving to UPN.

The whole concept behind this proposed series, which was to be a prequel to the movie, seems flawed to us. In *Manchester Prep*, Sebastian and Kathryn are supposed to be sophomores. In *Cruel Intentions*, the two are seniors. So even if *Manchester Prep* had been made a regular series, logically it would have been restricted to telling stories from a mere two years of these characters' lives. As it turned out, it didn't really matter.

After the quality-conscious people at Fox deemed the pilot unwatchable, Columbia TriStar retooled the pilot into a straight-to-video movie. That a majority of the pilot remains intact is obvious. It's equally obvious where the new material has been added. It's kind of like the *Twin Peaks* pilot that was released theatrically in other countries – a new ending was shot to create a sense of closure.

Sebastian Valmont (played by Phillippe in the movie, Robin Dunne here) leaves Illinois (?) to live with his father in New York City. His father has married into a super-rich family headed by Tiffany de Merteuil (Mimi Rogers), so Sebastian has a new school (Manchester Prep) and a new stepsister, Kathryn (played by Gellar in the movie, Amy Adams here).

Right off the bat the movie is an illogical mess. Sebastian seems to leave his old school at the end of the year (he somehow managed to print a nude picture of the principal's wife in the school yearbook), but after a cab ride to the airport and a plane ride to New York City, he arrives one day before the beginning of the new school year. Did the cab ride to the airport take three months? Sure, his cabby was a babe (on what planet does this movie take place?), but even a woman driver can probably find the airport in less than three months.

Sebastian and Kathryn take to each other like dogs and cats. Sebastian is better than Kathryn at nearly everything (except Sarah Michelle Gellar impersonation), but that isn't the end of the humiliations piled on the girl. The next day as Kathryn gives the orientation address to open the school year (she's president of the student body, of course), a girl named Cherie begins to choke on a piece of bubble gum. Cherie is saved by a quick application of the heimlich maneuver. Now, where do you think the gum ends up? Hint – it's somewhere funny! C'mon, guess.

If you guessed "Kathryn's hair," you can probably write a movie as good as this one.

Kathryn is also the head of the Manchester Tribunal, a secret society of popular kids who decide how best to humiliate the rest of the student populace. Those kids who spend their high-school years on the outside of the in-crowd probably suspect that something like this is going on, but the truth is even more disheartening. Teenagers are too selfish to bother with organized cruelty; like tornadoes, they pick their targets at random and without warning. It may make for a few good screen moments as the beautiful people cackle like Machiavelli, but the Tribunal is one of many subplots that never go anywhere because they were meant for later development in the TV series. Other non-starters include the "Sebastian's mother in rehab" plot and "Sebastian's father's naïve mistress plot."

For his part, Sebastian falls for Annette. . . er, *Danielle* (Sarah Thompson). You'll have to excuse our confusion, as the character's name was changed after the initial production and the name "Danielle" was dubbed in wherever necessary. For the most part, the film is edited to cover the change; we often see Danielle squirm at the moment her name is spoken, as if she is uncomfortable just hearing it. Other dialogue monkeying was performed in the editing room to add swear words, presumably to give the film a bit more "grit."

From this rich set-up the plot blooms. Sebastian tries to woo the chaste Danielle (who also happens to be the headmaster's daughter), while Kathryn tries to corrupt the gum-spitting virgin Cherie. Kathryn also begins attacking Sebastian with truly insidious schemes, the first of which is the **naked lesbian twin shower scene**. Hopefully this doesn't require an explanation. Sebastian takes a shower, and Kathryn sends **naked lesbian twins** to share the shower with him. As punishments go, it's right up there with the Spanish Inquisition's comfy chair. Are **naked lesbian twins** a male chauvinist fantasy? Hell yes! Did we love it? We're pretty sure the "woman driver" joke we made five paragraphs back should serve as our male chauvinist credentials.

So, the **naked lesbian twin shower scene**. How is it important? Well, there was probably dialogue, but we'll be darned if we can remember it. Obviously, this scene was added for the movie version, because Fox would never show **naked lesbian twins** on camera. For this reason, they will remain a second-tier network. But the **naked lesbian twins** do deliver some important exposition. For instance, they tell us that "Manchester Prep's a virtual whorehouse," even though we see precious little evidence to back this statement up. But who are we to disbelieve **naked lesbian twins**?

Right before this greatest of all scenes, the movie has our favorite dialogue bit. The Cambodian maid drops a platter and begins screaming hysterically. Sebastian comments, "Christ, it's like a f***in' Godzilla movie."

Hmm, that's not like any Godzilla movie *we've* seen. In any case, all of the dialogue in *Cruel Intentions 2* is as bad as that. The horrible acting just makes things worse. We tried to make the movie better by imagining Christopher Masterson (Francis from *Malcolm in the Middle*) as Sebastian. He might have been able to sell some of these lines. Amy Adams, however, is irredeemable as a faux Sarah Michele Gellar.

The most bizarre trait of *Cruel Intentions 2* is its outmoded use of stereotypes. Kathryn is the spoiled rich girl from every awful '80s comedy. The de Merteuil mansion has a full complement of embarrassingly out-of-date ethnic stereotypes for servants. The Asian maid goes into hysterical fits. The British butler is fatherly. The German chef kills squawking chickens with a cleaver within earshot of the dining room. And the footman is a slovenly Indian. What is this, a World War II Charlie Chan film?

To give the movie version some kind of closure the original episodes didn't have, the movie pulls out a "twist" ending. After falling in love with Danielle and renouncing his sexual predator ways, Sebastian finds out that it's all a set-up. Danielle is actually a slutty friend of Kathryn's pretending to be wholesome. This drives Sebastian into becoming the manipulative bastard we see in *Cruel Intentions*. There is some evidence that this coda was written and shot quickly, because the dialogue doesn't quite make sense:

Danielle (after sticking her tongue down Kathryn's throat): Don't tell me you bought that virgin bulls***.

Sebastian: No, I... I... I saw you, you were with your dad!

Wha...? Does Sebastian think there is a teenaged girl who *doesn't* act like a virgin in front of her father? That hardly seems like the reaction of such a cynical and manipulative person. And what could Kathryn's motivation possibly be for arranging such a scenario? The final scene depicts Cherie's seduction by Sebastian in the back of a limo as Kathryn and Danielle smile lasciviously from the front seat.

So the movie ends as it began, confusing and more than a little annoying. If the series wasn't good enough for TV, it's tough to imagine how the producers thought that adding a **naked lesbian twin shower scene** would make two pilot episodes into a compelling movie.

On the other hand, we encourage the producers of bad TV pilots to try adding **naked lesbian twin shower scenes** to their movies. We'll watch them all, just in case one of them accidentally turns out to be a movie worth watching for other reasons, too.

PART FOUR

I Wanted to Try Something Different

"I Wanted to Try Something Different"

Of course, the title above is more likely the excuse an actor uses afterwards to explain her presence in an unfortunate movie than the honest reason for doing it. Often there is a boat payment to be met, a favor to be repaid, or a studio contract to be fulfilled. Boredom may well inspire a few out-of-character career moves, but few people outside of Troma Studios ever set out to make a bad movie.

From a studio's perspective, an established star is often viewed as a panacea for a troubled project. Why delay a film's production with script re-writes when the mere inclusion of a household name will guarantee sufficient box office draw? We suspect that Robin Williams is the victim of several such studio crap shoots – the hope that his energetic improvisational talent will turn a script that could really use another month in the word processor into the next hit film must be a difficult temptation to resist. Studio execs (and Williams himself) never learn, though; for every *Mrs. Doubtfire* and *Good Will Hunting*, there seem to be four or five *Jumanji*s and *Being Human*s.

Making the decisions from the other side may be no less perilous. Bruce "Evil Dead" Campbell likes to play a game with his fans when they ask him about *Congo*, one of the more notorious stinkers with which he is associated. In the game, the fan plays the studio executive, and Campbell pitches *Congo* to them.

"I want to make a movie. It's based on a Michael Crichton novel, and adapted by John Patrick Shanley, who won an Academy Award for his screenplay *Moonstruck*. Sound good so far?"

"Of course," shrugs the fan, who realizes he is now the butt of a joke and is sorry he asked the original question.

"Also, I'm gonna get Frank Marhsall and the other producers of movies like *Raiders of the Lost Ark*, *Back to the Future*, and *Poltergeist* to produce and direct the film. That's exciting, right?"

"Well, yeah."

"Jerry Goldsmith will do the music, and Steven Spielberg's cinematographer will make sure it looks good. With all this talent working on the picture, does it sound like a movie you want to make?"

"Sure," the fan replies.

"*Sucker!*" yells Campbell with a grin.

Tentacles

(1977, Director: Ovidio G. Assonitis)

It's difficult not to generalize about movies, but we give every film we watch an opportunity to impress us. Chick flicks, Mexican wrestling movies, the complete works of Adam Sandler – sure, these film categories are all dark blots on the landscape of cinema, but we give them all a chance, and we even *like* some of them. But if there is a sub-genre that has a disproportionate number of bad films in its ranks, it is the *Jaws* rip-off. The vast majority of these ubiquitous flicks are unwatchable. Plus, we can unconditionally guarantee that there has never, ever been a good Italian *Jaws* rip-off.

Tentacles is an Italian *Jaws* rip-off, and therefore it is bad. Very bad. And bad in a boring way, not a funny way. It is not the kind of film you watch, it is the kind of film you survive. Clumsily made, incoherently edited, this movie fails to create even a moment of tension during its ninety tedious minutes.

The remarkable thing about *Tentacles* is that while it is obviously a low budget film, it has an astonishingly recognizable cast. John Huston, Shelly Winters (obviously riding high on her aquatic experiences in *The Poseidon Adventure*) and Claude Akins all put in time, and Henry Fonda is present for a couple of scenes. Yes, *that* Henry Fonda. What goes on here? Were these actors fulfilling their part of some bizarre Mafia pact? Only something of a shadowy, evil nature can explain the high-powered main cast thrown in with these low-statured Italian extras and producers' girlfriends.

To recount the plot seems pointless, but our dedication to our readers prevails. A seaside community called Solana Beach is plagued by mysterious deaths near the water. Reporter Ned Turner (Huston) investigates the case as bodies come bobbing up on shore. Is some human agency responsible, like the Trojan Construction Company owned by Whitehead (Fonda), or is it a giant octopus? Judging from the film's title, it's the octopus, but the creature is driven to madness by vibrations from the machinery Trojan is using to dig an underwater tunnel. Stop laughing – this is serious business!

None of the film's characters figure out what is happening in a timely manner. Instead, we must sit through an overwhelming number of scuba diving scenes. Few things are as boring as filmed scuba diving. People who are scuba diving must move slowly, and they can't talk to each other. All they can do is look at things and occasionally point at suspicious holes in the sea floor. We found ourselves rooting for the horrible man-eating creatures that (we hoped) were lurking at the bottoms of those holes.

Our patience went unrewarded. The divers are not eaten by terrifying monsters with a taste for human flesh, because *Tentacles* doesn't even have the budget to show the giant octopus that is nominally the focus of the film. Most of the octopus' scenes are created by filming a normal octopus at the bottom of an aquarium, then editing these shots into the action featuring Italian actors.

Notice that we say *Italian* actors. None of the American actors (except Bo Hopkins, who plays a marine biologist) ever interact with the octopus. We can only assume that Fonda, Huston, and the other Americans agreed to do this movie with the understanding that it was essentially a paid Italian vacation, and that they wouldn't have to go near the water. One way we tried to get through this film was by pretending that Huston was actually playing Gandalf, and that he was trying to defeat some sort of threat to Middle Earth. This worked until 55-year old Shelly Winters showed up in skintight satin pajamas. At this point we thought there might be two giant octopodes in the movie, but then we realized our mistake.

Huston, Winters, and Fonda disappear well before the film's conclusion, and none of them die at the tentacles of the monster, or even get a good look at it. This was a real disappointment, because the *Videohound's Golden Movie Retriever* promised us that we would "cheer when Winters is devoured by sea pest." Damn freelancers – we wish they'd watch those movies before they write the reviews.

The giant octopus is dispatched by its natural predators, a couple of convenient killer whales to whom Hopkins gives a pep talk before their release. One wonders if this is a reference to the fact that in *Jaws* the heroes' boat is named the *Orca,* but it seems unlikely that the people who made the film were even that clever. The scene in which the octopus dies is distracting for two reasons: The killer whales are played by hand puppets during most of the sequence, and we're pretty sure those hand puppets were tearing apart a real octopus during the film's climax. Apparently the Italian SPCA wasn't keeping an eye on filmmakers in those days.

We have read that octopodes are quite intelligent. Why, then, is there one in this movie? Did his agent promise him that it would advance his career? When asked why a giant octopus would suddenly become a predator of humans, one of the biologists offers the explanation that "it's an animal – disturbed by man's stupidity!"

We know exactly how the octopus feels.

What's that? Your appetite for killer sea beast movies has only been whetted by all this talk of murderous molluscs? Look no further than the list below, me hearties, for a sampling of the most terrifying films ever to feature finned furies and other underwater unspeakables!

Creature from the Black Lagoon – The 1954 classic can still scare audiences out of their bathing suits. We love the line in which the riverboat's captain describes the denizens of the Amazon as "keelers."

Piranha – Plucky investigators race killer fish downstream, hoping to avert disaster at a nearby summer camp. They don't entirely succeed. (Ulp.) The chattering noises made by the title critters may inspire nightmares. Be sure you pick up the original 1978 version.

Deep Blue Sea – This *Jaws* update throws in some genetic enhancement hocus pocus and convincing computer-generated sharks, but it fails to duplicate the sinister tension of Spielberg's masterpiece. Watch for the sudden and spectacular exit of Samuel L. Jackson.

Blood Beach – The action in this seashore flick comes not from the water, but from beneath the sand. Yeah, we thought it was lame too.

Humanoids from the Deep – Mutated experimental fish-men leave their ocean homes to forcibly mate with human women. Even more repulsive than it sounds, although it is hailed by some as a Corman horror "classic." Tellingly, the director is not one of those people.

More portholes (of varying quality) into the world of aqautic monsters: *Orca, Godzilla vs. the Sea Monster, Octaman, Monster from the Ocean Floor, Devilfish, Gorgo, They Bite, Alligator, Deepstar Six, Barracuda.*

Witchery

(1988, Director: Fabrizio Laurenti)

Finally, someone has made a movie that combines the excitement of watching paint dry on the wall of a theater showing a Steve Guttenburg film festival with the fun of witnessing David Hasselhoff's attempts to deflower a virgin. Gather the kids around the set and get ready for *Witchery!*

Strangely, the Internet Movie Database and other online sources often confuse *Witchery* with *Witchcraft* (1988), an American movie that has spawned an amazing eleven sequels to date, and another film named *Witchcraft* that was made in the '60s. Where this confusion comes from, we're not sure. Those other films may be bad, but it's unlikely that they plumb depths such as this.

On an island off the coast of Massachusetts, Leslie (Leslie Cumming) researches a famous witch incident that occurred there. She brings along her boyfriend Gary (David Hasselhoff), who is a photographer. Apparently there is a "witch light" on the island, and Leslie wants him to get a picture of it. Gary, meanwhile, is apparently only there to nail Leslie. Goody! We were worried that we wouldn't get to see the mating habits of David Hasselhoff.

We knew this was going to be a rough movie almost immediately. You could hit Leslie in the face repeatedly with a big stick and she wouldn't be able to act bruised. Compounding her total lack of acting ability is the fact that she's totally mush-mouthed. We could hardly tell what she was saying – which is a problem, given that her character handles most of the exposition.

As anyone familiar with horror films knows, when people show up with poor acting skills, it sometimes means that the movie is a foreign production filmed on U.S. shores without the benefit of professional actors. And because the filmmakers don't speak English well, they can't tell how bad the English performances are. That's the case here. Most of the behind the camera talent is Italian, but the film was shot on location around Boston. You can easily tell which actors are pros, and which were cast for their looks.

Anyhoo, Leslie fills us in on the background of the island, most of which is coming from an obscure German book she is translating. There were witches, they were burned at the stake. Attention horror filmmakers: No witches were burned at the stake in the U.S. Our ancestors subscribed to the hang 'em, drown 'em, or let-'em-rot-in-jail theories of witch disposal.

There is a hotel on the island now, and that was owned by a movie star who threw herself out a window. Or maybe a witch did that. *Witchery* is so boring that we quickly lost interest in anything that wasn't pushing the plot forward.

To get more victims on the island, we are introduced to a bunch of other characters. It seems that a rich family is going to buy the hotel and remodel it, so they decide to visit it, along with the real estate agent and an architect. The family is made up of Rose, the greedy matriarch; her husband Freddie, whose distinguishing characteristic is ugliness; their very young son Tommy, who can't act; and their grown and pregnant daughter Jane, played by Linda Blair. The real estate agent, Freddie, looks and talks like Robert F. Kennedy, and the architect, Linda, is a passably attractive woman, which (by dint of horror movie logic) means that she is a sex fiend.

Everyone is stranded on the island by a series of unlikely coincidences and pretty soon scenes of people wandering around the house are randomly edited between scenes of creepy things happening. Finally, there is a mysterious Woman in Black wandering around the house who seems to be running the show. Is she the movie star? A dead witch? A particularly bad Amway representative? It is never completely clear.

Some of the allegedly spooky events in the movie include: Jane drops her pills into a bathtub, then gets sucked into another dimension through the inky surface of the water. If only Linda Blair were so easily disposed! Jane is lucky enough to emerge from the creepy dimension, but the other residents are in for grimmer fates. Rose also gets sucked into another dimension through a wall safe before she is deposited in the chimney with her mouth sewn shut. Her mouth is stitched shut for the sole reason that it keeps her from screaming when her husband unknowingly lights a fire below her. Later Freddie and Linda are kidnapped into the alternate dimension and are crucified. And lastly, Leslie is raped by the devil.

The Woman in Black (hereafter WiB) occasionally talks about the "three doors to Hell," which, we soon learn, are avarice, lust, and ire. Those doors (represented by the people the Woman has killed), along with the blood of a virgin, will allow our dark-clad villainess to reincarnate herself as Jane's baby. And there's the moral of the story. Leslie's virgin blood was procured when she was raped, so she could have avoided that trauma if she had just had sex with the Hoffster. So ladies, if you're a virgin and David "Knight Rider" Hasselhoff says he wants to have sex with you, we would advise you to say yes. The alternative may be even worse.

Towards the end of the film the WiB seems to have taken over Jane instead of her unborn baby, as was her stated intention. But who knows how these possessions work? Jane *is* played by Linda Blair, so maybe she was possessed by simple force of habit.

Witchery is a miserable film; incompetence oozes from every frame. To explain why people would be trapped on the island, the characters talk about a huge storm that is engulfing the area. The problem is, there is no storm. We never hear a storm. Out the windows, we see no storm. We see footage of police cars on the mainland, driving down the street, with no storm in sight. Okay, the streets are wet, but that may just mean Ridley Scott was filming there the day before. The only evidence we see of the storm (other than lines of dialogue like "the wind is picking up" when it clearly isn't) is a repeated shot of some breakers, but not even very big breakers. Not since Ed Wood Jr. have we seen ineptitude on this scale.

(Our colleague Dr. Freex claims to have witnessed a similar level of uncooperative cinematic weather in his review of *Jack Frost* – no, not the Michael Keaton version – which we encourage you to read at www.badmoviereport.com.)

Witchery has strikes against it for including David Hasselhoff in one of his creepiest roles, but we must also give it kudos for all the nasty things that happen to him. It's not every day you get to see the star of *Baywatch* and a German singing sensation cough up blood, and *Witchery* delivers the goods when the chips are down. Does the sight of Michael Knight impaled on a candelabra make up for the missing story, the substandard acting, or the inane dialogue? No, but it sure gave us a few minutes of the giggles as we rewound and played that scene over a few more times.

> Sometimes even good actors can get caught in bad witchcraft films. Orson Welles, whose bad movie choices could probably fill a book of their own, found himself in the miserable film *The Witching* (aka *Necromancy*, aka *Rosemary's Disciples*). In it, the man who was Citizen Kane plays Cato, an occult leader in the town of Lilith, California. When a young couple moves to the town, they become instrumental in the cult's attempt to engineer the literal rebirth of Cato's son. The parallels to *Rosemary's Baby* are obvious, which is of course the reason it was tagged with the *Rosemary's Disciples* moniker.
>
> *The Witching* was masterminded by b-movie legend Bert I. Gordon, who is best known for giant creature films like *The Amazing Colossal Man* and *The Food of the Gods*. Unlike some of his simpler movies, this flick is nearly incoherent. This is partly because of the numerous versions that exist (scenes were added for a re-release in 1983), partly because of the incompetence exhibited by Gordon in his '70s films.
>
> *The Witching* is one of the few witchcraft movies that is actually worse than *Witchery*, which may explain why the actors involved have had fair to middling careers since. Pamela Franklin, who had an extremely promising early career, would further damage her reputation by reuniting with Gordon in *The Food of the Gods*, after which Franklin disappeared from feature films altogether. Lee Purcell made herself a fixture in TV movies and mainstream comedies like *Stir Crazy*, *Valley Girl*, and *The Incredible Hulk Returns*. Michael Ontkean hit a career high in the early '90s with *Postcards from the Edge* and his role as Sheriff Truman in the TV series *Twin Peaks*, but his fifteen minutes are clearly up. Roles in Lifetime Channel fare like *The Stepford Husbands* and *Nico the Unicorn* just don't quite compare.
>
> No matter how bad a witchcraft movie is, however, it is probably not to blame for the mediocre careers of its talent. More likely, the blame lies the other way. Still, it's fun to imagine Hollywood stars sitting around the campfire, scaring their kids with the tales of careers brought low by witchy movies: "And now, it's the story of Bette Midler and *Hocus Pocus!* OooooOOOOooooo!"

Carnosaur

(1993, Director: Adam Simon)

Roger Corman has long been the king of the rip-offs. During the past forty years, he has produced low budget films to capitalize on the success of every exploitation, horror, western, science fiction, and action film imaginable. From *X: the Man With X-Ray Eyes* to *Future Kick* to *Piranha* to *Stripped to Kill*, Corman fears no genre and spares every expense. The man even rips off his *own* films, recycling special effects from earlier movies to pad out the basic photography of his latest ultra-low budget opus.

All of this brings us to the summer of 1993, when a certain dinosaur movie directed by a certain Mr. Spielberg was scheduled to make box office history with some of the most realistic dinosaur effects ever created. Corman, seeing an opportunity, churned out his own dinosaur flick: *Carnosaur*, the small theatrical run of which started the week *before* that other dinosaur film made its bow.

Never one to miss out on a trick, Corman somehow shoehorned the otherwise competent Diane Ladd into the role of Dr. Tiptree, a mad scientist who genetically re-engineers dinosaurs into existence. We call this a "trick" because Ladd is mother to Laura Dern, who appeared in 1993's other dinosaur film. We don't know what dirt Corman had on Ladd to get her to appear in *Carnosaur*, but it probably involves someone's death, or sex with farm animals, or both.

Carnosaur claims to be based on the 1984 novel *Carnosaur* by Harry Adam Knight, but the film resembles the book only slightly. The novel is about a British reporter, Pascal, who thinks that a megarich local wildlife connoisseur named Penward has imported dangerous animals into the country. Pascal bravely seduces Penward's wife and learns the truth. In fact, Penward has been using gene splicing to turn chickens into dinosaurs, and pretty soon Deionychus and Tarbosaurus are roaming the British countryside, eating British citizens because even gamy old Britons are more appetizing than anything served in a British pub. Genre author John Brosnan, Knight's real identity, is credited with the movie's story treatment, but we suspect his work was largely ignored.

The movie *Carnosaur* takes place in a small town in the American southwest, populated by drunks, hippies, and Clint Howard. The drunks are represented by Raphael Sbarge, in the role of a disillusioned former medical student who passes the time raping the environment and slurrily spouting lines like, "Better a bottle in front of me than a frontal lobotomy." Doc's life turns around when he meets one of the hippies, a woman named Thrush (Jennifer Runyon). Meanwhile Clint Howard, represented by Clint Howard, tells gory stories to people who are trying to eat.

Then there are the dinosaurs. It seems local geneticist Dr. Tiptree is engineering chickens into dinosaurs because she has a beef with mankind in general. Boy, if there's one thing more evil than a scientist, it's a woman scientist. And if there's one thing more evil than a woman scientist, it's a woman scientist with an environmental agenda. But Tiptree has more up her sleeve than merely some lethal chickens. There's a nasty strain of the flu (revealed in the film as a series of pseudo-scientific captions) that she has invented which may spell the end of the human race – in one way or another.

Most of the film is the predictable "people get stalked by monster" scenes that have remained basically unchanged since *Alien*. The company that bankrolls Tiptree, a government subcontractor named Eunice, becomes aware of the fact that people are dying bloodily, and the saliva from the killer has the genetic markers associated with Eunice-improved chickens. Maybe the killer is eating Eunice chickens? "Either that, or the animal that killed these people was a chicken," one character opines with a straight face.

Movies like *Carnosaur* can be goofy and fun, but little of that comes into play here because the movie takes such a dark turn with the introduction of the disease and its gory results. The "government" as it is portrayed here is brutal and vicious, shooting first and asking no questions in its attempts to cover up the little project that they have inadvertently been funding. The movie starts out right with a few humorous lines and the use of Clint Howard, but *Carnosaur*'s final moments are so bleak and depressing that any fun we might have had quickly goes down the toilet.

Dooming *Carnosaur* to hellish mediocrity, however, are some very cheaply made dinosaurs. In a film titled after its creatures, those creatures need to be convincing, and these dinosaurs just aren't. Especially amusing was the article in *Dinosaur*, a magazine special printed by Starlog Telecommunications, which highlighted the various effects techniques in the movie:

> *... [Creature designer John] Buechler set about creating a series of different sized T. Rexes, including the full-sized, 16-foot-tall, pneumatically-operated creature, a 7-foot man-in-a-suit version, and a fully mechanical 3-foot beast with the ability to walk. For the Deionychus, Buechler created an 8-foot-man-in-a-suit model and a mechanized, walkable 1-foot mockup. Miniatures and hand puppets of both dinosaurs were also crafted.*

Needless to say, only the hand puppets (and a precious few seconds of animation) made the final cut of film. Yeesh, guys: if your hand puppet footage was the good stuff which made it into the actual feature, then you probably should have spent a few more bucks on R&D.

In more recent days, Roger Corman has taken to the ultimate in rip-off artistry: he rips off his own films in new ways. That's right: earlier Corman films that are now regrettably considered "classics" are ripe for the re-making, and Corman has done just that with updated versions of films like *Piranha* (with double the nostalgia potential for its inclusion of former *Punky Brewster* child star Soleil Moon Frye), *Humanoids from the Deep*, and *The Wasp Woman*.

Not that this should be particularly surprising. Where there's a dollar to be made in the budget film business, Corman will be there, palm extended. Nor can we claim that this is a particularly offensive practice, as Corman is only defacing his own "legacy" in much the same way that Disney churns out remakes of (and sequels to) films that have some actual nostalgia value. At least Roger Corman *admits* to milking his properties dry of every last dollar – without pretending that he does it for the good of families everywhere.

Starcrash

(1979, Director: Luigi Cozzi)

We'll give the Italians credit, they're fast. As we pointed out in our review of *Tentacles*, it was an Italian rip-off of 1975's Jaws, and hit theaters in 1977. *Starcrash*, an utterly amazing Italian rip-off of *Star Wars*, had a similar turnaround time. *Star Wars* was in theaters in 1977, and people desperate for another dose of space opera could go see *Starcrash* two years later.

But boy, you would have to be pretty desperate if you thought this compared to *Star Wars* in any way shape or form. *Star Wars* had Sir Alec Guinness and Harrison Ford; *Starcrash* has Christopher Plummer and David Hasselhoff. *Star Wars* built up a believable, if fantastic, universe; *Starcrash*'s alien planets are all too obviously Italian locations, given away by the fact that we've seen them all in many a Hercules film. With *Star Wars*, a new age of special effects began. With *Starcrash*, we were instantly transported back to the previous age, in which soda bottles suspended from fishing wire were somehow acceptable substitutes for spaceships.

The hero of *Starcrash* is interstellar rogue Stella, played by sexy Caroline Munro. She and her vapid, mystical sidekick Akton (Marjoe Gortner) are captured by the Empire (or somebody – it was never totally clear) and sent to an ore-mining prison colony.

Stella, who is made to wear a revealing and degrading prison outfit that is actually less revealing and degrading than what she wears when she has a choice in the matter, engineers a breakout. This is helped along by the fact that the ore processor fatally overloads after being shot once. After a few very welcome scenes of the scantily-clad Stella running around an Italian field, our heroine is picked up by Thor and Robot L, the law enforcement officers who captured and put her in prison in the first place. Thor tells Stella that the Emperor of the Galaxy wants to see her.

Sure enough, he does. The Emperor of the Galaxy (Christopher Plummer, who is dressed like he was waylaid into making this movie while on his way to play Marc Anthony for some other movie) charges Stella, Akton, Thor and L to find his son, whose ship was lost after it was attacked by red blob monsters. Stella and crew calculate three places that escape pods from the doomed ship may have landed.

The first planet is the planet of Amazons. We could really get behind this part of the film, as the scantily clad Amazons take Stella prisoner, and Stella fights her way out. Stella, it almost goes without saying, is wearing kick-ass knee-high boots.

The second planet is an ice planet. Stella wears a snow suit that covers her entire body. *Boring!* Let's move onto the next planet.

The last planet our heroes visit is populated by Neanderthals and David Hasselhoff. So we could have just said Neanderthals. Once Hasselhoff (who is the Emperor's son) is found we just have to wait for the good guys to defeat the bad guy for once and for all.

Oh wait, we didn't mention the bad guy. He's Count Zarth Arn (Joe Spinell), and he's out to do something really evil. We don't know what it is, but it involves his terrifying space fortress, which looks like a giant hand. When it goes into attack formation, naturally it makes a fist. Spinell is amazingly miscast – he's supposed to be dark and menacing, but compared to Darth Vader, Zarth Arn is a pizza delivery guy. Spinell was a fine actor who even appeared in *The Godfather,* but "galactic overlord" just isn't in his repertoire.

Starcrash is nearly unwatchable for many reasons. We love Caroline Munro, but for some reason her voice is dubbed by someone else. Everyone in the film is dubbed, except for Plummer and Hasselhoff – and even their voices were added in later, presumably over lunch one day, because the words rarely sync up to the actors' lips.

Starcrash is a typical Cormanesque hack job – recycled props and sets (note the costumes of the Imperial Guards, ripped straight from David Carradine's back after the filming of *Death Race 2000*), substandard effects, silly story, and a half-naked babe to hold it all together. If it weren't for the fact that she's been making similar trash all her career, we might even ask how Munro got roped into this movie.

The *coup de grâce* is the fact that all the dialogue is horribly written. Take, for instance, this actual passage of dialogue, with a few superflous bits taken out:

> "Get ready to ease out of orbit."
> "This doesn't make you nervous, does it?"
> "Well, leave it to me."
> "Build up maximum energy!"
> "OK, I'm ready."
> "All system prepare for full power!"
> "Let's lock in these controls..."
> "Let's go!"

This exchange prompted our friend Melanie to comment, "This really would have been more effective as a porn movie."

Melanie had many other choice comments, which we will quickly list here because she was so right about so many things.

- On the coherency of the plot: "What the hell? I have no idea what just happened!"
- On the protagonists: "They're morons."
- Regarding the special effects: "It's somebody's Lego collection!"
- Referring to Marjoe Gortner as Akton: "I think he's really convincing . . . as a *hairdresser*."
- And finally, Melanie's thoughts on *Starcrash* as a whole: "Not enough Wookiees in this movie. That's the problem."

We couldn't have said it better ourselves.

Alone in the Dark
(1982, Director: Jack Sholder)

There is a certain kind of actor who relishes the opportunity to play a crazy person. What better opportunity to overact and chew the scenery in ways that more buttoned-down roles won't allow? Several of those actors, including Jack Palance and Martin Landau, are featured prominently in *Alone in the Dark*. Donald Pleasence, no stranger to the less subtle aspects of the acting profession, is also in *Alone in the Dark*, playing the director of an insane asylum. But even for a character played by Donald Pleasence, he seems to be a few chairs short of a dinette set.

Pleasence is Leo Bane, the ditzy head of an unorthodox asylum known as The Haven, where the "voyagers" (don't call them patients!) are contained by doors held shut electrically. How exactly this is more humane than doors that lock mechanically isn't made clear, but neither are any of Dr. Bane's other methods. Dwight "A-Team" Schultz plays Dr. Potter, a psychiatrist whose wife wishes he would treat "neurotics, like everybody else." His only response is that he "just prefers psychopaths," and so he steps into a recently vacated position at The Haven. In his charge are several of the more violent patients, including ex-POW Hawke (Palance), church arsonist and former clergyman Byron (Landau), and a three hundred-plus pound child molester called Fatty (Erland van Lidth). Led by Hawke, the psychos decide that Potter must have murdered their previous doctor for his position and so decide to kill him in return.

One evening a citywide blackout allows these three patients, along with another mysterious killer known as the Bleeder (whose face we never see), to escape. Under the cover of the power outage and some unbelievably speedy civil unrest, Hawke, Byron, and Fatty pick up weapons and clothes at the scene of a local neighborhood looting, and head off to make some mischief.

The next day, the three psychos begin stalking Potter and his family. While Potter's wife and sister head off to protest at a local nuclear power plant (during a blackout?), Potter's young daughter is left alone. Then Fatty shows up in the house, claiming to be the babysitter. Note to Hollywood: Child molestation or the threat of such is never entertainment, and really has no place in a relatively frivolous movie like this one.

Happily, someone involved in the making of this movie had a little taste, and after a few uncomfortable scenes, nothing happens. But the real babysitter shows up while the daughter is asleep, and then has sex with her boyfriend . . . you can guess the rest.

The next night the power is still out, and Hawke, Byron, and Fatty surround Potter's house, intent on killing him. Trapped in the house is Potter, his family, and some guy named Tom Smith whom Toni picked up after the protest.

Whatever happened to the Bleeder? *Hmmm...*

Made in the wake of *Halloween* and its imitators, *Alone in the Dark* conforms slavishly to slasher movie conventions despite the fact that it's not about a solo slasher. And since there are an overabundance of villains, why not have a similar surplus of horror movie clichés? For instance, it is a well-known fact that in horror and sci-fi films, the token black guy is usually the first to die. In this film, once that occurs, they actually introduce *another* black guy, just so he can be the first to die in the second half of the film! *Alone in the Dark* also manages to give us two instances in which a car refuses to start in a crisis situation, and of course there are the aforementioned teens having sex who meet an unpleasant end. (We knew we'd be seeing more than a few of babysitter Carol Levy's physical assets because she was credited as "and Carol Levy as Bunky.")

The fact that this movie was ever committed to film, distributed, and shown in movie theaters should be a deep source of shame for most of the actors involved, but this is especially true for Martin Landau. Jack Palance we can understand – this is the guy who did one-armed pushups during his Oscar acceptance speech and embarrassed himself for generations to come with his performances in *Hawk the Slayer* and *Outlaw of Gor*. But Landau – he went toe-to-toe with Anjelica Huston in *Crimes and Misdemeanors!* What is he doing here, swinging a burning shirt over his head and aping the shrill, nervous laugh of a madman? It just goes to show that even a career like this one (*North by Northwest, Mission: Impossible*) can crash and burn (*Meteor, Harlem Globetrotters on Gilligan's Island*) before rebounding (*Crimes, Ed Wood*). True, Landau's 40-year career could be likened to a yo-yo, but we like to think that he's better than . . . *this*.

Topping off the shame like tepid whipped cream on a stale piece of pumpkin pie is one of the very worst *deus ex machina* endings you will ever witness. Just as Hawke is about to finish off Potter, the blackout ends. And hey, somebody left the TV on! And hey, the news is running a piece on the killers! And *hey*, the news guys are interviewing the *very doctor* who used to treat the loonies back at the Haven! He's not dead after all, and their little campaign of vengeance has all been a big misunderstanding! Whuttaya know about that?

If, after all this, we actually have to tell you not to rent *Alone in the Dark*, then you're beyond our help. We do hear there's a place for folks like you, though – where all the doors on all the cells are held shut by electricity.

If you watch as many bad movies as we do, you hope you won't have to watch the same bad movie more than once. If you *do* have to watch it again (usually because some schmuck made a newer version of the same story), you hope that at least it will be better the second time around. No such luck. *Angel* star David Boreanaz made his big-screen premiere in *Valentine* (2001), a breathtakingly inept slasher flick about high school friends murdered years after their school days as retribution for humiliating a nerdy classmate.

Valentine might have been merely forgettable (if only we *could* forget it!), except for the fact that the killer is actually revealed through the *exact same gag* that reveals the Bleeder's identity towards the end of *Alone in the Dark*. The revelation that apparent good guy Boreanaz was actually the killer might have been really surprising too, if his agent hadn't spoiled it in press releases months before the movie came out!

The Last Chase
(1981, Director: Martyn Burke)

By the time the last race is run, the human race is running on fumes. That's the apparent message behind *The Last Chase*, a strangely ambitious yet not-so-strangely horrible film about the future of America as imagined in the year 1981.

First comes the complicated set-up. What's a bad movie without the complicated set-up? Like the number of licks it takes to get to the center of Tootsie Pop, the world may never know. Lee Majors (fresh off *The Norseman*) plays Franklyn Hart, a race car driver who was on his way to setting some sort of record at an international racing championship when he was involved in a car crash. (Needless to say, Tiger Woods went on to win.) Because of this, Frank developed a psychological aversion to racing and can no longer drive in the speedy manner to which he became accustomed. In the years following the crash (which took place "in the '80s") the United States' supply of oil ran out, and the country was hit by a plague. Frank's wife and child died of the unidentified disease (judging by the wallpaper in Frank's '70s-style house, they were projectile vomiting), and Frank was made a spokesman for mass transit in the new order.

Precisely how the all-encompassing new order came about is never explained, but here's what we know: America only exists on the East Coast, with the majority of North America left unpopulated. California, however, exists as a "free republic" in opposition to the less laid-back America. The populated portions of the country are completely urban, and there is no fuel for cars or airplanes. Even more disturbing: Coca-Cola and McDonald's are things of the past. Surprisingly, the whole shebang is run from the Death Star's control room, by one guy who sits in the middle of the room with all the buttons, and a woman who looks at the big screen and asks questions for the other guy to answer. There are some vague hints that the disease

"I Wanted to Try Something Different"

and the gas crisis may have been contrived to facilitate the takeover, but that subject is never really explored.

After twenty years of being a spokesman, Hart has had enough. Truly, being a spokesman is backbreaking labor. Upon receiving a transmission from California he decides to make a run for it in his Porsche racer, which just happens to be buried under his garage. Psychological aversion or no, this is one boy who feels the need for speed.

Before Hart heads off on his cross-country odyssey, he somehow picks up a student named Ring. Ring is played by Chris Makepeace, who played a high school schlep who suffered many beatings by his classmates in the classic film *My Bodyguard*. In *The Last Chase*, he plays a high school schlep who suffers many beatings by his classmates. What a range, that Chris! (Given his performance here, it was difficult not to see the bullies' point of view.) Precisely how Ring hooks up with Hart is a very convoluted story, and quite contrived as well, so just take our word for it: Ring ends up riding shotgun as Hart makes a run for a border.

Needless to say, the totalitarian government can't stop Hart because all they have are electric golf carts. Faced with a PR disaster should gasoline succeed (huh?), Washington sends a bureaucrat named Hawkins (George Touliatos) to the Death Star's control room to oversee the recapture of Hart. If this were a particularly competent totalitarian regime they would simply impose a media blackout on the whole situation, so it wouldn't matter if Hart made it or not. But this doesn't seem to ever occur to anyone. Besides, "Radio Free California" keeps interrupting the *Leave it to Beaver* re-runs.

Now, you're a totalitarian regime that wants to catch a guy in a Porsche: What do you do – what do you do? If you answered, "Put Burgess Meredith in an old Sabre jet and send him after the car," you may have what it takes to impose your will upon a United States weakened by disease and lack of gas, because that's exactly what they do in *The Last Chase*. Meredith plays a Korean War-era fighter pilot who is apparently the only person qualified to fly anymore. Personally, we would have thought that they could have chosen some guy who was eighteen when the fuel ran out so that the pilot wouldn't be helplessly geriatric, but hey, we've never oppressed the population of any country, so what do we know?

In a token nod towards realism, Meredith's character, Captain Williams, enjoys his return to the skies so much that he merely toys with Hart, buzzing him menacingly and firing the odd machine-gun round in order to prolong the chase. Blithely ignoring the fact that the fuel in the jet can only last so long, Williams pursues Hart all the way to Arizona, where their shared love of speed and the extravagant waste of fossil fuels makes them brothers in spirit, especially after a lively game of chicken on the abandoned highway.

Oops, we forgot one other feature of the totalitarian order. They have "the laser," which is a smallish laser gun positioned on a small hill overlooking that abandoned highway in the middle of Arizona. Hawkins says it was put there to fight off the Russians, assuming the Russians tried to invade America by way of an abandoned highway in the middle of Arizona. Also, from what we see, the laser is not effective at hitting targets that move much faster than your average cactus, so if the Russians came in at even a slow trot America would be screwed.

The most depressing aspect of *The Last Chase* is that, if this is indeed the last motor chase in American history, it is rather pathetic. One guy in a racing Porsche pursued by men in electric golf carts and a geezer in a jet fighter does not make for gripping high-speed cinema. We prefer to think that the fascist anti-oil government in place might have invented speedy electric cars or even have a fleet of their own gas-guzzling automobiles stashed away in order to hunt down such lawbreakers as Hart. Even the makers of such lowbrow Corman efforts as *Grand Theft Auto* and *Death Race 2000* understood that chases need lots of cars so they can be cracked up and rolled over and generally destroyed in as flamboyant a manner as possible. Compared to these films, *The Last Chase* is downright soporific. To think that this is the end of the Great American Road is enough to make an assembly-line-hardened UAW member sit down on the factory floor and weep bitter, bitter tears.

Zardoz

(1974, Director: John Boorman)

Is there anyone with as varied a film career, quality-wise, as Sean Connery? Here is a man known world-wide as Secret Agent 007 James Bond, and yet two years after his last true Bond film (*Diamonds Are Forever*), here he is, running around in red underoos and calling himself Zed.

Not that there's anything *wrong* with that.

The film in which he does these things, however, is a terrific argument against the use of psychotropic chemicals. Far from the allegorical commentary it was probably intended to be, *Zardoz* is a muddle of surrealistic imagery and psuedo-intellectual twaddle intertwined with occasionally laughable moments. Connery's skimpy attire and sagging 43-year old physique aside, this is one movie that is just plain weird.

In the year 2293, the denizens of Earth worship the Big Giant Head from *3rd Rock from the Sun*. Finally, proof that NBC is making a bid to take over the world! If you want to get technical about it, they're actually worshipping Zardoz, their god and supplier of firearms. No, really. The big flying head descends upon the horse-riding masses, expostulates for a while on the good nature of guns versus the bad nature of penises, tosses out loads of weapons, and then departs. On second thought, maybe the big flying head is actually financed by the NRA. It even looks kind of like Charlton Heston playing Moses.

The point of all this flinging of ordnance is to fulfill Zardoz's plan: the unkempt and unwashed "Brutals" who live in the "Outlands" (as opposed to *Outland*, which is a totally different Sean Connery film) must be kept from multiplying. To this end, a race of kowtowing Exterminators has been developed to take the weapons from Zardoz and kill the other Brutals. Why the oppressed Brutals don't just hang around and grab up some of those guns for themselves when they're expelled willy-nilly from the mouth of Zardoz (complete with ammunition) is anyone's guess.

To get the plot moving, Zed hops aboard the Big Flying Head one day when it stops to collect a shipment of wheat. Once inside, Zed discovers that Zardoz is not a god, but rather a flying machine. After disposing of its pilot, Zed finds himself in the Vortex, an oasis of calm where the current ruling class of the planet holds a non-stop Renaissance festival.

The best thing about the Eternals, as they are called, is that many of them are played by perky '70s British actresses who don't feel the need for too much clothing. Connery must have had a terrific time frolicking about with these micromastic pretties, but they really don't make up for the assorted other British looneys we're subjected to during the course of the movie.

Weirdest of all is Friend, who looks like the genetic spawn of Eric Idle and Paul McCartney. He is apparently a bit of a bad egg, what with his thinking of bad thoughts and such. Through him we get to witness what happens when someone refuses to make leather mugs 24-7 like the rest of the Eternals. He becomes a Renegade, which means that he is artificially aged and then forced to wear an ill-fitting tux and hang out with other similarly dressed Renegades. They spend all their time dancing very slow waltzes. Oh, and the Vortex is also inhabited by the Apathetics, but they're *really* weird.

After 45 minutes of setup, the plot finally begins to fall together, and what a strange beast it turns out to be. You see, Zed is actually a super-brained mutant, and not the ruthless killer he seemed to be. He's the last hope for humanity or something, which is evidenced by his dialogue.

Zed: An old man calls me. The voice of the turtle is heard in the land.

We swear we are not making this up. Later on, the Eternals bequeath all of their collected wisdom to Zed, and because Zardoz is a film made in the '70s, this involves people having sex.

We've mentioned a couple of times before that science fiction films are rarely about ideas, which is strange because science fiction has its roots in idea-laden short stories. The saving grace of this movie is that it does have the occasional interesting idea, in particular the origin of the word Zardoz. Zed's quest does finally make some sort of twisted sense, which is a relief, but the plot is so buried in experimental filmmaking (the cinematographer's previous credits include *2001: A Space Odyssey*) and pretentious dialogue that it became difficult for us to care.

The only thing stranger than *Zardoz* (or Connery's attire in it) is the career of its director, John Boorman. Boorman made his mark a year before *Zardoz* with *Deliverance*, a film famous for causing psychological problems both in its stars and in a generation of moviegoers. He went on to direct an amazing variety of films, including the awful *Exorcist II*, *Excalibur*, *Emerald Forest*, and *Hope and Glory* (one of Chris' favorite movies). More recently, he brought us *Beyond Rangoon* with Patricia Arquette. We might have suspected that a director so firmly entrenched in the '70s super-cerebral science fiction genre during the making of *Zardoz* would go on to a bizarrely uneven career. . . much like Sean Connery, now that we think about it.

As super-weird '70s movies go, *Zardoz* could be worse. It could have starred someone less famous than Connery, which would have robbed us of the sight of James Bond wearing a full wedding dress.

Raise the Titanic!
(1980, Director: Jerry Jameson)

Obviously, the reason we originally went back and dug up this moldy oldie was because of the success of James Cameron's epic *Titanic*. Between the two of us we've seen *Titanic* five times, and we've seen *Titanic: the Exhibit* which toured many of the major U.S. museums. We've read the books, and we've visited the web sites. Heck, we've done everything but gone down to the wreck to see it ourselves.

Finally, we watched *Raise the Titanic!* Based on the pot-boiler by Clive Cussler, this movie would seem to be the perfect sequel to *Titanic*. Cameron spent three hours and fifteen minutes sinking the ship, and now we get to watch a cast of '80s character actors spend ninety minutes bringing it back up again.

First off, understand that *Raise the Titanic!* is a really big budget movie. The production values are lavish, the cast is all-star. Heck, they even got Alec Guinness to play a survivor of *Titanic*'s sinking. Jason Robards plays an Admiral and the venerable M. Emmet Walsh is also featured. Anne Archer shows up and demonstrates her nearly boundless ability to deliver annoying dialogue. ("I am a good fisherperson. I just can't get the wormy on the hooky!") John Barry provides the score, but that fact actually has a down side, because it inspires the irrational hope that James Bond will show up. The only person among the creative staff who doesn't seem to be a movie veteran is the director, Jerry Jameson. Pretty much everything he did before and after *Raise the Titanic!* has been for TV. That may go a long way towards explaining why so much of the drama in this movie plays like an old TV mini-series.

Why would anyone try to raise the *Titanic*? We're glad you asked. It seems that some secret organization in our government has designed an anti-missile shield (Salt II, anyone?) that will protect the

U.S., but they need a certain radioactive element to power it. That element is Byzanium, a made-up word that doesn't even sound real. Now it turns out that almost no Byzanium has ever been found, but then Dr. Gene Seagram (David Selby) discovers a possible source. It seems that a U.S. agent working on an arctic island discovers that an earlier group of American miners located a motherlode of Byzanium in the early years of the 20th century. The Byzanium was transported to England, where (you guessed it) it was put on the *Titanic* in a big vault for the last leg of its trip. If our heroes can get to the Byzanium, the government can activate their defense system. "If we're lucky," quips Seagram, "we can make nuclear warfare obselete."

So who can possibly raise the *Titanic*, thereby ensuring world peace? There is only one man up to this daunting task, and that man (and what a man!) is international man of action Dirk Pitt! Yes, Dirk Pitt! That's his name. Dirk Pitt! Doesn't the name Dirk Pitt! just scream to have an exclamation point after it? We think it does. Dirk Pitt!

Where were we? Oh yes, the *Titanic*. We got distracted by Dirk Pitt! So our heroes have to find *Titanic*. Rather than just raising the vault, or punching through the hull of the ship to get at the mineral, they decide to raise the entire darn thing from the bottom of the Atlantic. But with a man like Dirk Pitt! on their team, they can do it.

Unfortunately, the *Titanic* isn't at its last reported location. *D'oh!* Now they have to find it. As they search the sea floor in one of many long, boring, murky scenes where spotlights scan the ocean bottom, they find their first clue: A trophy congratulating a doctor for his three years of service on the ship *Olympic*. We are then informed that the same doctor was aboard *Titanic* when it went down. Uh huh. This begins a long line of historical and factual errors that could ruin your enjoyment of *Raise the Titanic*. *Olympic*, one of *Titanic*'s sister ships, was launched only eleven months before *Titanic*, so there is no way anybody aboard *Titanic* could have three years of experience on the other ship.

Our heroes, blissfully ignorant of history, continue on. Eventually, *Titanic* is found, ten miles from where it went down. Now wait a minute! *Titanic* sank in two miles of water, and when last seen it was heading straight down. How did it move horizontally ten miles from where it sank? It was a hunk of iron, and not hydrodynamically shaped. Also, when *Titanic* is found, it's in one piece. This is a problem because several survivors reported seeing her break in two. We'll forgive this, though, for the sake of the story – if you don't assume that the *Titanic* is essentially seaworthy once you get her up off the bottom, then you don't get those cool shots of her surfacing triumphantly after seventy years.

And surface she does: Dirk Pitt! (played by Richard Jordan) forms a plan to patch up the holes in the liner's hull, flush the water out of the lower decks with a buoyant foam, and float her to the top with some sort of compressed gas. If we give this movie credit for nothing else, we will say this: the scenes in which the ship actually surfaces are quite impressive. Even without today's fancy computer technology, the filmmakers have created not only a convincing model of the ship from afar, but also a darn good replica of the raised *Titanic*'s decks for the actors to walk around on afterwards. It's not completely seamless, of course, but certainly enough to convey the emotion involved as *Titanic* floats on the ocean once more.

It's too bad that the movie loses its momentum there. Once the *Titanic* does surface, the only thing left to do is sail it into New York to a huge crowd of onlookers (actually footage from the American Bicentennial celebration four years previous) and excavate the hold for the Byzanium. If they had done that in a timely manner, then this film would be getting a better review. Instead, there's an exercise in stupidity involving some Russians and a surprise "twist" ending involving the Byzanium. What this really does is extend the movie well beyond its climax, boring the audience to tears.

The problems with the ending reflect the problems with the film in general: too little of the action deals with the *Titanic* itself, and too much of it concentrates on the people involved. Do we care that Seagram's girlfriend, Dana (Anne Archer) used to be involved with Dirk Pitt!? No. Do we care that it inspires jealousy in Seagram? Not really. Are we interested to learn that Byzanium can be used for other weapons, thereby creating a moral quandry for Dirk Pitt! and

Seagram? Of course not! All we want is to see them raise the stinkin' ship.

What we have here is a shipwreck nearly as bad as the *Titanic*'s. A lot of money and effort went into this film, and we're sure that those who bankrolled it thought they had a surefire hit. Unfortunately, there was a large hidden iceberg in their way, one which could have been easily avoided by hiring better writers. OK, so we're beating this metaphor to death. Perhaps there is a deeper problem here. The story of the *Titanic* going down is one that speaks to everybody – that's why Cameron's *Titanic* was a worldwide hit. Maybe the story of the *Titanic* coming back up just doesn't hold the same appeal.

> Why a respected actor like Sir Alec Guinness would lend his credibility to *Raise the Titanic*, we're not sure. But it isn't the only time he's done work on a film that was outside his traditional genre. The mediocre woman-in-distress thriller *Mute Witness* (1995) includes just a brief bit of footage with Guinness, even though his character is central to the plot. The scene was actually shot ten years before the movie was completed, and was apparently the result of a chance encounter between Sir Alec and director Anthony Waller.
>
> Still, if Guinness hadn't been willing to take chances from time to time, we might never have known him as Obi-Wan Kenobi. Can you imagine someone else trying to pull off that "wretched hive of scum and villainy" line? *Brrrrr!*

The Star Wars Holiday Special
(1978, Directors: David Acomba, Steve Binder)

In the *Star Wars* films, you don't get much of a sense of what the characters do in their spare time. How does Darth Vader kick back? What does Obi Wan watch on TV? Is Grand Moff Tarkin a workaholic? Just about the only leisure activities we know of long ago in the *Star Wars* universe are weird holographic chess and Luke's forays into animal cruelty. ("I used to bull's-eye womp rats in my T-16 back home.")

Coming to the rescue of curious *Star Wars* fans like ourselves is *The Star Wars Holiday Special*, a TV offering that originally aired on November 17, 1978 (a long time ago in a galaxy far, far away, you might say), and shows us a day in the life of a *Star Wars* character's family, including a lot of what passes for popular entertainment across the galaxy. George Lucas himself was not involved in the actual production of the *Special*, though it does feature nearly every major character from the first *Star Wars* film, all played by the original actors. *The Star Wars Holiday Special* also introduces us to Chewbacca's family, and features the first ever appearance of Boba Fett. All this and numerous musical numbers fill up two hours of terminally cheesy '70s TV.

The *Special* takes place on the Wookiee holiday Life Day. At the Chewbacca household, Chewie's family nervously waits for the Wookiee alpha male to arrive. The Chewbacca household is made up of his wife Malla (played by Mickey Morton . . . hey! That's not a girl's name!), his son Lumpy, and Chewie's tragically ugly father Itchy. Yes, you read that last sentence correct, Chewie's closest family members are named Itchy and Lumpy.

Meanwhile, in stock footage culled from *Star Wars*, Han Solo and Chewie avoid Imperial Star Destroyers. ("Why do I always think gettin' you home for Life Day is gonna be easy?" moans Solo.) Malla

"I Wanted to Try Something Different"

and Itchy fret and then call various *Star Wars* characters on their video phones, including a transvestite Luke Skywalker (well, OK, maybe his stage makeup is just a bit overdone) and Princess Leia. Some Imperial troops search the Chewbacca residence, then leave. Chewbacca arrives, and the family celebrates Life Day with a ceremony that must be seen to be believed.

That's the entire plot – not really enough to fill two hours. Coming to the rescue are a raft of guest stars, including Art Carney, Beatrice Arthur, Diahann Carroll, Harvey Korman, and the musical talents of Jefferson Starship. They might as well have called it the *Star Wars Comedy Revue*, except for the fact that most of the really funny stuff is completely unintentional. Witness: the minutes-long "Wookiee"-dialogue scenes, consisting of nothing but that honking, moaning language they use. We're supposed to figure out what they're talking about by body language and context?

Lumpy: Haaaaarnk! Hooo hrrrrnk! (Mom! What did you get me for Life Day?)

Malla: Snort snrrnnk! Hrrrrrung! (Nothing, if you don't clean that bantha sty you call a room!)

Itchy: Hrunk hrunk hrunk hooot! (Hey kid! C'mere and pull my finger!)

The guest stars fill in the gaps between Wookiee conversations with short comedy sketches and musical numbers. You can tell this is science fiction, because the creators of the show try to make us believe that Bea Arthur can sing. Folks, we don't think any special effects budget is large enough for that. Nevertheless, Arthur croaks her way through a scene involving the Mos Eisley cantina, its cast of alien scum, and a giant rat.

Harvey Korman is the guest star most often on screen, with a faintly-amusing Galactic Julia Childs impression, an appearance as an alien on Tatooine who is smitten with the Bea Arthur barkeep character (again, this *is* fantasy), and a terminally unfunny "instruction video" bit that involves repeated video editing. Korman is most noted for the time he spent as a straight man to Carol Burnett and Tim Conway, and without them, his own comedic bits seem a bit – well, straight. He *can* be funny (see *Blazing Saddles*), but he isn't doing a very good job here.

The most offensive guest star, however, is the rank sentiment that pervades every scene. The original *Star Wars* movie had its moments of cheesy "I love you man" affection, but nothing can quite prepare you for the sight of Han Solo wrapping his arms around every Wookiee within reach. And how much more sympathetic could they make Lumpy? Look, they had a stormtrooper rip the head off his stuffed bantha!

And just when you think this video couldn't hurt you any more unless it popped out of the VCR at high speed and hit you straight in the face, Carrie Fisher begins to sing. Yes, she sings. And for a second you'll think, "Hey, they're dubbing her," and then you'll think, "No, if they were dubbing her it would sound better." The song itself is intended to be an inspirational variation on the *Star Wars* theme, but none of that intention shines through.

The one bright spot in this mess is the animated short that Lumpy watches on a portable TV thingy. Animated in a style similar to the movie *Heavy Metal*, it has neat designs and a story that moves at a good clip. Luke takes a Y-Wing to rendezvous with Chewie, who has inexplicably bound Han up and hung him by his feet from the ceiling. It turns out Han has contracted a deadly disease, and Chewie has to rely on the enigmatic Boba Fett to cure him. This was Boba Fett's first appearance, and it's pretty cool. Most surprising, it's actually consistent with his later appearances.

The worst thing about the *Special* is that after seeing it, we have come to hate Wookiees. We hate everything about them. (This was long after we reviewed *Starcrash*.) Malla is okay, but Itchy is the ugliest darn creature in the galaxy, and we wish someone would stuff Lumpy, that stunted little proto-Ewok, into a trash compactor. Why, of all the characters available, did the producers structure an entire two hours around stupid Wookiees?! And who the hell came up with that extra "e" at the end of the word "Wookiee?"

Like so many of the films we end up watching, *The Star Wars*

Holiday Special is a curiosity best left to extremely hard-core fans and to the corners of history. No matter how appealing it sounds to begin with, we guarantee this viewing experience can bring you little but pain. Fast forward to the animated sequence (let the Force be your guide) and turn the VCR off immediately after it ends. Trust in these words: you'll hate the rest of the special, and hate leads to the Dark Side.

Most Star Wars fans – heck, most people with a sense of curiosity – are now asking themselves, "where can *I* get a copy of this fine piece of Americana?" If you go to a store that sells or rents videos, prepare for disappointment. While you *can* find those unfortunate Ewok specials from years ago if you look hard enough, *The Star Wars Holiday Special* is harder to find than a Dewback on Hoth.

We got some personal insight into the reasons for this when we attended a talk by Steve Sansweet, head of fan relations at Lucasfilms. When asked about whether the *Holiday Special* might appear on DVD, Sansweet growled back, "Not on your life!"

In other words, Lucasfilms does not really acknowledge the special as part of *Star Wars* canon, and we are unlikely ever to see it released in an authorized form. In a rare example of negativity, the official Star Wars web site (www.starwars.com) calls the *Special* "regrettable" and a "heavily dated artifact of the late '70s [that] has only aired once, and is unlikely to ever surface again."

So an official release looks to be out of the question. Don't give in to despair, however: the *Special* has turned up on bootleg video tapes at dealer's tables in sci-fi conventions around the world, along with other curiosities like *The Phantom Edit*, which excises the annoying Jar-Jar Binks from much of *Episode I*, and countless underground films made by enthusiastic fans and imitators. Ain't capitalism grand?

APPENDICES

Movies Mentioned

Recommended Reading

B–Movie Web Sites

Movies Mentioned

One of the more frustrating experiences to have when reading about movies is to learn about a film you really want to see, but to find that there is more than one movie by that title, or that there is some other obstacle to finding the film that could be overcome if only you had just a *wee* bit more information. Here, then, is a complete list of the movies we mentioned in reviews and sidebars, with year and director information (indicated after the "D:"). Where whimsy dictated that we do so, we have included a capsule review.

2001: A Space Odyssey (1968) D: Stanley Kubrick.

A*P*E (1976) D: Paul Leder. Korean-American film about a 36 foot tall ape terrorizing the Korean countryside. The acting is basically on the same level as a middle school play, and the effects aren't much better.

Addiction, The (1995) D: Abel Ferrara. Pretentious, boring movie about a graduate student who becomes a vampire. She finds out life sucks, and tells us about it for minutes on end. Apparently the only thing worse than being a graduate student is being a graduate student who can't attend morning classes.

Air America (1990) D: Roger Spottiswoode.

Airplane! (1980) D: Jim Abrahams, David Zucker and Jerry Zucker.

Alien from L.A. (1987) D: Albert Pyun. How Pyun has managed to be so prolific yet always make such crap is one of the greatest unsolved mysteries on Earth. In this movie, Kathy Ireland discovers an underground population of Australian glam rockers.

Alligator (1980) D: Lewis Teague. John Sayles penned this *Jaws* rip-off with just a touch of an environmental message, but didn't lay it on too thick. Robert Forster plays the Chicago cop who finds himself dealing with a giant mutated alligator in the city's sewer system. An amusing and occasionally scary entry in the "killer beasts" sub-genre.

Amazing Colossal Man (1957) D: Bert I. Gordon Much-ballyhooed bad movie about a soldier exposed to the radiation of a "plutonium bomb blast." Radiation, as we've learned from Godzilla movies, makes things grow, and grow he does, until he's sixty feet tall. The pace is a little slower than you might expect. Director Gordon was obsessed with giant creatures; he followed this film with *War of the Colossal Beast*.

American Pie (1999) D: Paul Weitz.

Amityville Horror, The (1979) D: Stuart Rosenberg. Allegedly based on a true story, a house on Long Island is haunted, much to the chagrin of the current owners. Seven sequels followed.

Amityville II (1982) D: Damiano Damiani. Whether this is supposed to be a prequel or a sequel to the original film is not exactly clear, although it seems to be based on the real-life DeFeo murders. A new resident of the haunted house is possessed by a demon and goes crazy.

Angel Dust (1994) D: Sogo Ishii. At a certain time every week a woman is murdered in public, but the police have no leads. A female investigator thinks the slayings might have something to do with a cult that has been accused of

Appendix: Movies Mentioned **153**

brainwashing.
Annie Hall (1977) D: Woody Allen.
As Good As it Gets (1997) D: James L. Brooks.
Assault of the Killer Bimbos (1987) D: Anita Rosenberg. Sleazy movie about go-go dancers framed for murders by a gangster.
Baby (1985) D: Bill L. Norton. During the '80s, the theory that there might be sauropods still living in central Africa became quite popular. True, today it seems a little silly because we know sauropods didn't live in swamps (as these theories presupposed), but now you can see African dinosaurs in this Disney film. Two Americans find dinosaurs and try to save them from hunters, especially the cute baby one.
Babysitter, The (1995) D: Guy Ferland.
Back to the Future (1985) D: Robert Zemeckis.
Barracuda (1978) D: Wayne Crawford and Harry Kerwin. Slower, more ponderous version of *Piranha*, without even the distinction of the summer-camp lake swim scene. A strange population-control experiment goes awry and barracuda become more aggressive when they encounter the experiment's chemicals in the sea. A few *Jaws* in-jokes fail to make the film enjoyable.
Basic Instinct (1992) D: Paul Verhoeven.
Batman & Robin (1997) D: Joel Schumacher. Two hours of our lives we'll never get back. While predecessor Tim Burton knew enough to make dark films in this comic-book series, this installment practically has "Bang!" and "Pow!" balloons over the fights.
Beach, The (2000) D: Danny Boyle.
Beautician and the Beast, The (1997) D: Ken Kwapis.
Being Human (1993) D: Bill Forsyth. Robin Williams tries desperately to be a serious actor, and a tragically bad film results. Williams plays the role of multiple men throughout history, and nothing interesting happens to any of them. At least it features an appearance by the gorgeous Anna Galiena.
Ben Hur (1959) D: William Wyler.
Beverly Hills Bodysnatchers (1989) D: Jonathan Mostow. Campy comedy about mortician creating zombies with money stolen from mobsters.
Beyond Control: The Amy Fisher Story (1993) D: Andy Tennant.
Bikini Summer (1991) D: Robert Veze.
Blade Runner (1982) D: Ridley Scott.
Blazing Saddles (1974) D: Mel Brooks.
Blob, The (1958) D: Irvin S. Yeaworth Jr. Steve McQueen fights a voracious alien blob. It's actually much better than it sounds.
Blood Beach (1981) D: Jeffrey Bloom.
Blood of Dracula (1957) D: Herbert L. Strock. Hypnotic therapy turns a woman into a vampire. Next time, go to a strict Freudian.
Blood Surf (2000) D: James D. R. Hickox. A documentary crew on location to film people surfing with sharks run afoul of a giant crocodile.
Bodyguard, The (1992) D: Mick Jackson.
Buffy the Vampire Slayer (1992) D: Fran Rubel Kuzui.
Bull Durham (1988) D: Ron Shelton.
Butterfly (1981) D: Matt Cimber.
Captain America (1992) D: Albert Pyun. Pyun despoils the image of popular comic book hero Captain America. We're so bitter that we can't even talk about this film.
Captain Eo (1986) D: Francis Ford Coppola.
Car Wash (1976) D: Michael Schultz.
Casablanca (1942) D: Michael Curtiz.
Cast Away (2000) D: Robert Zemeckis.
Cat-Women of the Moon (1953) D: Arthur Hilton.
Charlie's Angels (2000) D: McG.
Chill Factor (1999) D: Hugh Johnson.
Citizen Kane (1941) D: Orson Welles.
Clockwatchers (1997) D: Jill Sprecher.
Coma (1978) D: Michael Crichton.

Congo (1995) D: Frank Marshall. Despite the award-heavy production crew and an early cameo by Bruce Campbell, *Congo* is one of the most disappointing cinematic conversions of a Michael Crichton novel yet. We're all for monkeys in the movies, but these sinister simians were pointless.

Crash and Burn (1990) D: Charles Band. In the future an evil corporation has taken over the world, and the only thing that can safeguard liberty is a giant robot. Don't get too excited, the robot only shows up for a few minutes at the end of the movie, and it isn't very good.

Creature from the Black Lagoon (1954) D: Jack Arnold.

Critters (1986) D: Stephen Herek. Alien bounty hunters come to Earth looking for dangerous little furballs that eat everything.

Critters 2: the Main Course (1988) D: Mick Garris. The critters come back and disrupt Easter festivities in a small town.

Crocodile (2000) D: Tobe Hooper.

Crocodile Dundee (1986) D: Peter Fairman.

Crossing, The (1990) D: George Ogilvie.

Cruel Intentions (1999) D: Roger Kumble.

Crush, The (1993) D: Alan Shapiro.

Curse, The (1987) D: David Keith. A relatively faithful adaptation of H. P. Lovecraft's *Colour Out of Space*, but badly shot and acted. Hard to watch, but not because it's scary.

Curse II: The Bite (1988) D: Frederico Prosperi. A man's hand turns into a snake. This has nothing to do with *The Curse* (1987).

Curse of the Pink Panther (1983) D: Blake Edwards.

CyberTracker (1994) D: Richard Pepin. If you want a little martial arts with your *Terminator* (1984) rip-off, you could do worse than this film with Don "The Dragon" Wilson.

Cyborg (1989) D: Albert Pyun. Albert Pyun teams with Jean Claude Van Damme (who does *not* play the titular half-robot) to create some movie magic.

Dances With Wolves (1990) D: Kevin Costner.

Dangerous Liaisons (1988) D: Stephen Frears.

Dazed and Confused (1993) D: Richard Linklater.

Death Race 2000 (1975) D: Paul Bartel. A perennial favorite of b-movie fans. Vicious race car drivers compete for points by mowing down pedestrians, with a little slap-and-tickle thrown in for good measure. Some fine exploitation starring David Carradine and Sylvester Stallone, and produced by Roger Corman, of course.

Deep Blue Sea (1999) D: Renny Harlin.

Deepstar Six (1989) D: Sean S. Cunningham. Low-budget predecessor to *Leviathan* and *The Abyss* manages to provide enjoyable underwater adventure despite its humble origins. A heretofore-unknown predatory aquatic creature munches on the crew of a sea-bottom heavy construction vessel when they disturb its home. Try not to focus on the scientific mistakes and you'll probably enjoy yourself.

Devil Fish (1984) D: Lamberto Bava. If you recognized the director as the son of acclaimed Italian horror director Mario Bava, you might expect some good things from *Devil Fish*. Sadly, you'll get none of them. Goofy gore effects do little to help this tedious tale of a watery predator run amok. Of course, the creature was created by a nearby monolithic evil company to kill people for no good reason, and only the bumbling local law enforcement and a few stalwart scientists can stop it. Sounds familiar, but we just can't think where we've seen it before.

Diamonds Are Forever (1971) D: Guy Hamilton.

Die Hard (1988) D: John McTiernan.

Appendix: Movies Mentioned **155**

Mathematicians have had to coin the term "gigazillion" to describe the number of rip-offs of this action film. Bruce Willis stars as the sardonic L.A. cop accidentally caught up in the evil-doings of a band of thugs. Alan Rickman gives one of his best performances as the villain.

Dinosaurus! (1960) D: Irvin S. Yeaworth Jr.. Explosions release two dinosaurs and a cave man from suspended animation near an island.

Don't Answer the Phone (1980) D: Robert Hammer.

Don't Be Afraid of the Dark (1973) D: John Newland.

Don't Go in the House (1980) D: Joseph Ellison.

Don't Go to Sleep (1982) D: Richard Lang.

Don't Mess with My Sister! (1985) D: Meir Zarchi. Director Zarchi's only follow-up to *I Spit on Your Grave* (1978) is a boring, simplistic story about guy who cheats on his wife, raising the ire of his wife's family.

Donnie Brasco (1997) D: Mike Newell.

Dr. Dolittle (1998) D: Betty Thomas.

Dungeonmaster (1985) D: Dave Allen, Charles Band, et al.

E.T. the Extra-Terrestrial (1982) D: Steven Spielberg.

Earth vs. the Spider (1958) D: Bert I. Gordon. Director Gordon continues his obsession with really big animals, in this case a humongous spider.

Ed (1996) D: Bill Coutrurié.

Ed Wood (1994) D: Tim Burton. It may not resemble what really happened very much, but Tim Burton's biopic of grade Z filmmaker is heartfelt. Watching the talented Burton recreate Wood's films to perfection is a hoot.

Emerald Forest (1985) D: John Boorman.

Everyone Says I Love You (1996) D: Woody Allen.

Evil Dead, The (1982) D: Sam Raimi. Sam Raimi and Bruce Campbell exploded on to the horror scene with this film, although it took Hollywood a few years to notice. Highly original stuff at the time, and on a dark night it can still generate fear in a way that few of its imitators have been able to duplicate.

Ewok Adventure, The (1984) D: John Korty.

Ewoks: The Battle for Endor (1985) D: Jim & Ken Wheat.

Excalibur (1981) D: John Boorman.

Exorcist II: The Heretic (1977) D: John Boorman.

Fade to Black (1980) D: Vernon Zimmerman. A film nerd starts dressing up as movie monsters and killing people. Do a remake about a *Star Trek* nerd and we'll be the first people in line.

Fake Out (1982) D: Matt Cimber.

Fantastic Voyage (1966) D: Richard Fleischer. Fabulous special effects highlight this tale of a group of scientists shrunk to microscopic size to perform surgery inside a dying diplomat.

Fast Times at Ridgemont High (1982) D: Amy Heckerling.

Faster, Pussycat! Kill! Kill! (1965) D: Russ Meyer. Russ Meyer's greatest film. Violent female gangsters kidnap a woman and try to sell her to a horrible old man and his sons. Cleavage is exposed, people are killed. These girls drive fast, too.

Fathom (1967) D: Leslie H. Martinson. A skydiver is recruited to reclaim a nuclear weapon. Hey, more excuses to get Raquel Welch into a skin tight suit!

Field of Dreams (1989) D: Phil Alden Robinson.

First Kid (1996) D: David M. Evans.

Flesh for Frankenstein (1974) D: Paul Morrissey. Udo Kier plays the good Baron in this gory film. Frankenstein wants to create a new race, and he doesn't care who he has to kill to do it.

Flight of the Navigator (1986) D: Randal Kleiser. A young boy becomes the pilot of an alien ship.

Food of the Gods, The (1976) D: Bert I. Gordon. Gordon once again displays a

love for abnormally large creatures, this time farm animals (mostly rats, but there is a giant chicken) who terrorize the luckless inhabitants of an island off the coast of Canada, including Marjoe Gortner. One might ask why our characters don't hightail it off the island, but one might as well ask why Pamela Franklin spends the entire film wearing a hat that perfectly resembles a dead cat.
Fools Rush In (1997) D: Andy Tennant.
For Love of the Game (1999) D: Sam Raimi.
Forever Young (1992) D: Steve Miner.
Free Willy 3 (1997) D: Sam Pillsbury.
French Connection (1971) D: William Freidkin.
Friday the 13th 3-D (1982) D: Steve Miner. Famous movie serial killer Jason actually got his trademark hockey mask in this film. Jason targets horny teenagers and bikers at a farm near Crystal Lake.
Fried Green Tomatoes (1991) D: Jon Avnet.
Future Kick (1991) D: Damian Klaus. Recipe for a lame sci-fi thriller: take one b-movie actress (Meg Foster), add one kickboxer-turned-actor (Don "The Dragon" Wilson), put them on a series of dark, urban sets. Mix with incoherent script involving virtual reality and robots. Garnish liberally with strippers. Don't expect tasty results.
Get Over It (2001) Tommy O'Haver.
Glengarry Glen Ross (1992) D: James Foley.
Go (1999) D: Doug Liman.
God Told Me To (1977) D: Larry Cohen.
Godfather, The (1972) D: Francis Ford Coppola.
Godzilla (1998) D: Roland Emmerich.
Godzilla vs the Sea Monster (1966) D: Jun Fukuda. Spunky dance contestants find themselves aboard a hijacked boat while searching for a friend lost at sea. The boat has been stolen by a bank robber on the lam, but at least he's useful when they stumble upon a mysterious island whose natives have been enslaved by a terrorist syndicate! Godzilla and Mothra guest-star in this campy tale of intrigue which also happens to feature a giant shrimp monster that does the terrorists' bidding. Classic '60s story and style.
Good Will Hunting (1997) D: Gus Van Sant.
Gorgo (1961) D: Eugene Lourié. It might seem a bit odd that acclaimed French director Lourie would be involved with a monster movie, but the resulting 78-minute film at least knows its limitations. British treasure-hunters off the coast of Ireland capture a dinosaur and haul it back to a buyer in London, who puts it on display at his circus. The only problem: Gorgo's a baby, and mama wants him back! A good-natured tale of giant lizards running roughshod over familiar London landmarks.
Grand Theft Auto (1977) D: Ron Howard.
Gremlins (1984) D: Joe Dante.
Greystoke: The Legend of Tarzan (1984) D: Hugh Hudson.
Hairspray (1988) D: John Waters.
Halloween (1978) D: John Carpenter. The teen slasher flick started here. A mute killer named Michael Myers escapes from a mental hospital on Halloween Eve and slaughters high school students. Jamie Lee Curtis plays one victim who won't go quietly.
Harlem Globetrotters on Gilligan's Island (1981) D: Peter Baldwin. TV movie in which the castaways have been rescued from the island and returned to it to start a beach resort. Lamebrain plot (as if another kind existed on the show) involves an unscrupulous millionaire (Martin Landau) who wants to buy the resort. It all comes down to a showdown match between the Globetrotters and a team of robots. The scene you're imagining right now is better than the way it really looks.
Hawk the Slayer (1980) D: Terry Marcel.

Appendix: Movies Mentioned **157**

No, he's not related to Buffy. Medieval fantasy Hawk (John Terry) gathers a band of warriors to fight his evil brother (Jack Palance), who threatens to extinguish a small town and nunnery. J.R.R. Tolkien may never stop spinning in his grave.
Heathers (1989) D: Michael Lehmann.
Heatseeker (1995) D: Albert Pyun. Albert Pyun returns to his favorite theme, low-budget cyborgs.
Heavy Metal (1981) D: Gerald Potterton.
Highlander (1986) D: Russell Mulcahy. Visually flashy but empty movie about immortal swordsmen competing for a mystical prize. Still, compared to any of its three sequels, it's nearly *Citizen Kane*.
Highlander II: The Quickening (1991) D: Russell Mulcahy. Incredibly inept sequel to *Highlander* (1986). Ignoring that there should be no immortals left after the first film, *Highlander II* posits that the immortals were actually prisoners exiled from either the past or another planet, depending on which version you see. Set in the near future, Lambert's character must dismantle a solar shield run by a corrupt corporation.
Hocus Pocus (1993) D: Kenny Ortega.
Honkytonk Man (1982) D: Clint Eastwood.
Hope and Glory (1987) D: John Boorman.
Humanoids from the Deep (1980) D: Barbara Peters.
Humanoids from the Deep (1996) D: Jeff Yonis. A slight improvement to the original film, but still pretty pointless. Director Yonis has re-written the original script extensively, but it's still a repulsive premise, even for a horror film.
I Know What You Did Last Summer (1997) D: Jim Gillespie.
I Still Know What You Did Last Summer (1998) D: Danny Cannon.
I Was a Teenage Werewolf (1957) D: Gene Fowler Jr. With a title like that, what else do you need to know? Okay, it stars Michael Landon.
Incredible Hulk Returns, The (1988) D: Bill Bixby and Nicholas Corea. The world may think David Bruce Banner dead, but the *Hulk* superhero franchise lives on in this TV movie. Bixby and Lou Ferrigno return as Banner and his giant green alter-ego, but this time they are joined by Steve Levitt and Eric Allen Kramer as Donald Blake and his doppelganger from Norse mythology, Thor. Watch for Tim Thomerson as a Cajun mercenary with a bad accent.
Independence Day (1996) D: Roland Emmerich.
International Stewardesses (1974) D: Al Silliman Jr.
It Came from Outer Space (1953) D: Jack Arnold.
Jack Frost (1997) D: Michael Cooney. The first of two killer-snowman movies features a serial murderer dissolved by "experimental acid" into a snowbank. The acid bonds his DNA to the snow molecules and presto! A snowman with a penchant for slaughter is born. Features the occasional snappy one-liner and a remarkable dearth of snow.
Jack Frost (1998) D: Troy Miller. Michael Keaton is the inattentive father who dies on Christmas Eve and whose spirit is summoned a year later by a magic harmonica to inhabit the body of a snowman to spend time with his son. No, you didn't imagine that sentence, and that's really the plot of the movie. Unsurprisingly, it's one of the most repulsive creations yet to grace the silver screen.
Jack the Bear (1993) D: Marshall Hersovitz.
Jaws (1975) D: Steven Spielberg.
Jaws 3-D (1983) D: Joe Alves. A giant shark kills people at an ocean-themed amusement park.
Jerry Maguire (1996) D: Cameron Crowe.
JFK (1991) D: Oliver Stone.
Jumanji (1995) D: Joe Johnston.
Jurassic Park (1993) D: Steven Spielberg.
Jurassic Park III (2001) D: Joe Johnston.
Kill, Baby, Kill (1966) D: Mario Bava.
King Cobra (1999) D: David and Scott Hillenbrand.

King Dinosaur (1955) D: Bert I. Gordon. Four astronauts land on an alien planet populated by snakes, lemurs, and "dinosaurs" that look suspiciously like lizards magnified with trick photography.
King Kong (1933) D: Merian C. Cooper and Ernest B. Schoedsack.
Knights (1993) D: Albert Pyun. Another Albert Pyun film. We haven't seen it, and we aren't knocking down the door of the local rental store to rectify that situation.
Komodo (1999) D: Michael Lantieri. Komodo dragons run rampant on a small American island.
L.A. Confidential (1997) D: Curtis Hanson.
L.A. Story (1991) D: Mick Jackson. Steve Martin parodies L.A. culture as a TV weatherman who wants more out of life. Quite possibly Martin's best work.
Land Before Time (1998) D: Don Bluth.
Leprechaun (1993) D: Mark Jones.
Legend of Billie Jean, The (1985) D: Matthew Robbins.
Let's Scare Jessica to Death (1971) D: John Hancock.
Lost Continent, The (1951) D: Sam Newfield. Scientists travel to an island looking for a fallen satellite and find poorly animated dinosaurs.
Lost in Space (1998) D: Stephen Hopkins.
Lost World: Jurassic Park, The (1997) D: Steven Spielberg.
Love Potion No. 9 (1992) D: Dale Launer.
Lucky Numbers (2000) D: Nora Ephron.
Mad Max (1979) D: George Miller.
Malibu Bikini Shop, The (1985) D: David Wechter.
Mallrats (1995) D: Kevin Smith. Smith's much maligned sequel to *Clerks* follows two young men (Jeremy London, Jason Lee) who have girlfriend problems and wander a mall, in that order. It's not as bad as some people said at the time, though it does have problems. Some guy named Ben Affleck plays the villain.
Massacre at Central High (1976) D: Rene Daadler. A creepy teenager is maimed by some kids at school, so he responds by going on a killing spree. Not really a slasher flick, despite the title.
Masters of the Universe (1987) D: Gary Goddard.
Metalstorm: The Destruction of Jared-Syn (1983) D: Charles Band.
Meteor (1979) D: Ronald Neame. Sean Connery and Natalie Wood team up to stop a runaway asteroid from destroying the Earth. Yes, really.
Miami Hustle (1996) D: Lawrence Lanoff. Kathy Ireland stars as a confidence trickster (quit laughing) who goes undercover to bilk an unwitting heiress (Audie England) out of her fortune. Did we mention the heiress works in a strip club?
Midsummer Night's Dream, A (1968) D: Peter Hall.
Mod Squad, The (1999) D: Scott Silver.
Modern Times (1936) D: Charles Chaplin.
Monkey Business (1952) D: Howard Hawks.
Monster from the Ocean Floor (1954) D: Wyott Ordung. Beautiful young American on vacation in Mexico encounters a sea beast. Only the improbably handsome marine biologist and his one-man submarine can beat back the amoebic beast, enlarged by nuclear fallout. Not exactly a classic, but it is one of Roger Corman's very first productions.
Moonstruck (1987) D: Norman Jewison.
Mr. Peek-A-Boo's Playmates (1962) D: Ronald V. Ashcroft.
Mrs. Doubtfire (1993) D: Chris Columbus.
Muppets Take Manhattan, The (1984) D: Frank Oz. The Muppets set out to produce a Broadway play.
Mute Witness (1994) D: Anthony Waller.
My Bodyguard (1980) D: Tony Bill.
My Tutor (1983) D: George Bowers.
Myra Breckinridge (1970) D: Michael Sarne. Raquel Welch plays the result of a sex change operation on film critic Rex Reed. Yes, it's camp.
Naked Gun 33 1/3 (1994) D: Peter Segal.
Nemesis (1993) D: Albert Pyun. Incoherent cyberpunk thriller from director Al-

Appendix: Movies Mentioned 159

bert Pyun. Somehow he got the money to make three sequels.

Nemesis 2: Nebula (1995) D: Albert Pyun. Built around the dubious star power of female bodybuilder Sue Price, this Pyun film is worse than most of his output.

Nemesis 3: Prey Harder (1995) D: Albert Pyun. Filmed back-to-back with *Nemesis 2* (1995), the disturbing muscled protagonist of the later *Nemesis* films continues to wander around a desert wasteland.

Nemesis 4: Death Angel (1995) D: Albert Pyun. More Albert Pyun goodness with Sue Price killing androids.

Nico the Unicorn (1998) D: Graeme Campbell.

Night of the Living Dead (1968) D: George Romero. The original movie about people trapped in a house with monsters outside. Romero's low-budget classic is still scary even though there isn't much gore by modern standards.

Night Strangler, The (1973) D: Dan Curtis. Carl Kolchak (Darren McGavin) is back and now working in Seattle. He hunts for a killer who drains women of a small amount of blood before breaking their necks with superhuman strength. No, it isn't a vampire, which makes things just that much more interesting.

Nightmare on Elm Street, A (1984) D: Wes Craven. Wes Craven created a memorable bogeyman in Freddy Kruger, a spectral child molester who can appear in teenagers' dreams. There were seven sequels, none of them as good as the original.

North by Northwest (1959) D: Alfred Hitchcock.

Octaman (1971) D: Harry Essex. Title creature waves its tentacles at the principal actors for eighty minutes, supposedly as revenge for the "scientific" interest they have in his regular eight-armed brethren. Relentlessly boring, since the monster is seen from the film's first minutes and doesn't do much after that.

Omega Doom (1996) D: Albert Pyun.

Does your cat need a bath? Do that instead of watching this Albert Pyun film, you'll be happier. Rutger Hauer stars as the robotic antihero in this *Yojimbo* (1961) remake.

One Million Years B.C. (1966) D: Don Chaffey. Ray Harryhausen created the dinosaurs in this story of star-crossed prehistoric lovers. Lots of monsters and Raquel Welch in the famous fur bikini.

Orca (1977) D: Michael Anderson. A killer whale takes its revenge on the sailor (Richard Harris) who killed its mate while trying to capture a specimen for an aquarium. If you can swallow the premise that a killer whale is intelligent enough to a) desire vengeance and b) recognize and hunt down the man who caused its misery, you might have a chance at enjoying this movie. Most famous for the scene in which Bo Derek loses her broken leg (cast and all!) to the voracious sea critter.

Osterman Weekend, The (1983) D: Sam Peckinpah.

Out of Sight (1998) D: Steven Soderbergh.

Outland (1981) D: Peter Hyams.

Outlaw of Gor (1989) D: John "Bud" Cardos.

Pajama Tops (1984) D: Rob Iscove

Pallbearer, The (1996) D: Matt Reeves.

Party at Kitty and Stud's, The (1970) D: Morton Lewis.

Piranha (1978) D: Joe Dante.

Playgirls and the Bellboy, The (1962) D: Fritz Umgelter.

Poison Ivy II (1995) D: Anne Goursaud.

Poison Ivy: The New Seduction (1997) D: Kurt Voss.

Police Academy (1984) D: Hugh Wilson.

Poltergeist (1982) D: Tobe Hooper.

Porky's (1981) D: Bob Clark.

Poseidon Adventure, The (1972) D: Ronald Neame.

Postcards from the Edge (1990) D: Mike Nichols.

Postman, The (1997) D: Kevin Costner.

Prehysteria! (1993) D: Albert Band and

Charles Band.
Prom Night (1980) D: Paul Lynch. The past haunts the prom when a killer offs partying teens to deal with childhood trauma. Jamie Lee Curtis stars.
Prom Night IV: Deliver Us from Evil (1992) D: Clay Borris. It takes place on prom night, but not at the prom. Four high school students in a secluded cabin are stalked by a religious zealot. *Star Trek* fans may want to see this movie for Nicole de Boer's underwear scenes, but everyone else should avoid it.
Protector, The (1985) D: Jackie Chan and James Glickenhaus.
Psycho (1998) D: Gus Van Sant.
Pumpkinhead II: Blood Wings (1994) D: Jeff Burr. The bigheaded demon is back on a tear through rural America. The monster is still cool, but this is a concept that loses its appeal quickly.
Python (2000) D: Richard Clabaugh.
Quick and the Dead, The (1995) D: Sam Raimi.
Quiz Show (1994) D: Robert Redford.
Raging Bull (1980) D: Martin Scorsese.
Raiders of the Lost Ark (1981) D: Steven Spielberg.
Rebel Without a Cause (1955) D: Nicholas Ray. James Dean plays a teenager ready to rebel at whatever adults happen to be around. Great drama, even if the attempts to explain juvenile delinquency seem quaint today.
Road Trip (2000) D: Todd Phillips.
Robin Hood: Prince of Thieves (1991) D: Kevin Reynolds.
Romeo + Juliet (1996) D: Baz Luhrmann.
Romy and Michele's High School Reunion (1997) D: David Mirkin.
Ruthless People (1986) D: Jim Abrahams and David Zucker.
Santa Claus Conquers the Martians (1964) D: Nicholas Webster. This low-budget kiddie film is a bit of a cult classic today. Martians abduct Santa Claus because their children are obsessed with TV shows from Earth. Once on the red planet, St. Nick turns the tables on his cut-rate kidnappers.
Satan's School for Girls (1973) D: David Lowell Rich. TV movie stars '70s TV regular Pamela Franklin as the woman who goes undercover in a girl's boarding school to discover who murdered her sister. Franklin is appealing enough, but the fresh-faced, pretty Kate Jackson steals the show. Lloyd Bochner is the wacked-out Skinnerian teacher who may or may not be sacrificing his students to Satan. Cheryl Ladd is also present, presaging her *Charlie's Angels* connection to Jackson.
Satan's School for Girls (2000) D: Christopher Leitch. Kate Jackson returns for the remake, but this time she's part of the school's creepy faculty. Shannen Doherty and Julie Benz provide the perky-young-thing portion of the program. A few more special effects are in this TV film than were in its predecessor, but overall not much of an improvement.
School Spirit (1985) D: Alan Holleb.
Scream (1996) D: Wes Craven.
Shadows of Desire (1994) D: Sam Pillsbury.
Showgirls (1995) D: Paul Verhoven. Often condemned by modern critics as the worst film ever made, in truth it's too glitzy and (unintentionally) entertaining to be hailed as such. "Trashiest" ever, perhaps.
Silence of the Lambs (1991) D: Jonathan Demme.
Singin' in the Rain (1952) D: Stanley Donen and Gene Kelly.
Sins of Silence (1996) D: Sam Pillsbury.
Six Days, Seven Nights (1998) D: Ivan Reitman.
Slaughter High (1986) D: George Dugdale. A group of friends respond to an invitation to their high school reunion, only to find it's a trap laid by a nerd they wronged in school. Very violent, and the ending is painfully confusing.
Sorry, Wrong Number (1989) D: Tony

Appendix: Movies Mentioned **161**

Wharmby.
Spacehunter: Adventures in the Forbidden Zone (1983) D: Lamont Johnson. An intergalactic garbage man strives to rescue three women from the evil Overdog. More *Mad Max* (1979) than *Star Wars* (1977).
Speed (1994) D: Jan de Bont.
SSSSSSS (1973) D: Bernard L. Kowalski.
Star Wars: Episode I - The Phantom Menace (1999) D: George Lucas.
Star Wars: Episode IV - A New Hope (1977) D: George Lucas.
Stepford Husbands, The (1996) D: Fred Walton. Payback's a bitch – literally. This time the men are transformed into perfect hubbies by women who are sick of barbecues and football. The fourth in a muddled series.
Stepford Wives, The (1975) D: Bryan Forbes.
Stewardesses, The (1969) D: Al Silliman Jr.
Stir Crazy (1980) D: Sidney Poitier.
Stripped to Kill (1987) D: Katt Shea. A psycho's out there, killing strippers. A cop goes undercover as a dancer to solve the case. Haven't we seen this one before – about a million times? Watch for Norman "Mr. Roper" Fell as the club manager.
Sunset Boulevard (1950) D: Billy Wilder.
Supergirl (1984) D: Jeannot Szwarc.
Superman II (1980) D: Richard Lester. Christopher Reeves plays Clark Kent/Superman for the second time. This time the man of steel has to take on three Kryptonian criminals, but only after he reveals his real identity to Lois Lane. The action scenes are the reason to see this film. Never have super-powered combatants looked so good in live-action.
Superman IV: The Quest for Peace (1987) D: Sidney J. Furie. How low can you go? Superman fights a nuclear powered villain created by Lex Luthor, but is eventually K.O.'d by shoddy special effects.
Swingers (1996) D: Doug Liman.
Tails You Live, Heads You're Dead (1995) D: Tim Matheson.
Teenage Mutant Ninja Turtles (1990) D: Steve Barron.
Terminator, The (1984) D: James Cameron.
Texas Chain Saw Massacre, The (1974) D: Tobe Hooper.
There's Nothing Out There (1991) D: Rolfe Kanefsky. Well, there's not *much* out there anyway. A very short monster kills teens on Spring Break at a remote house. Mostly noteworthy for featuring a character who knows the rules of the horror film, five years before *Scream* (1996).
They Bite (1994) D: Brett Piper. A surprisingly funny spoof of the killer sea critter flick, *They Bite* features not only horror movie in-jokes but also porn movie in-jokes. A case of mistaken identity brings a scientist-turned-tabloid-reporter together with the director of a porn film as a slimy beast consumes half-naked lovelies for lunch. With ubiquitous-yet-ridiculous Ron Jeremy as one of the crew working for the porn director.
Tin Cup (1996) D: Ron Shelton.
Titanic (1997) D: James Cameron. Mildly successful prequel to *Raise the Titanic*.
Trancers 4: Jack of Swords (1994) D: David Nutter.
Trancers 5 (1995) D: David Nutter.
Troop Beverly Hills (1989) D: Jeff Kanew and John Kricfalusi.
Twister (1996) D: Jan de Bont. Helen Hunt is menaced by an artificial construction of computer generated polygons... and that's just Bill Paxton.
Unforgiven (1992) D: Clint Eastwood.
Untouchables, The (1987) D: Brian De Palma.
Valentine (2001) D: Jamie Blanks.
Valley Girl (1983) D: Martha Coolidge. Early Nick Cage vehicle involves star-cross'd lovers, affected speech, and big, big hair. Somehow it holds viewers in its thrall – perhaps it's the fact that Cage's chest hair has been shaved into a perfect V.
Valley of Gwangi, The (1969) D: Jim

O'Connolly. Dinosaurs and cowboys! A western show captures an allosaur and displays it until, inevitably, it escapes. More Ray Harryhausen goodness.
Virtuosity (1995) D: Brett Leonard.
Volunteers (1985) D: Nicholas Meyer.
Voyage of the Rock Aliens (1988) D: James Fargo.
Wasp Woman, The (1960) D: Roger Corman. Cosmetics queen uses youth serum concocted from wasp jelly to regain her youth, but at the cost of transformation into a wasp creature who feeds on human blood by night. Hey, it's called *The Wasp Woman* – you wanted a plot synopsis that wasn't ridiculous? Some of Corman's best work, with fave actress Susan Cabot.
Waterworld (1995) D: Kevin Reynolds.
Waxwork II: Lost In Time (1992) D: Anthony Hickox. Part-spoof, part-homage to wacky horror films with plots that make no sense. Time-travel, zombies, disembodied hands, a Bruce Campbell cameo – this film has it all.
Wedding Singer, The (1998) D: Frank Coraci.
Weird Science (1985) D: John Hughes.
West Side Story (1961) D: Jerome Robbins and Robert Wise.
What Ever Happened to Baby Jane? (1962) D: Robert Aldrich.
What's Eating Gilbert Grape? (1993) D: Lasse Hallström.
What's the Matter with Helen? (1971) D: Curtis Harrington.
Who's That Girl? (1987) D: James Foley. Madonna stars in this modern remake of *Bringing Up Baby*. It has none of the charm of its model.
Whole Nine Yards, The (2000) D: Jonathan Lynn.
Wild Things (1988) D: John McNaughton. Pros: Denise Richards topless. Cons: Kevin Bacon bottomless.
Witchcraft (1988) D: Rob Spera. Often compared to the classic "devil's-child" flick *Rosemary's Baby*, mostly because it features a woman who has just given birth and the sinister connection her husband has with the occult. Don't expect the same level of atmosphere or talent, though. For some reason, this film has been confused with *Witchery* (1988), reviewed on page 124.
Witching, The (1974) aka *Necromancy* aka *Rosemary's Disciples*. D: Bert I. Gordon.
Wolf (1994) D: Mike Nichols.
World Is Not Enough, The (1999) D: Michael Apted. Denise Richards plays a nuclear physicist in one of the greatest tests of suspension of disbelief ever asked of an audience. You know what would make a great movie? Richards' character from this movie should team up with Keanu Reeves' character from *Chain Reaction* (1996). We'd pay to see that.
X: The Man With X-Ray Eyes (1963) D: Roger Corman. Ray Milland is the scientist obsessed with enabling humans to see a wider spectrum of radiation. His experiments (on himself, naturally) work a little too well, at first with comical results which later turn tragic. A Corman classic.

Appendix: Movies Mentioned

Appendix B: Recommended Reading

Selected entries by Ken Begg (www.jabootu.com)

Reel Shame has shown you many of Hollywood's disasters, but many more await you in the pages of these books.

The Gross. Peter Bart. St. Martin's Press, 1999. A former studio executive and now a columnist for *Variety*, few know the movie business like Bart. Here he examines the films that came out in the summer of 1998: *Godzilla, There's Something About Mary, Saving Private Ryan, Armageddon,* etc. Those wondering how studios went from making films to generic 'product' will find this book invaluable. Sections include a look at each studio's slate, chapters on individual major films, and a week-by-week examination of how the movies fared at the box office. The only problem with this marvelous book is that Bart didn't follow it up every year with a similar volume.

If Chins Could Kill: Confessions of a B-Movie Actor. Bruce Campbell. St. Martin's Press, 2001. The autobiography of perhaps the most prominent modern cult movie actor, *If Chins Could Kill* is a treat for fans. It is also, alternately, a near-homage to those fans and a subtle joke on them. Aside from the humorous treatment of Campbell's life and career, the book contains eye-opening material on the creation and subsequent marketing of independent movies, as well as the actor's thoughts on the Hollywood studio system, his friends and colleagues, and the benefits of a regular job in TV versus the more glamorous film roles. A solid read, although obviously more captivating if you are already a fan of his work (*Evil Dead, Army of Darkness, The Adventures of Brisco County, Jr.*).

How I Made a Hundred Movies in Hollywood and Never Lost a Dime. Roger Corman with Jim Jerome. Da Capo Press, 1998. Corman's own stories about his career are nowhere near as interesting as the ones told about him, but the book includes a good number of those as well. The story begins at the beginning and recounts the story of the most influential producer in b-movies up to 1990, stopping along the way to collect anecdotes from the people – some of them now the most powerful people in Hollywood – Corman used and abused along the way. You may find yourself skipping Mr. Corman's rather dry retelling of the accounting details of each film in favor of the stories from other people, which are helpfully set apart in bold text.

I Hated, Hated, Hated This Movie. Roger Ebert. Andrews McNeel, 2000. Renowned film critic Roger Ebert dives into his review archives and surfaces with over two hundred movies that were awarded two stars or fewer out of four. The title is lifted from his review of *North*, but there are dozens of scathing phrases in the book that would have served as well. As he says himself of the movies presented, "The degree of their badness ranges from those that are deplorable to others that are merely hilariously misguided." A good read in either case.

Cult Horror Films. Welch Everman. Citadel Press, 1993. From the mouthwatering list of films featured – covering not only horror but also sci-fi titles from the '50s through the '80s – a seeming must-purchase. Unfortunately, the author's penchant for affixing a repetitive 'political' message to every film quickly becomes tiresome. Worse, this 'analysis' is often imposed on the movie whether it fits or not. Heavily illustrated, the book works best as a wonderfully varied roster of genre films to hunt down and watch. Just don't bother actually reading it. Everman also produced the very similar *Cult Sci-Fi Movies*.

Horror Film Directors, 1931-1990. Dennis Fischer. McFarland & Co., 1991. The single best guide to horror movie directors, foreign and domestic. A healthy 800 pages plus, most directors associated with the genre are represented here. B-movie fans will particularly enjoy the second part of the book, dedicated to more minor figures. Although shorter, these chapters cover such essential characters as Al Adamson, Larry Buchanan and Ed Wood. A classic of its kind. A brilliant short history of the horror genre during the period covered is another definite plus.

Science Fiction Filmmaking in the '80s. Lee Goldberg, Randy Lofficier, Jean-Marc Lofficier, and William Rabkin,. McFarland & Co., 1995. A slim compilation of interviews with the makers of a dozen films, including *Aliens, Dune, Blade Runner* and the *Mad Max* and *Star Trek* series. Not a comprehensive look at '80s genre filmmaking, and update interviews may have deepened the book's appeal. The pieces themselves, conducted during or shortly after the making of the films, are fairly solid. Not a bad reference book, but specifically useful only if you're interested in one of the limited number of titles featured here.

Which Lie Did I Tell? William Goldman. Pantheon Books, 2000. Novelist and screenwriter Goldman (*The Princess Bride*) is also one of Hollywood's most trenchant observers. Here he continues documenting his experiences in the movie trade. He discusses movies he worked on, and why they were successful (*Misery*) or not (*Year of the Comet*), as well as favorite scenes from classic movies. Perhaps the best part of the book is a short screenplay he wrote specifically for it. This he shows to other filmmakers, and we see how the input of others radically changes the nature of a project. Everyone's views are interesting, but when they're done the script is generally completely different. Great stuff.

Nightmare of Ecstasy: The Life and Art of Edward D. Wood, Jr. Rudolph Grey. Feral House, 1994. The only biography currently available on the renowned "Worst Director Ever." Grey, fittingly, sought to create a book as unusual as its subject's films. Attempting to recreate the, shall we say, non-linear aspects of Wood's oeuvre, Grey's book is a oral history that follows few of the normal structural rules. It hops around from subject to subject almost at random, grouping together statements by those who knew Wood both professionally and personally. Interesting, if sometimes annoying.

Incredibly Strange Films. Re/Search Publications, 1986. Re/Search produced a series of books on various baroque subjects. Like the others, this is an assembly of pieces by different writers. There are interviews with a satisfying range of prominent b-movie names (Russ Meyer, Ted V. Mikels, Doris Wishman, etc.), articles on weird little genres, essays on a small number of titles and further miscellaneous pieces. The separate parts are extremely solid. All in all, it's difficult to think of a more satisfying primer volume for the beginning b-movie fan.

Invasion of the B-Girls. Jewel Shepard. Eclipse Books, 1992. B-movie goddess Shepard conducts a series of interviews with other such actresses. The range of subjects is particularly good, including well-known genre actresses from the '50s and the most prominent 'scream queens' of the '80s. Yvette Vickers, Caroline Munro, Martine Beswicke, Mary Woronov, Michelle Bauer, Linnea Quigley and P.J. Soles are among the interviewees here. Unfortunately, Shepard isn't a journalist, and sometimes lets interesting subjects get glossed over. The tone is chatty. Remarks range from amusing to defensive, especially regarding the 'bimbo' image many consider themselves to labor under. Unsurprisingly, the older actresses, who often appeared in at least some high-end films, provide the best material.

The Essential Monster Movie Guide. Stephen Jones. Billboard Books, 2000. Yet another capsule review guide, the book suffers from several flaws. The reviews can be brusque, with some films rating a single descriptive line. Odd gaps occur, even for this sort of book. Skipping *Them!* in a 'horror' movie guide is one thing. Skipping it in a 'monster' movie guide is criminal. Most useful for its extensive coverage of obscure material, including cartoon shorts, sex films and TV show episodes with putatively supernatural themes. Not essential, but a useful supplement to other, more comprehensive books.

The Phantom Ultimate Video Guide. Joe Kane. Dell Books, 1989. Kane, aka the Phantom of the Movies, is the only serious rival to Michael "Psychotronic" Weldon as a knowing and wry commentator on the b-movie scene. This is his first collection of capsule reviews, and can safely be considered essential for those planning to journey through the more obscure shelves of their local video store. The sequel, *The Phantom of the Movies' Videoscope*, followed in 2000. If you buy both of Kane's books and both of Weldon's, you will have the solid beginnings of a fine b-movie library.

Bad Movies We Love. Edward Margulies and Stephen Rubello. Penguin Books, 1993. Compiled from many years' worth of a column by the same name in the pages of *Movieline* magazine, this book holds aloft a number of Hollywood's biggest movie mistakes. Then it holds their makers responsible for their crimes. Reviews are brief, but sharply witty. The authors score extra points for their inclusion of two Pia Zadora films.

Videohound's Horror Show: 999 Hair-Raising, Hellish, and Humorous Movies. Mike Mayo. Visible Ink Press, 1998. Like the other genre-oriented Videohound tomes, *Horror Show* contains a bevy of longer-than-average capsule reviews, punctuated by photos, personality profiles, and sidebars. The author has an obvious love for the subject matter. Much of this material is lifted (albeit in reworded form) from Mayo's other Videohound work (such as *Video Premieres*), so beware of overlap if that sort of thing irks you.

Roger Corman: Best of the Cheap Acts. Mark Thomas McGee. McFarland & Company, 1988. This slim but packed volume is composed of four parts. The first is a primer on Corman's career, perhaps the length of a long magazine article. The second and meatiest section examines each of the films Corman personally directed. These write-ups are highly informative and come complete with cast and crew information. Third is a section on members of Corman's stock company, each afforded their own entry. A list of films Corman produced closes things out. Heavily illustrated. McGee also wrote the more extensive AIP history *Faster and Furiouser.*

The Fifty Worst Films of All Time. Harry Medved and Randy Dreyfuss. [Michael Medved uncredited.] Fawcett Columbine Books, 1978. The four 'bad movie' books written by the Medved Brothers created what has become a popular field of study, particularly on the Internet. This is the first, with the Medveds and co-author Dreyfuss identifying fifty films ranging from cheesy dime sci-fi pictures to laughably pretentious arthouse fare. Each film is given its own chapter, with elements such as plot holes and bad dialogue examined to great comic effect. Also hilarious are the sections titled "The Critics Rave," quoting especially pungent critical response to the films. A classic.

The Golden Turkey Awards. Harry and Michael Medved. Perigee Book, 1980. This, the Medveds' second volume, is the seminal one. By proclaiming an "official" Worst Film and Director - the 'winners' chosen by the votes of readers - the idea of 'bad' movies was given momentum and focus. Those winners, needless to say, were *Plan 9 from Outer Space* and Ed Wood, Jr. The rest of the book nominates titles for various categories, for instance, Worst Casting of All Time, before choosing a winner. Twenty-plus years later, the Medveds' trenchant humor still more than holds its own.

The Hollywood Hall of Shame. Harry and Michael Medved. Perigee Books, 1984. The third of the Medveds' four volumes on bad movies goes in another direction. Instead of just poking fun at films of dubious quality, we are treated to detailed production histories of films that went horribly awry. Most of these are, suitably, well-budgeted major studio disasters, such as Liberace's *Sincerely Yours* or the insane Clint Eastwood/Lee Marvin musical *Paint Your Wagon.* Elizabeth Taylor, meanwhile, gets her own 'wing.' Well researched and often fascinating stuff.

Son of Golden Turkey Awards. Harry and Michael Medved. Villard Books, 1986. With their fourth and final book, the Medveds decided to revisit the formula that works best for them. However, a wide new range of categories is proffered (The Most Embarrassing Nude Scene in Hollywood History, The Most Insufferable Kiddie movie ever), nominees presented, and a winner chosen. The victors in the above categories, for those interested, are an aged Burgess Meredith (!) in *Such Good Friends* and *Pinocchio in Outer Space.* Also includes a relatively short but incisive "Who's Who in Bad Movies."

The Lurker in the Lobby. Andrew Migliore and John Strysik. Armitage House, 2000. New England horror writer H. P. Lovecraft may not be well known outside is devoted following, but his influence is broad. This book covers the two dozen or so movies that have been made from Lovecraft's stories, plus TV episodes and some amateur films that have been shown at Lovecraft festivals. However, that coverage is limited to summaries of the plots with some small amount of commentary. There are also some interviews with behind the scenes talent like Dan O'Bannon and John Carpenter.

Mike Nelson's Movie Megacheese. Mike J. Nelson. Harper, 2000. Nelson, famously the head writer and eventual host of cable TV's *Mystery Science Theater 3000*, returns to business with this slim volume of essays attacking various recent dumb movies. While hardly weighty, Nelson's penchant for snarky and esoteric barbs remains much in evidence: "Pinkett's scenes [in *A Low Down Dirty Shame*] go on longer than you can imagine, stretching far into the event horizon. Though I don't understand the physics involved, I know that you can watch her scenes in a moving car and come back home just in time to see yourself leaving."

Paul Blaisdell, Monster Maker. Randy Palmer. McFarland & Co., 1997. Blaisdell is an obscure figure but one beloved by fans of '50s schlock sci-fi. He was the designer of the monster suits for such classic flicks as *It Conquered the World*, *Invasion of the Saucer Men*, and *From Hell It Came*. Moreover, and for almost no money – he worked mostly often for legendary skinflints Roger Corman and Bert I. Gordon – he usually built the suits and even played the monsters. An in-depth tribute to one man's unique contribution to movie history. Aficionados will find this fascinating stuff.

Black Action Films. James Robert Parish and George H. Hill. McFarland & Co., 1989. Perhaps the only systematic examination of the oddly neglected Blaxploitation cycle. The book covers over two hundred films from the '50s through the late '80s. Obviously, though, the focus is on the '70s, when seemingly hundreds of films like *Shaft* and *Cotton Comes to Harlem* played to packed urban theaters. Entries include credits, plot descriptions and background information. The more important films receive a more detailed look. Heavily illustrated. More books on this subject wait to be written, but this is a very handy primer.

Cult Movies. Danny Peary. Dell Publishing, 1981. Film historian Peary examines a hundred films sporting intense fan followings. These span the gamut of genres and era: musicals, westerns, horror, sci-fi, exploitation fare, Hollywood classics. Peary's strength is to provide intelligent commentary on his subjects without resorting to the sort of pseudo-academic theorizing that defines so much film criticism. If you didn't think anyone had anything interesting to say anymore about *Citizen Kane* or *King Kong* or *The*

Maltese Falcon, this is the book for you. Followed by two smaller volumes, this series is an essential addition to any film buff's home library.

Cult Movie Stars. Danny Peary. Simon & Schuster, 1991. Peary adds another indispensable title to his list of film-related books. Unsurprisingly, this volume examines not individual movies but rather actors who have a deeply entrenched fan following. Over seven hundred thespians are covered, from old time character actors to the obligatory horror movie stars and scream queens to especially prominent porno stars. Entries include a brief description of what accounts for the actor's appeal, followed by lists of his or her notable films, grouped from "Cult Favorites" to "Also of Interest." Very solid stuff.

Slimetime. Steven Puchalski. Headpress, 1996. "A guide to sleazy, mindless, movie entertainment." A compilation of longer than normal capsule reviews, generally running from between a third to half a page, covering mostly exploitation fare from the '60s through the '80s. Collected from a British b-movie magazine, the reviews are usually vulgar but always lively and often quite funny. Not a book for kids, but well-written enough to entertain adults who don't mind a little mindless profanity.

Confessions of a Cineplex Heckler. Joe Queenan. Hyperion, 2000. Queenan's articles generally fall into two categories. First, he'll examine a series of bad films containing a common thread. Examples would be bad accents, nuns or films in which ears are sliced off. The others are stunt-related pieces. He might, for instance, privately hand out refunds to patrons who have seen a bad movies. Queenan can be a bit of a jerk - the title piece records his adventures heckling a movie, apparently just to see how far he can go in annoying his fellow viewers without being beaten up - but taken in measured doses his stuff is rather funny. Besides, the chapter mocking Barbra Streisand is worth buying the book all by itself.

Japan's Favorite Mon-star: The Unauthorized Biography of "The Big G." Steve Ryfle. ECW Press, 1998. Though Toho's fanatical protection of their most famous property prohibited Ryfle even from including the word "Godzilla" in the title of his creation, this book (a monster in its own right at four hundred pages) is probably the best history to date of Japan's most famous movie monster. Ryfle, a journalist who has written on Godzilla and other monster movies for a number of years, has his own humorous perspective on the evolution of the Big G and his friends. In the book's pages can be found countless interviews, fascinating archive photos, and reviews of every Godzilla movie ever made – and even a few that weren't.

The Devil's Candy. Julie Salamon. Houghton Mifflin, 1991. Ever wonder how a film goes bad? This will answer many of your questions. Critic Salamon was allowed to chronicle the making of what was assumed to be a can't-miss movie, Brian DePalma's adaptation of Tom Wolfe's novel *Bonfire of the Vanities*. There from the very beginning to the bitter end, Salamon records the numerous small decisions that snowballed into a catastrophically bad movie. Given what happened here, the chances of another journalist ever again being given this sort of access are practically nil. One of the most fascinating and informative books on the filmmaking process ever written.

The Worst Movies of All Time, Or: What Were They Thinking? Michael Sauter. Citadel Press, 1995, 1999 (Revised). While covering much of the same ground as the Medved Brother's volumes, Sauter's book is an amusing and succinct examination of bad movies ranging from the silent era to such modern titles as *The Postman* and *Armageddon*. Each film receives roughly three to four pages of coverage. Also included are side articles on various fads, such as the disaster movies of the '70s. While major studio product is covered in the main articles, appendixes provide coverage of the more typical b-movie fare. A very solid choice.

"Bold! Daring! Shocking! True!" Eric Schaefer. Duke University Press, 1999. A lengthy, in-depth history of the social menace exploitation film of the '20s through the '50s. In order to escape the censors, producers would create supposed morality tales that just happened to feature the sex, crime and drug use mainstream movies could not. The gimmick was to make sure to show all the horrible consequences that inevitably followed the lovingly detailed scenes of debauchery. Schaefer's text can be a tad academic in tone. Moreover, the book is more social history than film history. Readers looking for a guide to the movies themselves should look elsewhere.

For Reel. Harold Schechter and David Everitt. Berkley Boulevard Books, 2000. *For Reel* covers the true stories behind certain movies in a series of short essays. Most of the entries cover movies based on real people or real historical events, though a few cover the real stories behind the people who made films, like the producers of *King Kong*. A list of historical sources would have been nice, especially for some of the more outrageous stories, like the 15th century cannibal clan that was the alleged inspiration for *The Hills Have Eyes*.

Videohound's Cult Flicks and Trash Pics. Carol Schwartz [Editor]. Visible Ink Press, 2001. This second edition of the Videhound b-movie reference is lent further credibility with the inclusion of a foreword by Bruce Campbell, but the hundreds of meaty capsule reviews ought to be enough for any fan of schlock movies. Photos and entertaining sidebars abound, though the most useful feature is the index arranged by category.

Cyborgs, Santa Claus and Satan. Fraser A. Sherman. McFarland & Co., 2000. One of the more obscure corners of b-moviedom gets its own book as author Sherman examines the world of made-for-TV horror, sci-fi and fantasy films and mini-series. Remember seeing Burl Ives getting killed by a giant turtle? The title's here: *Bermuda Depths*, 1978. Entries include the original broadcast date, what broadcast or cable network the film first appeared on, cast listings and a brief synopsis and notes. Includes a lengthy appendix listing many other films featuring more marginal genre content. A unique resource.

Creature Features. John Stanley. Berkley Boulevard Group, 1997, 2000. Former TV horror host Stanley's book stands, more or less, as a Leonard Maltin-esque capsule guide for horror and sci-fi movies. *Creature Features* tends to be more inclusive than many others similar tomes, largely due to the fact that revised editions generally come out every year or two. Like Maltin's movie guides, part of the fun is seeing whether you agree or disagree with Stanley's rating of each film from one to five stars. A useful general interest guide.

The Encyclopedia of Bad Taste. Jane and Michael Stern. HarperCollins, 1990. The Sterns have made a career of analyzing pop culture in sharply-written books, but none of them resonates with b-movie fans quite so well as this one. The Sterns don't write entire entries on particular movies, preferring instead to single out people and trends. However, so many of those people and trends become the focus of bad movies that there's a film recommendation to be found every few pages. For example, the entry on "breasts, enormous" features a full-page photo of b-movie queen Chesty Morgan. Other entries include bikers, Weeki Wachee mermaids, bodybuilding, Jayne Mansfield, and professional wrestling. A perfect coffee table tome.

The Encyclopedia of Pop Culture. Jane and Michael Stern. HarperCollins, 1992. Though not as scandalously appealing as their *Encyclopedia of Bad Taste*, this Stern volume still contains some irresistable material concerning movies that most folks would rather forget. Though it includes the mandatory entries on the Beatles, Disney World, Frank Sinatra, and *The Simpsons*, b-movie buffs will quickly zero in on articles about beach party flicks, biker movies, and *Twin Peaks*. The Sterns even devote two full pages to the history of the TV remote control.

The Psychotronic Encyclopedia of Film. Michael Weldon. Ballentine Books, 1983. One of the handful of books no B-movie fan should be without, Weldon's book is perhaps the closest thing to a 'bible' for the cult movie enthusiast. A wide range of genres is covered by the always-knowledgeable Weldon, including horror, sci-fi, biker, spy and exploitation films. Those looking for a definitive capsule review book need look no further. Profusely illustrated, and covering over 3,000 movies, the even more immense follow-up volume was Weldon's *Psychotronic Video Guide*.

B-Movie Web Sites

Much of the material in this book was first published on the world wide web, so we think it's proper to point you to web sites that cater to the tastes of b-movie buffs. Some are review sites (including ours), others are companies that specialize in releasing b-movies to video. A listing here does not necessarily represent our endorsement of a particular site, product, or company. Sites do disappear from time to time, however, so if you're reading this in the year 2050 and the links are dead, don't say we didn't warn you.

Anchor Bay Entertainment
   http://www.anchorbayentertainment.com/

And You Call Yourself a Scientist!
   http://twtd.bluemountains.net.au/Rick/liz.htm

Astounding B-Monster, The
   http://www.bmonster.com/

Attack of the 50 Foot DVD!
   http://www.50footdvd.com/

B-Masters Cabal, The
   http://www.b-masters.org/

B-Movie Message Board
   http://www.badmoviezone.com/

B-Notes
   http://www.jabootu.com/acolytes/bnotes/

Bad Cinema Diary
   http://www.cathuria.com/bcd/

Bad Movie Planet
   http://www.badmovieplanet.com/

Bad Movie Review Website, The
   http://www.badmovies.org/

Bad Movie Report, The
http://www.badmoviereport.com/

Braineater
http://www.braineater.com/

Brian's Drive-In Theater
http://www.briansdriveintheater.com/

Brotherhood of Bad Movies
http://www.geocities.com/sporkatron/

Cavalcade of Schlock, The
http://www.geocities.com/tyrannorabbit/

Celebrity Nudity Database
http://www.cndb.com/

Cold Fusion Video Reviews
http://www.coldfusionvideo.com/

Horror-Wood
http://www.horror-wood.com/

Jabootu's Bad Movie Dimension
http://www.jabootu.com/

Joe Bob Report, The
http://www.joebobbriggs.com/bmovieguide/

Losman's Lair of Horror
http://www.losman.com/

Mr. Skin - Celebrity Nude Movie Reviews
http://www.mrskin.com/

Movie Mistakes
http://www.movie-mistakes.co.uk/

Opposable Thumb Films
http://www.opposablethumbfims.com/

Appendix: B-Movie Web Sites **175**

Prison Flicks
    http://www.prisonflicks.com/

Razzies, The
    http://www.razzies.com/

Sinister Cinema
    http://www.sinistercinema.com/

Something Weird
    http://www.somethingweird.com/

Stinkers, The
    http://www.thestinkers.com/

Stomp Tokyo
    http://www.stomptokyo.com/

Tapes of Terror
    http://www.morticiasmorgue.com/tot.html

Teleport City
    http://www.teleport-city.com/

Unknown Movies, The
    http://www.unknownmovies.com/

WilliamGirdler.com
    http://www.williamgirdler.com/

You can always find the latest addenda, updates, corrections, and other information about this book at the *Reel Shame* web site.

Reel Shame
    http://www.reelshame.com/

Index

!, names requiring, 144

A
Aames, Willie, in *Zapped!*, 94–96
Academy Awards
  for Cuba Gooding, Jr., 47
  for Dino DeLaurentis, 42
  for Gene Hackman, 47
  for Helen Hunt, 5, 61
  for John Patrick Shanley, 119
  for Kevin Costner, 100
  for Rick Baker, 42
  for Sean Connery, 47
  winning, despite system, 3
Acey, Robert, in *Sizzle Beach U.S.A.*, 97–100
Acomba, David, *The Star Wars Holiday Special* directed by, 147–150
acting
  bad, paragon of, 13
  breasts as substitute for, 89
  dignity in, 3–4
actor(s)
  hazing of, 3
  qualifications of, 3
  script quality judged by, 47–48
Adams, Amy, in *Cruel Intentions 2*, 111–114
The Addiction, 10, 153
adult movies, 3-D presentation of, 54
Air America, 60, 153
Airplane!, 153
Akins, Claude, in *Tentacles*, 121–123
alcoholic clowns, movies about, 73–75
Alfonso, Kristian, in *Blindfold: Acts of Obsession*, 89–90
Alien from L.A., 60, 153
Aliens, *Carnosaur* spoof of, 19
Allen, Karen, in *The Turning*, 81–82
Allen, Woody, singing of, 25
Alligator, 123, 153
Ally McBeal (television series), Tim Thomerson in, 60
Alone in the Dark, 134–136
The Amazing Colossal Man, 127, 153
Amazing Yo-Yo Snake Action™, 65–66
American Pie, 91, 153
The Amityville Horror, 52, 153
Amityville II, 52, 153
Amityville 3-D, 52–54
Anaconda, 64–66
Anderson, Erika, in *Zandalee*, 104–105
Anderson, Gillian, nudity by, 79, 81–82
Anderson, Pamela, in *Barb Wire*, 108–109
Angel (television series), 136
Angel Dust, 71, 153–154
Aniston, Jennifer, in *Leprechaun*, 51, 104
Annie Hall, 85, 154
apartment tenants, stereotypes of, 26
A*P*E, 54, 153
Aquaman (comic series), Peter David writing for, 63
Archer, Anne, in *Raise the Titanic!*, 143–146
Are You In the House Alone?, 14–16
Arquette, Patricia, 142
Arthur, Bea, in *The Star Wars Holiday Special*, 148–150
As Good As It Gets, 5, 61, 154
Assault of the Killer Bimbos, 27, 154
Assonitis, Ovidio, *Tentacles* directed by, 121–123
The A-Team, Dwight Schultz in, 107
Auberjonois, Rene, in *King Kong*, 41–42
Austrian Army, fresh meat in, 23

Azito, Tony, in *Private Resort*, 92–93

B
Baby, 19, 154
The Babysitter, 106, 154
babysitting, pizza method for, 6
Back to the Future, 119, 154
bad boys, criteria for, 8
Bad Movies We Love (book), 167
Baio, Scott, in *Zapped!*, 94–96
Baker, Rick
  Academy Awards of, 42
  King Kong special effects by, 40–41
Band, Charles
  Metalstorm: The Destruction of Jared-Syn directed by, 60
  Trancers directed by, 55–57
  Trancers II directed by, 58–60
Baranski, Christine, in *Getting In*, 49–50
Barb Wire, 108–109
Barracuda, 123, 154
Barry, horror movie characters named, 29–30, 37
Barry, John, *Raise the Titanic!* score by, 143
Barry, Raymond J., in *The Turning*, 81–82
Barrymore, Drew
  nudity by, 79
  in *Poison Ivy*, 101–103
  singing of, dubbed, 25
Bart, Peter, *The Gross* (book), 164
Basic Instinct, 106, 154
Batman, limited range of motion of, 18
Batman & Robin, 18, 28, 154
Baywatch (television series), Tim Thomerson in, 60
The Beach, 28, 154
The Beautician and the Beast, 71, 154
Being Human, 119, 154
Beller, Kathleen, in *Are You In the House Alone?*, 14–16
Ben Hur, 84, 154
Benedict, Dirk, in *SSSSSSS*, 66
Berkeley, Elizabeth, nudity by, 79
Beverly Hills 90210 (television series), Shannen Doherty on, 5, 88
Beverly Hills Bodysnatchers, 27, 154
Beyond Control: The Amy Fisher Story, 101, 154
Beyond Rangoon, 142
big flying head, National Rifle Association and, 140
bikini movies, 93
Bikini Summer, 93, 154
Binder, Steve, *The Star Wars Holiday Special* directed by, 147–150
Black Action Films (book), 169
Black characters, stereotypes of, 17
Blade Runner, 20, 22, 154
Blair, Linda, in *Witchery*, 125–127
blank pages, strange, 115–116
Blazing Saddles, 149, 154
Blessed, Brian, in *Robin Hood: Prince of Thieves*, 64
Blindfold: Acts of Obsession, 88–90
The Blob, 10, 154
Blood Beach, 123, 154
Blood of Dracula, 10, 154
Blood Surf, 66, 154
Bochner, Lloyd
  in *The Lonely Lady*, 11–12
  in *Mazes & Monsters*, 34
The Bodyguard, 100, 154
"Bold! Daring! Shocking! True!" (book), 171
Bond girl, Denise Richards as, 19
Boorman, John, *Zardoz* directed by, 140–142
boots, kick-ass knee-high, 132
Boreanaz, David, 136
Bosom Buddies, Tom Hanks in, 32
Bowers, George, *Private Resort* directed by, 91–93

178 Reel Shame

Boyle, Lara Flynn, in *The Temp*, 106–107
The Brain, in *Ed Wood*, 25
Brander, Leslie, in *Sizzle Beach U.S.A.*, 97–100
Brander, Richard, *Sizzle Beach U.S.A.* directed by, 97–100
Brass, Tinto, *Caligula* directed by, 83–84
breasts
  awards for, 109
  movies created around, 108–109
  as separate characters, 88–89, 91–92
  synonyms for, 91
Bridges, Jeff, in *King Kong*, 40–42
Broderick, Matthew, luck of, 5
Brosnan, John, 129
Brown, Julie, in *Shakes the Clown*, 74–75
Buechler, John, creature effects of, 130
Buffy the Vampire Slayer, 110, 154
buildings, killer, 67–69
Bull Durham, 100, 154
Bullock, Sandra, in *Love Potion No. 9*, 96
Burke, Martyn, *The Last Chase* directed by, 137–139
Burnett, Carol, 149
Buscemi, Steve, in *Zandalee*, 104–105
business, breaking into, 3
Butterfly, 12, 154

C
Cage, Nicholas, in *Zandalee*, 104–105
Caligula, 83–84
Cameron, James, 143
Campbell, Bruce
  in *Congo*, 64, 119–120
  If Chins Could Kill: Confessions of a B-Movie Actor (book), 164
cannibalism, among hillbillies, 29
Cappello, Frank
  No Way Back directed by, 70–72
  other careers of, 72
Captain America, 60, 154
Captain Eo, 3-D presentation of, 54, 154
Captain Marvel (comic series), Peter David writing for, 63
Car Wash, 60, 154
Carney, Art, in *The Star Wars Holiday Special*, 148–150
Carnosaur, 19, 128–130
Carradine, David, costuming of, 132
Carroll, Diahann, in *The Star Wars Holiday Special*, 148–150
Casablanca, 154
  remake of, 108–109
Cast Away, 34, 154
catchphrase, inadvisability of using at crime scene, 105
Catholic school uniforms, on Guam, 6
Cattrall, Kim, relative merits of as best friend, 7
Cat-Women of the Moon, 54, 154
Chapelle, Dave, in *Getting In*, 49–51
character names, in cyborg movies, 21
Charles in Charge (television series), 94
Charlie's Angels, 51, 101, 154
Charmed (television series), Shannen Doherty in, 90
Chill Factor, 47, 154
Citizen Kane, 154
  remake of, 109
Clark, Blake, in *Shakes the Clown*, 73–75
Clark, Candy, in *Amityville 3-D*, 52–53
Clay, Andrew Dice, in *Private Resort*, 93
Clockwatchers, 51, 154
Clooney, George, limited range of motion of, 18
Close, Glenn, Andie MacDowell dubbed by, 25
clowns, alcoholic, movies about,

73–75
Colomby, Scott, in *Are You In the House Alone?*, 14
Coma, 38, 154
comedy, tardiness of, in *Hercules Goes Bananas*, 24
comic books, movies based on, 108–109
Cone, Tyler, in *Texas Chainsaw Massacre: The Next Generation*, 29–30
Confessions of a Cineplex Heckler (book), 170
Congie, Terry, in *Sizzle Beach U.S.A.*, 97–100
Congo, 64, 119–120, 155
Connery, Sean
  bad movies of, 47
  in *Zardoz*, 140–142
Conway, Tim, 149
Cops (television series), 110
Corman, Roger
  dinosaur movies of, 19, 128–130
  How I Made a Hundred Movies in Hollywood and Never Lost a Dime (book), 164–165
  rip-off artistry of, 130
  Roger Corman: Best of the Cheap Acts (book) (McGee), 167–168
Cort, Bud, in *Theodore Rex*, 19
Costner, Kevin
  career of, 100
  in *Sizzle Beach U.S.A.*, 97–100
Cox, Courteney, movie career of, 51
Cox, Richard, in *Zombie High*, 37–38
Cozzi, Luigi, *Starcrash* directed by, 131–133
Crash and Burn, 55, 155
Creature Features (book), 172
Creature from the Black Lagoon, 155
  3-D presentation of, 54
  John Voight inspired by, 64
  killer sea beast in, 123

Crewson, Wendy, in *Mazes & Monsters*, 33–34
Crichton, Michael, 119
Crimes and Misdemeanors, 136
Critters, 26, 155
Critters 2: The Main Course, 26, 155
Critters 3, 26–28
Crocodile, 66, 155
Crocodile Dundee, 25, 155
The Crossing, 70, 155
Crothers, Scatman, in *Zapped!*, 95–96
Crowe, Russell, in *No Way Back*, 70–72
Cruel Intentions, 110, 155
Cruel Intentions 2, 110–114
The Crush, 106, 155
Cult Horror Films (book), 165
Cult Movie Stars (book), 170
Cult Movies (book), 169–170
Cumming, Leslie, in *Witchery*, 124–127
The Curse, 66, 155
Curse II: The Bite, 66, 155
Curse of the Pink Panther, dubbing in, 25
Cussler, Clive, *Raise the Titanic!* adapted from novel by, 143
custodians, of destiny, 9
Cutting Class, 8–10
  existentialism of, 9–10
CyberTracker, 22, 155
Cyborg, 22, 155
Cyborg 2, 20–22
cyborg movies
  benefits of making, 22
  character names in, 21
  post-apocalyptic
    flaws in premise of, 20
    Terminator and, 22
  prostitutes in, 20
  soldiers in, 20
Cyborgs, Santa Claus and Satan (book), 172

D

Dances With Wolves, 100, 155
Danes, Claire, bad movies of, 47
Dangerous Liaisons, 110, 155
Danner, Blythe, in *Are You In the House Alone?*, 14
Dark Angel (television series), David Nutter directing for, 63
Dark Horse Comics, 108–109
Daviau, Allen, cinematography of, 120
David, Peter, career of, 63
Dazed and Confused, 37, 155
Dear, William, role-playing theories of, 32
Death Race 2000, 155
 costumes in, 132
 The Last Chase compared to, 139
decent movies. See *Trancers*
Deep Blue Sea, 123, 155
Deepstar Six, 123, 155
DeLaurentis, Dino, lifetime achievement award for, 42
Deliverance, 142
Dench, Judi, nudity of, 79
DeNiro, Robert, other, 21
Depp, Johnny
 nudity of, 80
 in *Private Resort*, 91–93
Dern, Laura, 128
destiny, janitors as custodians of, 9
Devilfish, 123, 155
The Devil's Candy (book), 171
Diamonds Are Forever, 140, 155
DiCaprio, Leo
 in *Critters 3*, 26–28
 death in success of, 28
Die Hard, 27, 69, 155–156
dignity, 3–4
 maintaining, 47–48
 starting out with, 3–4
dinosaur(s)
 absence of, in *King Kong*, 42
 movie craze for, 19, 128
 robotic, 17–19
Dinosaurus!, 19, 156
Disney, Roger Corman compared to, 130
Dr. Dolittle, 72, 156
dogs, filmic homicide of, 11
Doherty, Shannen
 asymmetrical features of, 5, 88, 90
 in *Blindfold: Acts of Obsession*, 88–90
 in *Girls Just Want To Have Fun*, 5–7
 killed (as Heather Duke) by Winona Ryder, 5
 nudity by, 79
 in prime-time television, 5
Dolan, Michael, in *The Turning*, 81–82
Dollman, Tim Thomerson in, 59–60
Donnie Brasco, 91, 156
D'Onofrio, Vincent, dubbed by Maurice LeMarche, 25
Donovan, Tate, in *Love Potion No. 9*, 96
Don't Answer the Phone, 16, 156
Don't Be Afraid of the Dark, 16, 156
Don't Go in the House, 16, 156
Don't Go to Sleep, 16, 156
Don't Mess With My Sister!, 16, 156
Dooley, Paul, in *Shakes the Clown*, 73–75
Drago, Billy, in *Cyborg 2*, 21–22
Dreyfuss, Randy, and Harry Medved, *The Fifty Worst Films of All Time* (book), 168
dubbing, 25
dues, paying, 49
The Dukes of Hazzard (television series), and *Zombie High*, 38
dull surprise, popularity of, in acting, 12
Dunaway, Faye, in *The Temp*, 107
Dungeonmaster, 55, 156
Dungeons & Dragons, 32, 33

Index **181**

Dunne, Robin, in *Cruel Intentions 2*, 111–114
Duran Duran, talent of, 36

E
Earth vs. the Spider, 10, 156
Easterbrook, Leslie, in *Private Resort*, 92–93
eating, by Calista Flockhart, 50
Ebert, Roger, *I Hated, Hated, Hated This Movie* (book), 165
Ed, 51, 156
Ed Wood, 91, 156
  dubbing in, 25
  Martin Landau in, 136
Egbert, Dallas, III, *Mazes & Monsters* inspired by, 32
80s
  soundtracks of, 5–6
  stereotypes of, 26, 53
  teen sex comedies of, 91, 94, 96
  3-D craze of, 54
  TV movies of, love in, 33
Einstein, Albert, in *Zapped!*, 95
Elizondo, Hector, in *Private Resort*, 92–93
Elmer Fudd, Julie Brown impersonation of, 74
Embrace of the Vampire, 85–87
Emerald Forest, 142, 156
The Encyclopedia of Bad Taste (book), 172
The Encyclopedia of Pop Culture (book), 172
Englund, Robert, in *Python*, 66
erotic thrillers, 105
The Essential Monster Movie Guide (book), 167
Estrada, Erik, in *King Cobra*, 66
E.T.: The Extra-Terrestrial, 101, 156
Everitt, David, and Harold Schechter, *For Reel* (book), 171
Everman, Welch, *Cult Horror Films* (book), 165
Everyone Says I Love You, 156
  Drew Barrymore in, 101
  dubbing in, 25
evil, ultimate, 52–53
Ewok(s), specials about, 150
The Ewok Adventure, 156
Ewoks: The Battle for Endor, 156
Excalibur, 142, 156
Exorcist II: The Heretic, 142, 156

F
Fade to Black, 60, 156
Fake Out, 13, 156
Fantastic Voyage, 47, 156
Farr, Jamie, in *Curse II: The Bite*, 66
Fast Times at Ridgemont High, 94, 156
Faster, Pussycat! Kill! Kill!, 16, 156
Fathom, 47, 156
Felony (rock band), in *Graduation Day*, 36
femme fatale movies, 106
Fenn, Sherilyn, in *Zombie High*, 37
Field of Dreams, 100, 156
The Fifty Worst Films of All Time (book), 168
filmmaking
  guerilla, 49
  rules of, in *The Lonely Lady*, 11
First Kid, 62, 156
Fischer, Dennis, *Horror Film Directors, 1931-1990* (book), 165
Fisher, Carrie, in *The Star Wars Holiday Special*, 148–150
Fleischer, Richard, *Amityville 3-D* directed by, 52–54
Flesh for Frankenstein, 54, 156
flies, Ultimate Evil's love of, 53
Flight of the Navigator, 5, 156
Flockhart, Calista, in *Getting In*, 49–50
Fly Girls, Jennifer Lopez in, 65
Fonda, Henry, in *Tentacles*, 121–123

The Food of the Gods, 127, 156–157
Fools Rush In, 51, 157
Footloose, soundtrack of, 6
For Reel (book), 171
For the Love of the Game, Kevin Costner in, 100, 157
Ford, Harrison
   in *Star Wars*, 131
   in *The Star Wars Holiday Special*, 147–150
Forever Young, 62, 157
Forsett, Theo, in *Tammy and the T-Rex*, 17
Fox television network, quality of programming on, 110
Franklin, Pamela, work with Bert I. Gordon, 127
Free Willy 3, 105, 157
Freed, Herb, *Graduation Day* directed by, 35–36
French Connection, 47, 157
Friday the 13th 3-D, 54, 157
Fried Green Tomatoes, 28, 157
Friends (television series), cast of, movie success of, 51
Fromage, Marty. See Williams, Robin
Frye, Soleil Moon, in *Piranha*, 130
Fudd, Elmer, Julie Brown impersonation of, 74
Full House (television series), Lori Loughlin on, 53
Full Moon Entertainment, in dinosaur movie craze, 19
Full Moon Video Zone, 59
Future Kick, 128, 157

G
Gale, James, in *Texas Chainsaw Massacre: The Next Generation*, 30–31
Garfield, Allen, in *Cyborg 2*, 20
Gellar, Sarah Michelle, in *Cruel Intentions*, 110

Get Over It!, 91, 157
Getting In, 49–51
Gibson, Mel, dubbing of, in *Mad Max*, 25
Gielgud, John, in *Caligula*, 84
Gilbert, Sara, in *Poison Ivy*, 101–103
Girls Just Want To Have Fun, 5–7
Glengarry Glen Ross, 88, 157
Go, 49, 157
God Told Me To, 16, 157
The Godfather, 132, 157
Godzilla, 157
   in dinosaur movie craze, 19
   and King Kong, 39
Godzilla vs. the Sea Monster, 123, 157
Goldberg, Lee, et al., *Science Fiction Filmmaking in the '80s* (book), 165
Goldberg, Whoopi, in *Theodore Rex*, 19
Golden Globe Award, for Pia Zadora, 12
Golden Raspberry Awards
   for Faye Dunaway, 107
   for *The Lonely Lady*, 13
   for Pamela Anderson's breasts, 109
   for *Showgirls*, 13
The Golden Turkey Awards (book), 168
Goldman, William, *Which Lie Did I Tell?* (book), 166
Goldsmith, Jerry, 120
Goldthwait, Bob, in *Shakes the Clown*, 73–75
Good Will Hunting, 119, 157
Gooding, Cuba, Jr., bad movies of, 47
Goodman, Dody, in *Private Resort*, 92–93
Gordon, Bert I., *The Witching* by, 127
Gorgo, 123, 157
Gortner, Marjoe, in *Starcrash*, 131–133
Goursaud, Anne
   Embrace of the Vampire directed by, 85–87

Poison Ivy II directed by, 103
Graduation Day, 35–36
Grand Theft Auto, 139, 157
grasshoppers, as hats, 7
Grauman, Walter, *Are You In the House Alone?* directed by, 14–16
Gremlins, 27, 157
Grey, Rudolph, *Nightmare of Ecstasy: The Life of Edward D. Wood, Jr.* (book), 166
Greystoke: The Legend of Tarzan, 25, 157
Grodin, Charles, in *King Kong*, 40–42
The Gross (book), 164
Guam, Catholic school uniforms on, 6
Guccione, Bob, *Caligula* and, 83
guerilla filmmaking, 49, 99
Guillermin, John, *King Kong* directed by, 39–42
Guinness, Alec
  career of, 146
  in *Raise the Titanic!*, 143–146
  in *Star Wars*, 131

H
Hackman, Gene, bad movies of, 47
Hairspray, 13, 157
Hall, Anthony Michael, in *Weird Science*, 96
Halloween, 10, 135, 157
ham, exploding, condiments for, 59
Hamill, Mark, in *The Star Wars Holiday Special*, 148–150
Hanks, Tom, in *Mazes & Monsters*, 32–34
Harlem Globetrotters on Gilligan's Island, 136, 157
Harper, Tess
  in *Amityville 3-D*, 52–53
  in *The Turning*, 81–82
Harrison, John, in *Texas Chainsaw Massacre: The Next Generation*, 29–30

Harryhausen, Ray, dinosaur movies of, 19
Hasselhoff, David
  in *Starcrash*, 131–133
  in *Witchery*, 124–127
Hawk the Slayer, 135, 157–158
hazing, of actors, 3
Heathers, 5, 90, 158
Heatseeker, 22, 158
Heavy Metal, 149, 158
Henkel, Kim, *Texas Chainsaw Massacre: The Next Generation* directed by, 29–31
Hercules Goes Bananas, 23–24
heterosexual perverts, Roddy McDowell as, 8
high schools, horror movies set in, 10, 35
  absence of titular events in, 35
  death sequences of, 36
  nudity in, 36
Highlander, 47, 158
Highlander II: The Quickening, 47, 158
Hill, George H., and James Robert Parish, *Black Action Films* (book), 169
Hill Street Blues (television series), Tim Thomerson on, 60
Hillbillies, cannibalistic, 29
Hillenbrand, David, and Scott Hildebrand, *King Cobra* by, 66
Hocus Pocus, 127, 158
Hogan, David, *Barb Wire* directed by, 108–109
Holland, Tom, *The Temp* directed by, 106–107
The Hollywood Hall of Shame (book), 168
Home Fires Burning (play), *The Turning* based on, 81
homosexual characters, stereotypes of, 17

Honkytonk Man, 60, 158
Hope and Glory, 142, 158
Hopkins, Bo, in *Tentacles*, 122–123
Horror Film Directors, 1931-1990 (book), 165
horror movies
  in high schools, 10
    absence of titular events in, 35
    death sequences of, 36
    nudity in, 36
  sequel settings for, 26
  titles for, 16
How I Made a Hundred Movies in Hollywood and Never Lost a Dime (book), 164–165
Howard, Clint
  in *Barb Wire*, 108–109
  in *Carnosaur*, 129–130
Hu, Kelly, in *No Way Back*, 70–71
Humanoids from the Deep, 123, 158
  update of, 130
Hunt, Helen
  career of, 5
  in *Girls Just Want To Have Fun*, 5–7
  relative merits of, as best friend, 7
  in *Trancers*, 55–57
  in *Trancers II*, 58–60
  in *Trancers III: Deth Lives*, 61
Huston, Anjelica, 136
Huston, John, in *Tentacles*, 121–123
Hutton, Timothy, in *The Temp*, 106–107
Hyde, Jonathan, in *Anaconda*, 64–66

I
I Hated, Hated, Hated This Movie (book), 165
I Know What You Did Last Summer, 16, 158
I Still Know What You Did Last Summer, 16, 158
I Was a Teenage Werewolf, 10, 158
Ice Cube, in *Anaconda*, 64–66

If Chins Could Kill: Confessions of a B-Movie Actor (book), 164
IMAX features, 3-D presentation of, 54
The Incredible Hulk (comic series), Peter David writing for, 63
The Incredible Hulk Returns, 127, 158
Incredibly Strange Films (book), 166
Independence Day, 72, 158
International Stewardesses, 54, 158
Invasion of the B-Girls (book), 166
Ireland, Kathy
  acting method of, 12
  in *Miami Hustle*, 109
It Came From Outer Space, 54, 158

J
Jack Frost, 126, 158
Jack the Bear, 62, 158
Jackson, Samuel L., in *Deep Blue Sea*, 123
James, Henry, bikini works of, 97
Jameson, Jerry, *Raise the Titanic!* directed by, 143–146
janitors, as custodians of destiny, 9
Japan's Favorite Mon-star: The Unauthorized Biography of "The Big G" (book), 170
Jar-Jar Binks, excision of, 150
Jaws, 158
  movie rip-offs of, 121, 123
Jaws 3-D, 54, 158
Jefferson Starship, in *The Star Wars Holiday Special*, 148–150
Jerry Maguire, 158
  Cuba Gooding, Jr. in, 47
  and *Texas Chainsaw Massacre: The Next Generation*, 31
JFK, 100, 158
The Johns Hopkins University, getting into, 49–51
Jolie, Angelina, in *Cyborg 2*, 21–22
Jones, Stephen, *The Essential Monster*

Movie Guide (book), 167
Jordan, Richard, in *Raise the Titanic!*, 144–146
Joy, Robert, in *Amityville 3-D*, 53
Joyner, C. Courtney, *Trancers III: Deth Lives* directed by, 61–63
Jumanji, 119, 158
Jurassic Park, 12, 19, 158
Jurassic Park III, 19, 158

K
Kane, Carole, in *Theodore Rex*, 19
Kane, Joel, *The Phantom Ultimate Video Guide* (book), 167
Kaufman, Lloyd, and *Sizzle Beach U.S.A.*, 97
Kelly, Gene, on dignity (as Don Lockwood), 3–4
Kemp, Martin, in *Embrace of the Vampire*, 85–87
Kenny, Tom, in *Shakes the Clown*, 73–75
Kill, Baby, Kill, 16, 158
killers, obvious choices for, 9
King Cobra, 66, 158
King Dinosaur, 19, 158–159
King Kong, 39–42, 159
  dinosaurs in, 19
  and Godzilla, 39
Kiser, Terry, in *Tammy and the T-Rex*, 17
Kletter, Richard, *The Tower* directed by, 67–69
Knight, Harry Adam, *Carnosaur* based on novel by, 128–129
Knights, 22, 159
Komodo, 66, 159
Korman, Harvey, in *The Star Wars Holiday Special*, 148–150
Koteas, Elias, in *Cyborg 2*, 21–22
Kudrow, Lisa, movie career of, 51
Kumble, Roger, *Cruel Intentions 2* directed by, 110–114

Kusaba, Craig, *Sizzle Beach U.S.A.* written by, 97

L
L.A. Confidential, 70, 159
L.A. Story, 5, 159
Ladd, Cheryl, in *Poison Ivy*, 101–103
Ladd, Diane, in *Carnosaur*, 128–130
Ladd, Jordan, in *Embrace of the Vampire*, 86–87
LaFleur, Art, in *Trancers* movies, 62
LaMarche, Maurice, Vincent D'Onofrio dubbed by, 25
Land Before Time movies, 19, 159
Landau, Juliet, in *Theodore Rex*, 19
Landau, Martin
  in *Alone in the Dark*, 134–136
  career of, 135–136
Langdon, Sue Ann, in *Zapped!*, 95–96
Lange, Jessica, in *King Kong*, 39–42
The Last Chase, 137–139
Lauper, Cyndi, and *Girls Just Want To Have Fun*, 5
Laurenti, Fabrizio, *Witchery* directed by, 124–127
Laverne & Shirley (television series), Tim Thomerson in, 60
Le Cinema de Tit, 92. See also sex, teen comedies about
LeBlanc, Matt, movie career of, 51
LeBrock, Kelly, in *Weird Science*, 96
The Legend of Billie Jean, 70, 159
Legion of Doom, in Shakespearean drama, 28
Leitch, Donovan, Jr., in *Cutting Class*, 8–10
Leprechaun, 51, 104, 159
Lerner, Michael, in *No Way Back*, 71–72
lesbian twins, naked, 112
Let's Scare Jessica to Death, 16, 159
Levy, Carol, in *Alone in the Dark*, 135
Liman, Doug, *Getting In* directed by,

49–51
Link, Ron, *Zombie High* directed by, 37–38
Liotta, Ray, in *The Lonely Lady*, 11
Little, Rich, David Niven dubbed by, 25
Llosa, Luis, *Anaconda* directed by, 64–66
loan sharking, primer for, 105
The Lonely Lady, 11–13
   Golden Raspberry Awards for, 13
Loomis, Deborah, in *Hercules Goes Bananas*, 24
Lopez, Jennifer, in *Anaconda*, 64–66
The Lost Continent, 19, 159
Lost in Space, 51, 159
The Lost World: Jurassic Park, 19, 159
Loughlin, Lori, in *Amityville 3-D*, 52–53
love
   in 80s TV movies, 33
   reincarnation and, 85
Love Potion No. 9, 96, 159
Lucasfilms, on *The Star Wars Holiday Special*, 150
Lucky Numbers, 51, 159
The Lurker in the Lobby (book), 168–169

M
MacDowell, Andie, dubbing of, in *Greystoke: The Legend of Tarzan*, 25
Mad About You (television series), Helen Hunt on, 5, 61
Mad Max, 25, 159
Madonna, film career of, 48
Madsen, Virginia, in *Zombie High*, 37–38
maguppies. *See* breasts
Mailer, Stephen, in *Getting In*, 49–51
Majors, Lee, in *The Last Chase*, 137–139
Makepeace, Chris
   in *The Last Chase*, 138–139
   in *Mazes & Monsters*, 33–34
male chauvinism, examples of, 111, 112, 129
Malibu Bikini Shop, 93, 159
Malibu Hot Summer, 97
Mallrats, 5, 90, 159
Manchester Prep (television series), 110
Margulies, Edward, and Stephen Rubello, *Bad Movies We Love* (book), 167
Marshall, Frank, producing credits of, 119
Martial Law (television series), Kelly Hu in, 70
Massacre at Central High, 10, 159
Masters of the Universe, 51, 159
Masterson, Christopher, 113
Mayo, Mike, *Videohound's Horror Show: 999 Hair-Raising, Hellish, and Humorous Movies* (book), 167
Mazes & Monsters, 32–34
McCarthy, Andrew, in *Getting In*, 49
McConaughey, Matthew, in *Texas Chainsaw Massacre: The Next Generation*, 30–31
McDowall, Roddy, heterosexual perversity of, 8
McDowell, Malcolm, in *Caligula*, 83–84
McGee, Mark Thomas, *Roger Corman: Best of the Cheap Acts* (book), 167–168
meat, fresh, Austrian Army as source of, 23
Medved, Harry
   and Michael Medved
      The Golden Turkey Awards (book), 168
      The Hollywood Hall of Shame (book), 168
      Son of Golden Turkey Awards(book), 168

and Randy Dreyfuss, *The Fifty Worst Film of All Time* (book), 168
Medved, Michael, and Harry Medved
  The Golden Turkey Awards (book), 168
  The Hollywood Hall of Shame (book), 168
  Son of Golden Turkey Awards (book), 168
Meredith, Burgess, in *The Last Chase*, 138–139
Metalstorm: The Destruction of Jared-Syn, 60, 159
Meteor, 159
  Martin Landau in, 136
  Sean Connery in, 47
Metter, Alan, *Girls Just Want To Have Fun* directed by, 5–7
Miami Hustle, 109, 159
Miami Vice (television series), set design of, 37
Midler, Bette, witchcraft movie work of, 127
A Midsummer Night's Dream, 79, 159
Migliore, Andrew, and John Strysik, *The Lurker in the Lobby* (book), 168–169
Mike Nelson's Movie Megacheese (book), 169
Milano, Alyssa
  in *Embrace of the Vampire*, 85–87
  nudity by, 79
  in *Poison Ivy II*, 103
Millennium (television series), David Nutter directing for, 63
Mirren, Helen, in *Caligula*, 84
misopedia, 89
Mission: Impossible, 136
Mrs. Doubtfire, 119, 159
Mr. Universe, as Hercules, 23
Mr. Peek-A-Boo's Playmates, 54, 159
Mitchell-Smith, Ilan, in *Weird Science*, 96

The Mod Squad, 47, 159
Modern Times, 85, 159
Monkey Business, 95, 159
Monster from the Ocean Floor, 123, 159
monster movies
  killer sea beasts in, 121–123
  monster effects in, 65–66
  updates of, 39
Montgomery, Lee, in *Girls Just Want To Have Fun*, 6–7
Moonlighting (television series), Tim Thomerson on, 60
Moonstruck, 119, 159
Morita, Pat, in *King Cobra*, 66
Morrow, Rob, in *Private Resort*, 91–93
Morton, Mickey, in *The Star Wars Holiday Special*, 147–150
movies, decent. See *Trancers*
Mull, Martin, in *Cutting Class*, 8–10
Munro, Caroline, in *Starcrash*, 131–133
Muppet Babies, *Girls Just Want To Have Fun* compared to, 6
The Muppets Take Manhattan, 6, 159
murderer, as occupation, benefits of, 9
mustard, for exploding ham, 59
Mute Witness, 146, 159
My Bodyguard, 33, 138
My Tutor, 94, 159
Myra Breckinridge, 47, 159
mythology, butchered, 23–24

N

Naked Gun 33 1/3, 13, 159
naked lesbian twins, 112
National Rifle Association, big flying head financed by, 140
Necromancy, 127
Nelson, Judd, in *Blindfold: Acts of Obsession*, 88–90
Nelson, Mike J., *Mike Nelson's Movie Megacheese* (book), 169
Nemesis, 22, 159

Nemesis 2: Nebula, 22, 159–160
Nemesis 3: Prey Harder, 22, 160
Nemesis 4: Death Angel, 22, 160
nepotism, in *Trancers II*, 59
Newmyer, Lisa Marie, in *Texas Chainsaw Massacre: The Next Generation*, 29–30
Nicholson, Jack, as love object, in *As Good As It Gets*, 5, 61
Nico the Unicorn, 127, 160
Night of the Living Dead, 37, 160
The Night Strangler, 38, 160
Nightmare of Ecstasy: The Life of Edward D. Wood, Jr. (book), 166
A Nightmare on Elm Street, 10, 160
Niven, David, dubbing of, 25
Nixon, Marni, Natalie Wood dubbed by, 25
"no concept" film, 99
No Way Back, 70–72
Nolan, Tom, in *School Spirit*, 96
The Norseman, 137
North by Northwest, 136, 160
Northern Exposure (television series), 91
novels, film adaptations of
 of Clive Cussler, 143
 of Harold Robbins, 11
 of Harry Adam Knight, 128–129
 of Michael Crichton, 119
nudity, career advancement from, 79
Nutter, David, career of, 63

O
Octaman, 123, 160
Odious Comic Relief™, Martin Mull as, 9
O'Donnell, Chris, filmic death of, 28
O'Halloran, Jack, in *King Kong*, 41–42
Omega Doom, 22, 160
One Million Years B.C., 47, 160
Ontkean, Michael, work of, 127
Opper, Don, in *Critters 3*, 26–28

Orca, 123, 160
Oscars. *See* Academy Awards
The Osterman Weekend, 60, 160
O'Toole, Peter, in *Caligula*, 83
Out of Sight, 65, 160
Outland, 140, 160
Outlaw of Gor, 135, 160

P
Pajama Tops, 13, 160
Palance, Jack
 in *Alone in the Dark*, 134–136
 in *Cyborg 2*, 20–22
The Pallbearer, 51, 160
Pallenberg, Rospo, *Cutting Class* directed by, 8–10
Palmer, Randy, *Paul Blaisdell, Monster Maker* (book), 169
Palsley, Ray. *See* Reiser, Paul
Parish, James Robert, and George H. Hill, *Black Action Films* (book), 169
Parker, Sarah Jessica, in *Girls Just Want To Have Fun*, 5–7
The Party at Kitty and Stud's, 104, 160
Paul Blaisdell, Monster Maker (book), 169
Peary, Danny
 Cult Movie Stars (book), 170
 Cult Movies (book), 169–170
Peet, Amanda, in *The Whole Nine Yards*, 51
Perensky, Tonie, in *Texas Chainsaw Massacre: The Next Generation*, 29–31
Perlman, Ron, *other*, 52
Perry, Matthew
 in *Getting In*, 49–50
 movie success of, 51
personality, optionality of, in B-movies, 98–99
perverts, heterosexual, Roddy McDowell as, 8

Index **189**

Peterson, Kristine, *Critters 3* directed by, 26–28
The Phantom Edit, 150
The Phantom Menace, 162
The Phantom Ultimate Video Guide (book), 167
Phillipe, Ryan, in *Cruel Intentions*, 110
Pilgrim, George, in *Tammy and the T-Rex*, 17
Pillsbury, Sam, Zandalee directed by, 104–105
Pinky and the Brain, and *Ed Wood*, 25
Piranha, 123, 128, 160
  update of, 130
Pitt, Brad, in *Cutting Class*, 8–10
pizza method, for babysitting, 6
Playboy (magazine), Drew Barrymore in, 101
The Playgirls and the Bellboy, 54, 160
Pleasance, Donald, in *Alone in the Dark*, 134–136
Plummer, Christopher, in *Starcrash*, 131–133
Poison Ivy, 101–103, 106
Poison Ivy: The New Seduction, 103, 160
Poison Ivy II, 103, 160
Police Academy, 92, 160
Poltergeist, 119, 160
Porky's, 91, 94, 160
The Poseidon Adventure, 121, 160
Postcards from the Edge, 127, 160
The Postman, Kevin Costner in, 100
The Practice, Lara Flynn Boyle in, 106
Prehysteria!, 19, 160
Pressly, Jaime, in *Poison Ivy: The New Seduction*, 103
Private Resort, 91–93
Prom Night, 10, 160–161
Prom Night IV: Deliver Us from Evil, 10, 161
prostitutes, in cyborg movies, 20
The Protector, 109, 161

Pruett, Harrison, in *Embrace of the Vampire*, 86–87
Psycho, 47, 161
The Psychotronic Encyclopedia of Film (book), 173
Puchalski, Steven, *Slimetime* (book), 170
Pumpkinhead II: Blood Wings, 10, 161
Puopolo, L.A., *The Turning* directed by, 81–82
puppetry
  in *Carnosaur*, 130
  shoddy, 27
Purcell, Lee, work of, 127
Python, 66, 161
Pyun, Albert
  niceness of, 60
  post-apocalyptic cyborg movies of, 22

Q
Quaid, Dennis, in *Are You In the House Alone?*, 15–16
Queenan, Joe, *Confessions of a Cineplex Heckler* (book), 170
The Quick and the Dead, 28, 70, 161
Quigley, Linnea, nudity of, 36
Quiz Show, 91, 161

R
Raffill, Stewart, *Tammy and the T-Rex* directed by, 17–19
Raging Bull, 85, 161
Raiders of the Lost Ark, 119, 161
Raimi, Sam
  For the Love of the Game directed by, 100
  The Quick and the Dead directed by, 70
Raise the Titanic!, 143–146
rape
  disgusting morals about, 15
  gratuitously graphic depiction of, 16

rapists, screen debuts as, 11, 15
Razzie Awards. *See* Golden Raspberry Awards
Rebel Without a Cause, 10, 161
Reeves, Steve, as Hercules, 23
reincarnation
  love and, 85
  of witches, virginity in, 126
Reinhold, Judge, in *Zandalee*, 104–105
Reiser, Paul
  Helen Hunt and, 5
  in *The Tower*, 67–69
Rice, Anne, vampires of, 87
Richards, Denise, in *Tammy and the T-Rex*, 17–19
Road Trip, 91, 161
Robards, Jason, in *Raise the Titanic!*, 143–146
Robbins, Harold, novels of, adapted to film, 11
Roberts, Julia, singing of, 25
Roberts, Tony, in *Amityville 3-D*, 52–53
Robin Hood: Prince of Thieves, 64, 100, 161
Robinson, Andy, in *Trancers III*, 62
Roger Corman: Best of the Cheap Acts (book), 167–168
Rogers, Mimi, in *Cruel Intentions 2*, 111–114
role-playing games, 32–34
Romeo + Juliet, 28, 47, 161
Romy and Michele's High School Reunion, 51, 161
Roseanne (television series), Sara Gilbert on, 101
Rosemary's Disciples, 127
Rosenthal, Robert J., *Zapped!* directed by, 94–96
Royce, Roselyn, in *Sizzle Beach U.S.A.*, 97–100
Rubello, Stephen, and Edward Margulies, *Bad Movies We Love* (book), 167
Runyon, Jennifer, in *Carnosaur*, 129–130
Ruthless People, 70, 161
Ryan, Meg, in *Amityville 3-D*, 53
Ryfle, Steve, *Japan's Favorite Mon-star: The Unauthorized Biography of "The Big G"* (book), 170

S
St. Elsewhere (television series), Tim Thomerson on, 60
Salamon, Julie, *The Devil's Candy* (book), 171
Sandler, Adam, in *Shakes the Clown*, 73–75
Sansweet, Steve, on *The Star Wars Holiday Special*, 150
Santa Claus Conquers the Martians, 13, 161
Sasdy, Peter, *The Lonely Lady* directed by, 11–13
Satan's School for Girls, 90, 161
Sauter, Michael, *The Worst Movies of All Time, Or: What Were They Thinking?* (book), 171
Sbarge, Raphael, in *Carnosaur*, 129–130
Schachter, Felice, in *Zapped!*, 95–96
Schechter, Harold, and David Everitt, *For Reel* (book), 171
Schoelen, Jill, in *Cutting Class*, 8–10
School Spirit, 96, 161
Schroeder, Michael, *Cyborg 2* directed by, 20–22
Schultz, Dwight
  in *Alone in the Dark*, 134–136
  in *The Temp*, 107
Schwartz, Carol, *Videohound's Cult Flicks and Trash Pics* (book), 171–172
Schwarzenegger, Arnold, in *Hercules*

Goes Bananas, 23–24
Schwimmer, David, movie career of, 51
Science Fiction Filmmaking in the '80s (book), 165
Scolari, Peter, in *Bosom Buddies*, 32
Scream, 161
    Courteney Cox in, 51
    deconstruction of horror genre in, 10
    Drew Barrymore in, 101
screen debuts, as rapists, 11, 15
scripts, quality of, actors as judges of, 47–48
sea beasts, killer, 121–123
Seidelman, Arthur Allan, *Hercules Goes Bananas* directed by, 23–24
Selby, David, in *Raise the Titanic!*, 144–146
sex
    in bequeathal of knowledge, 141
    and Dungeons & Dragons, 33
    hardcore, in *Caligula*, 83
    skanky, in *The Lonely Lady*, 12–13
    teen comedies about, 91, 94, 96
    vomit and, 71
Sex and the City (television series), Sarah Jessica Parker in, 5
Shadows of Desire, 105, 161
Shaefer, Eric, *"Bold! Daring! Shocking! True!"* (book), 171
Shakes the Clown, 73–75
Shakespearean drama, Legion of Doom in, 28
Shanley, John Patrick, Academy Award for, 119
Shea, Katt, *Poison Ivy* directed by, 101–103
Shepard, Jewel, *Invasion of the B-Girls* (book), 166
Sheperd, Karen, in *Cyborg 2*, 20
Sherman, Fraser A., *Cyborgs, Santa Claus and Satan* (book), 172
Sholder, Jack, *Alone in the Dark* directed by, 134–136
shower scenes, with **naked lesbian twins**, 112
Showgirls, 11, 13, 161
Silence of the Lambs, 12, 161
Silverman, Jonathan, in *Girls Just Want To Have Fun*, 6
Simon, Adam, *Carnosaur* directed by, 128–130
Singin' in the Rain, 3–4, 161
Sins of Silence, 105, 161
Six Days, Seven Nights, 51, 161
Sizzle Beach U.S.A., 97–100
Skerritt, Tom, in *Poison Ivy*, 101–103
skin flicks, 93
Slater, Helen, in *No Way Back*, 70–72
Slaughter High, 10, 161
Slimetime (book), 170
Smith, Kevin, and redemption of Shannen Doherty, 5
Smith, Melanie, in *Trancers III*, 62–63
snake movies, 64–66
soldiers, in cyborg movies, 20
Son of Golden Turkey Awards (book), 168
Sorry, Wrong Number, 16, 161
soundtracks
    in the 80s, 5–6
Spacehunter: Adventures in the Forbidden Zone, 54, 161–162
Speed, 47, 162
Spinell, Joe, in *Starcrash*, 132–133
Square Pegs (television series), Sarah Jessica Parker on, 5
SSSSSSS, 66, 162
Stallone, Sylvester, in *The Party at Kitty and Stud's*, 104
Stang, Arnold, in *Hercules Goes Bananas*, 24
Stanley, John, *Creature Features* (book), 172
Star Trek: Deep Space Nine
    Andy Robinson in, 62

Rene Auberjonois in, 42
Star Wars: Episode I - The Phantom Menace, 150, 162
Star Wars: Episode IV - A New Hope, 131–133, 162
The Star Wars Holiday Special, 147–150
Starcrash, 131–133
Starsky and Hutch (television series), Tim Thomerson on, 60
The Stepford Husbands, 127, 162
The Stepford Wives, 38, 162
stereotypes, combined, in single character, 17
Stern, Jane, and Michael Stern
  The Encyclopedia of Bad Taste (book), 172
  The Encyclopedia of Pop Culture (book), 172
Stern, Steven Hilliard, *Mazes & Monsters* directed by, 32–34
The Stewardesses, 54, 162
Stir Crazy, 127, 162
Stoltz, Eric, in *Anaconda*, 65–66
stoners, zombies compared to, 37
strange blank pages, 115–116
The Streets of San Francisco (television series), and *Zombie High*, 38
Stripped to Kill, 128, 162
Strong, Arnold. *See* Schwarzenegger, Arnold
Strysik, John, and Andrew Migliore, *The Lurker in the Lobby* (book), 168–169
success, television vs. movie, 51
Sunset Boulevard, 85, 162
Supergirl, 70, 162
Supergirl (comic series), Peter David writing for, 63
Superman II, 41, 162
Superman IV: The Quest for Peace, 47, 162
surprise, dull, popularity of, in acting, 12
suspense movies, titles for, 16
Swanson, Kristy, in *Getting In*, 49–50
Swingers, 47, 49, 162

T
Tails You Live, Heads You're Dead, 16, 162
Tammy and the T-Rex, 17–19
Teenage Mutant Ninja Turtles, 162
teenagers
  cruelty of, 111–112
  horror movie focus on, 10
  sex comedies about, 91, 94, 96
television, control over, 58–59
The Temp, 106–107
Temptation Island (television series), 110
Tentacles, 121–123
The Terminator, 22, 162
The Texas Chain Saw Massacre, 29, 162
Texas Chainsaw Massacre: The Next Generation, 29–31
Theodore Rex, in dinosaur movie craze, 19
There's Nothing Out There, 16, 162
They Bite, 123, 162
Thomas, Heather, in *Zapped!*, 95–96
Thomerson, Tim
  career of, 60
  cost to employ, 55
  in *Trancers*, 55–57
  in *Trancers II*, 58–60
  in *Trancers III: Deth Lives*, 61–63
Thompson, Sarah, in *Cruel Intentions 2*, 112–114
3-D movie craze, 52, 54
Tilly, Jennifer, in *Embrace of the Vampire*, 86–87
time travel, in *Trancers*, 55–57
Tin Cup, 100, 162
Titanic, 28, 143, 162

Touliatos, George, in *The Last Chase*, 138–139
The Tower, 67–69
Toyokawa, Etsushi, in *No Way Back*, 71–72
Trancers, 5, 55–57
Trancers II, 58–60
Trancers III: Deth Lives, 61-63
Trancers 4: Jack of Swords, 62, 63, 162
Trancers 5, 62, 63, 162
Trancers 6, 62
Trancers 7, 62
Trancers 8, 62
Trancers 9, 62
Trancers 10, 62
Trancers 11, 62
Trancers 12, 62
Trancers 13, 62
Trancers 14, 62
Trancers 15, 62
Trancers 16, 62
Trancers 17, 62
Trancers 18, 62
Trancers 19, 62
Trancers 20, 62
Travolta, John, as 70s cultural commodity, 98
Trejo, Danny, in *Anaconda*, 64
Troma Studios, and *Sizzle Beach U.S.A.*, 97
Troop Beverly Hills, 13, 162
True, Rachel, in *Embrace of the Vampire*, 86–87
The Turning, 79, 81–82
Twin Peaks (television series), 106, 127
twins, naked lesbian, 112
Twister, 61, 162
2001: A Space Odyssey, 142, 153

U
ultimate evil, 52–53
Unforgiven, 47, 162

The Untouchables, 162
  Kevin Costner in, 100
  Sean Connery in, 47

V
Valentine, 136, 162
Valley Girl, 127, 162
The Valley of Gwangi, 19, 162
Van Damme, Jean-Claude, in *Cyborg*, 22
Van Dien, Casper, in *Python*, 66
van Lidth, Erland, in *Alone in the Dark*, 134–136
Vaughan, Vince, bad movies of, 47
Vidal, Gore, *Caligula* and, 83
Videohound's Cult Flicks and Trash Pics (book), 171–172
Videohound's Horror Show: 999 Hair-Raising, Hellish, and Humorous Movies (book), 167
virginity, necessity of
  in vampire love, 85–86
  in witch reincarnation, 126
Virtuosity, 70, 163
voices, dubbed, 25
Voight, John, in *Anaconda*, 64–66
Volunteers, 60, 163
vomit, and sex, 71
Voyage of the Rock Aliens, 13, 163

W
Walker, Paul, in *Tammy and the T-Rex*, 17
Wallace, David, in *Mazes & Monsters*, 33–34
Walsh, M. Emmet, in *Raise the Titanic!*, 143–146
Ward, Megan, in *Trancers II*, 58–60
wardrobe, slutty, 17–18
The Wasp Woman, 163
  update of, 130
Waterworld, 100, 163
Waxwork II: Lost in Time, 101, 163

weather, uncooperative nature of, 126
The Wedding Singer, 101, 163
Weird Science, 96, 163
Welch, Raquel, bad movies of, 47
Weldon, Michael, *The Psychotronic Encyclopedia of Film* (book), 173
Welles, Orson, witchcraft movie of, 127
West Side Story, 25, 163
What Ever Happened to Baby Jane, 16, 163
What's Eating Gilbert Grape?, 27, 163
What's the Matter With Helen, 16, 163
When Good Pets Go Bad (television series), 110
Which Lie Did I Tell? (book), 166
White, Vanna, in *Graduation Day*, 36
The Whole Nine Yards, 51, 163
Who's That Girl, 48, 163
Wild Things, 19, 163
Williams, Robin
  in *Shakes the Clown*, 74
  studio crap shoots with, 119
Winfrey, Oprah, dieting habits of, 47
Winters, Shelly, in *Tentacles*, 121–123
Wisberg, Aubrey, *Hercules Goes Bananas* written by, 24
Witchcraft, 124–127, 163
Witchery, 124–127
The Witching, 127, 163
Witherspoon, Reese, 110
Wolf, 51, 163
Wood, Ed. *See also* Ed Wood
  Nightmare of Ecstasy: The Life of Edward D. Wood, Jr. (book) (Grey), 166
Wood, Natalie, singing of, dubbed, 25
Woods, Michael, in *Blindfold: Acts of Obsession*, 88–90
Wookiees
  family life of, 147–150
  lack of, 133
The World Is Not Enough, 19, 163

The Worst Movies of All Time, Or: What Were They Thinking? (book), 171
Wuhrer, Kari, in *Anaconda*, 65–66

X
X: the Man With the X-Ray Eyes, 128, 163
Xena: Warrior Princess (television series), Tim Thomerson in, 60
The X-Files (television series)
  David Nutter directing for, 63
  Gillian Anderson in, 81–82

Z
Zadora, Pia, 11–13, 13
Zandalee, 104–105
Zapped!, 94–96
Zardoz, 140–142
Zellweger, Renee, in *Texas Chainsaw Massacre: The Next Generation*, 29–31
Zombie High, 10, 37–38
zombies. *See also Trancers* movies
  stoners compared to, 37

About the Authors

Scott Hamilton and Christopher Holland have been writing about movies together for nearly ten years, at first in their college newspaper, and later in magazines like *SFX* and *The Radio Times*, and on the web. In 1996 they created Stomp Tokyo, a web site designed to focus on all kinds of movies on home video, but which quickly became synonymous with b-movies, cult flicks, and genre films. (With a name like Stomp Tokyo, it was bound to happen.)

Since then, Stomp Tokyo has evolved to include a number of side projects and sub-sites by other authors, including The Bad Movie Report, Attack of the 50 Foot DVD, and Bad Movie Planet. In 2000, Chris and Scott wrote a number of reviews for *The Radio Times Guide to Film*. The *New York Times* called Stomp Tokyo "a place to indulge your questionable cinematic taste," and *Entertainment Weekly* has dubbed it "trash movie paradise." The site has also been featured in The *St. Petersburg Times*, The *San Francisco Chronicle*, and a number of "site of the day" web sites, including the original Cool Site of the Day and PCWorld Online.

The authors live in St. Petersburg, Florida, where they maintain Stomp Tokyo as a publishing business for their online and print endeavors. *Reel Shame* is their first book.

Give yourself or someone you know the gift of

REEL SHAME

Ask your local bookseller or use this order form!
(Of *course* we accept photocopies. We wouldn't ask you to rip the page out of your book!)

YES, I want _____ copies of *Reel Shame: Bad Movies and the Hollywood Stars Who Made Them* at $14.99 each, plus $4 shipping for the first book and $1 for each additional book. (Florida residents please add $1.05 sales tax per book.) Canadian orders must be accompanied by a postal money order in U.S. funds. Allow 15 days for delivery.

My check or money order for $ _____ is enclosed.

To order by credit card, please visit our web site:

http://www.reelshame.com/

Name _____

Address _____

City _____ State _____ Zip _____

Phone _____ E-mail _____

Please make your check payable and return to:

Stomp Tokyo
6822 22nd Ave N, #278
St. Petersburg, FL 33710
e-mail: books@stomptokyo.com